Ford Total PERFORMANCE

FORD'S LEGENDARY HIGH-PERFORMANCE STREET AND RACE CARS

MARTYN L. SCHORR

motorbooks

© 2015 Quarto Publishing Group USA Inc.
Text © 2015 Martyn L. Schorr

First published in 2015 by Motorbooks, an imprint of Quarto Publishing Group USA Inc., 400 First Avenue North, Suite 400, Minneapolis, MN 55401 USA.
Telephone: (612) 344-8100 Fax: (612) 344-8692

quartoknows.com
Visit our blogs at quartoknows.com

Motorbooks titles are also available at discounts in bulk quantity for industrial or sales-promotional use. For details contact the Special Sales Manager at Quarto Publishing Group USA Inc., 400 First Avenue North, Suite 400, Minneapolis, MN 55401 USA.

10 9 8 7 6 5 4 3 2

ISBN: 978-0-7603-4858-1

Library of Congress Cataloging-in-Publication Data

Schorr, Martyn L., author.
  Ford total performance : Ford's legendary high-performance street and race cars / Martyn L. Schorr.
    pages cm
  Includes index.
  Summary: "An illustrated history of the Ford Motor Company's classic race and street cars, including Cobras and Shelby Mustangs, from 1961 to 1971"--Provided by publisher.
  ISBN 978-0-7603-4858-1 (hc w/jacket)
  1. Ford automobile--Performance. 2. Ford automobile--History. 3. Automobiles, Racing. 4. Automobiles, Racing--History. 5. Ford Motor Company--History. I. Title.
  TL215.F7S364 2015
  629.222--dc23
                    2015019364

Acquiring Editor: Darwin Holmstrom
Project Manager: Madeleine Vasaly
Art Director: Cindy Samargia Laun
Cover and Book Designer: John Sticha

ACKNOWLEDGMENTS

A book, like a car, is not created in a vacuum. The author wishes to acknowledge help and support from the following: Wes Allison, Dick Brannan, Peter Brock, John Craft, Warren Crone (fordimages.com), Joe Curley, Scott Davies, Martin Godbey (Sarasota Classic Car Museum), Charlie Gray Jr., Brent Hajek (Hajek Motorsports Museum), Randy Hernandez (Fran Hernandez Collection), Lee Holman, Gary Jean, Al Joniec, Bill Kolb Jr., Rick Kopec (SAAC), Roy Lunn, Fred Mackerodt, Mike Matune, Bob McClurg, Mike McGuire, John Gardner and Jeremy Henrie (Larry H. Miller Total Performance Museum, Miller Motorsports Park), Claus Mueller (Iron Age Garage), Mose Nowland, Joe Oldham, Larry "Mario" Parker, Mike Perlini (Tasca Family Archives), Jim Reep, Michael Alan Ross, Stuart Schorr, Ned Scudder, Nick Smith (Factory Lightweight Collection), and Archie Urciuoli.

Special thanks go to:

Sharon Schorr, my editor, who kept me "on point" through tens of thousands of words.

Jim Farley, executive vice president, and president, Europe, Middle East, and Africa, Ford Motor Company.

Dean Weber and Aimee Plante, Ford Motor Company Archives.

Jim Padilla, president and COO, Ford Motor Company, 2004–2006.

Darwin Holmstrom and the Motorbooks team, who turned tens of thousands of my words and hundreds of images into this book.

Dedicated to my granddaughter, Azra Naz Schorr.

CONTENTS

FOREWORD

The history of Ford Motor Company is connected, from one success to the next, by racing. From the beginning, Ford developed, tested, proved, and promoted its products through performance events primarily in the United States. Participation in competitive events worldwide would come later.

The history of Ford racing, celebrated in this book, put my father, John Holman, in the right place at the right time. Holman & Moody was an integral part of most of Ford's racing history. My dad worked with Zora Arkus-Duntov on flathead engine projects and they became great personal friends, often fishing together. John worked with Don Sullivan, the engineer who helped Henry Ford design the first V-8 and the 427 engine that gave Ford a one-two-three victory at Le Mans in 1966.

John was on Bill Stroppe's winning Lincoln team at the Carrera Panamericana race across Mexico and on the pit crew at Indy with Bill Vukovich. They built cars (and engines) that won at Daytona, Indy, Sebring, Le Mans, and racing circuits all over the world. In the 1960s, Holman & Moody Fords raced and won in every major category, including quarter-mile drags, 12- and 24-hour GT endurance races, and grueling international road rallies.

As the son of a racing legend, I was able to participate in Ford's rich competition heritage. I got to roll around on a creeper and *play* under the 1953–1954 Lincolns at Bill Stroppe's race shop on Signal Hill in Long Beach, California. I met Zora Arkus-Duntov, Peter DePaolo, Henry Ford II, Edsel Ford II, and all the major race-car drivers of the day. I worked in the pits with Joe Weatherly when he won at Darlington in 1960, fueled the Cobra Daytona Coupes with Alan Mann Racing at Le Mans and Nürburgring in 1965, timed the GT40 Mark IIs at Daytona in 1966, and worked on the winning Indy engines at Ford Engineering in Dearborn. I am proud to have had a small part in the most successful racing factory in the world.

Now, as president of Holman & Moody, I have become the caretaker of this history. The book you are about to read showcases Ford's performance and racing history, which, in many ways, is also the history of Holman & Moody. During the mid- to late 1960s, Ford *owned* the racing world. Ford-powered vehicles won the Daytona 500 four times, the 24 Hours of Le Mans four times, and the Indianapolis 500 five times, and they dominated NHRA/AHRA drag racing.

Ford Total Performance focuses on how Ford put America on the road and racetracks and how that heritage led to years of motorsports domination and powerful production muscle cars that ruled the roads. Consummate examples of Ford's racing heritage and horsepower include Model T and A speedsters, 1932 Ford V-8s, aluminum-paneled 1957 *Battlebirds*, Le Mans–winning GT Mark IV, Tour de France–winning Mustangs, and the 1969 NASCAR champion Torino Talladega.

Now that historic racing has developed into a major attraction on the motorsports calendar, Ford's rich history of racing can be seen in action. Vintage Ford race cars can be found at popular venues like Daytona, the Le Mans Classic 24-hour race, Goodwood Revival, and the Monterey Historics.

Major car collections and museums here and abroad, along with high-profile concours at Amelia Island and Pebble Beach, often feature iconic Ford race cars.

On display at a recent vintage race at Laguna Seca was one of two original 1957 *Battlebirds* sitting next to the Le Mans–winning 1967 GT Mark IV. The differences are startling. The 1957 Thunderbird racer is a steel-framed, front-engine/rear-wheel drive, altered-production car with a 400-horsepower, 312-cubic-inch, Y-block V-8. The Mark IV GT is a sophisticated, purpose-built race car with an aluminum chassis and a midmounted, dry-sump, 427-cubic-inch FE big-block. Over a period of ten years, Ford racing had progressed at the speed of light. Holman & Moody raced both of these outstanding machines in their day—the *Battlebird* at Daytona and the GT at Le Mans. Ralph Moody and Fireball Roberts drove the two *Battlebirds* at Daytona.

Holman & Moody continues to build vintage GT Mark II Le Mans race cars with original chassis, bodies from the original molds, and 427 Holman & Moody engines. We also build "continuation" 1964 Fairlane road racers powered by 427 engines and, for the first time, TdF (Tour de France) special-edition Mustangs for the road. The history of Holman & Moody and Ford racing, celebrated in *Ford Total Performance*, continues today stronger than ever in Charlotte, North Carolina. Just as our TdF Mustang is based on the race-winning 1964 Mustang, our GT is based on the winning 1966 GT Mark II and certified for historic racing.

The best is yet to come!

Lee Holman
President, Holman & Moody

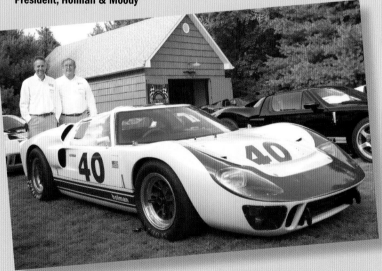

Lee Holman with Holman & Moody engineer Bob D'Amato, left, and one of the company's GT40 Mark II continuation cars. Holman uses original chassis, bodies from original molds, and H&M 427 engines. It's surrounded by 2005–2006 Ford GTs. *Bob D'Amato*

INTRODUCTION

If you could read Ford's DNA, it would spell out "racing and performance."

Before there was a Ford Motor Company, there was a Ford race car. Henry Ford's remarkable upset victory over odds-on favorite Alexander Winton in a ten-lap, ten-mile race in Grosse Pointe, Michigan, on October 10, 1901, set off a chain of events that led to the formation of the Ford Motor Company in 1903. Winton was a successful racer who built the most technologically advanced, most powerful cars of the period, but on the eighth lap of the race, Ford caught up and passed him to win the $1,000 purse and a cut-glass punch bowl. The rest is history.

At a celebration of the company's motorsports centennial in 2001, Henry Ford's great-grandson, Edsel Ford II, said: "Not only is our racing tradition older than our company, but there might not even have been a Ford Motor Company without racing. My grandfather needed to get the world's attention—and he knew how. Henry Ford built a race car."

Sixty-five years after his grandfather became a record-holding race-car driver and upscale auto manufacturer, Henry Ford II watched as his Anglo-American GT40s ended Enzo Ferrari's reign at Le Mans in 1966. Ford then returned to Le Mans in 1967 with all-American Mark IVs and captured a second win at the world's most prestigious sports-car endurance race. Following the win in 1967, a GT40 (P/1075) won again in 1968 and 1969. At Ford, racing and winning had become synonymous.

For *Ford Total Performance*, I was able to connect and reconnect with people, cars, and priceless experiences from my youth spent as a hot rodder in New York City and as an automotive journalist.

My career paralleled Ford's golden era of high performance and motorsports. I started out as the publicity director of the Draggin' Wheels in 1955, and by 1965, I was editor of *CARS* and changed the magazine's title to *Hi-Performance CARS*. Subsequently, I became the automotive group's editorial director.

I had incredible experiences researching this book. I was able to meet and talk with some of the true heroes of Ford's golden age of high-performance cars and racing—men who helped turn Ford's marketing mantra of "Total Performance" into the realization of Henry Ford II's dream of motorsports domination. I hadn't seen or talked with many of these people in four or five decades; others I had known about but never met. Many of the great Ford engineers, product planners, marketers, race-team principals, and racers are no longer with us. I hope I've done justice to their places in Ford history.

One of my personal heroes is Roy Lunn, who, during his almost-fifteen-year career at Ford, led the teams that created the Mustang I Experimental Sports Car and, with John Wyer, brought the original GT to life. Still a brilliant engineer and car designer at age ninety, Lunn has become a futurist and since 2003 has written a number of books, including *Globalization: A Worldwide Quest*

for a Sustainable Future in 2008. He and I talked for hours about race cars and racing in the 1960s and his thought-provoking ideas and designs for environmentally sound cars of the future. Among his many prized possessions from his career is a letter he received when he was Advanced Concepts Manager at Ford, dated June 28, 1966: "Dear Roy: For the record, I want to congratulate you on your creative role in the historic Ford victory at Le Mans. This victory and the World GT Championship attained by machinery created largely at your direction are a great tribute to your planning and your design and engineering resourcefulness. Sincerely, Don Frey, Vice-President and General Manager, Ford Division."

I've also had a number of conversations with Mose Nowland, a true legend whom I have, unfortunately, never met in person. He retired as senior motorsports engineer in 2012 after spending fifty-seven years at Ford. Right up to his retirement, he was involved in Ford race engine development. He says, "My biggest thrill while working for Ford was receiving the Spirit of Ford Award, the highest honor Ford bestows for lifetime achievement in auto racing, on or off the track. Edsel Ford II presented it to me at a special event at the Waldorf Astoria in New York City prior to the annual NASCAR banquet in 2005."

Even though I covered Ford performance cars and racing as a photojournalist and magazine editor in the 1960s and 1970s, writing this book gave me new insight into what was going on behind the scenes. No other carmaker before, during, or since, has been able to match Ford's meteoric motorsport successes. Ford Motor Company is truly unique among domestic and worldwide automakers—even though it's been a public corporation since January 17, 1956, Ford family members own special Class B shares giving them 40 percent voting rights and a powerful voice in determining the future of the company. If that were not the case, it's a good chance that Ford would not have supported racing from 1962 until 1970 . . . and probably this book would never have been written!

I talked with my friend and retired Ford president and chief operating officer Jim Padilla at a Sarasota Café Racers lunch in Sarasota, Florida, about the family-company connection. "To better understand how Ford operates, you first have to understand the blurred line between the Ford family and Ford Motor Company," he said.

That blurred line between the Ford company and the Ford family continues. When the production '05 Ford GT was introduced, J Mays, then vice president of design, said, "The car is a hero. It's the car that put Ford on the map in terms of international racing, and it signaled to the world that the Ford family doesn't settle for the status quo."

Enjoy the ride.

HERITAGE AND HORSEPOWER

Fours That Roar!

Henry Ford's Model T and Model A started a racing revolution that today continues stronger than ever in prewar historic racing in America and abroad.

Thanks to Henry Ford, going fast at the turn of the century and well into the 1920s was not the exclusive domain of wealthy sportsmen. Between 1909 and 1927, Ford built more than fifteen million affordable Model Ts, changing travel and the American landscape forever. It was the first truly affordable automobile manufactured in America. In the 1920s, you could buy a Model T for as little as $260! Powering the Model T was a 177-cubic-inch, L-head four-cylinder engine producing 20 horsepower. Enthusiasts wanting to go fast for very little money flocked to Henry's Tin Lizzies.

Ford replaced the ultra-successful Model T with the much-improved Model A, building almost five million between 1928 and 1931. The Model A L-head four-cylinder, displacing 201 cubic inches, doubled the Model T's horsepower to 40. Actual production lasted until March 1932 when it was replaced by the Model B, which showcased an improved 50-horsepower four-cylinder and the game-changing V-8 flathead engine. With more power, the Model A continued Ford's appeal to performance enthusiasts looking to go fast on a budget. In 1929, you could buy a Model A roadster for under $400!

At the time, thousands of speed and performance garages dotted the map from coast to coast. They specialized in coaxing more power from popular

Claus Mueller competes in vintage races and road rallies in Europe with his handcrafted, aluminum-body speedster. Originally built in Argentina, it's powered by a 70-horsepower Model B Four, built to H&H Super Touring specs. *Claus Mueller/Iron Age Garage*

The ultimate power conversion for Model A Fours is the vintage HAL DOHC conversion, boasting overhead valves with four per cylinder and dual camshafts. The first sixteen-valve dual-cam conversion was the Frontenac (Fronty) developed by the Chevrolet brothers for pure race engines. *Claus Mueller/ Iron Age Garage*

This stunning '29 Model A speedster was built in Europe for road racing, found in Sweden, and brought to the United States in 2008. Its unique body with extensive louvers and streamlining is powered by a mild L-Head Model B Four, owned and raced by Ford Heacock. *Ford Heacock*

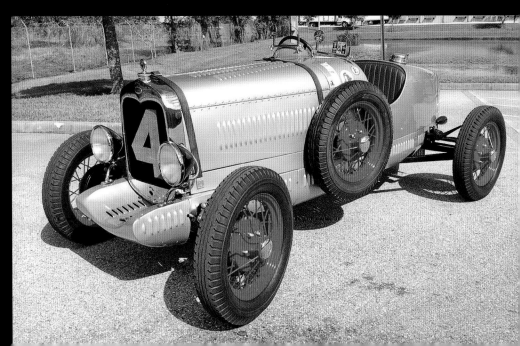

Bill Stelcher has been road racing since the 1960s and campaigns a picture-perfect speedster built on a '29 Ford chassis fitted with a Rootleib boattail body. Here he leads the pack during the 2014 Historics at Indianapolis Speedway. *M. M. "Mike" Matune Jr.*

four-cylinder Fords. New-car dealers got into the action as well. They converted used Model Ts and later Model As into sporty cars, hot rods, and race cars using Mercury and Langdon speedster bodies, Ruckstell two-speed rear ends, Franklin steering, Buffalo 20-inch wire wheels, and modified engines.

Ford enthusiasts could choose from overhead valve (OHV), single overhead cam (SOHC), or dual overhead cam (DOHC) conversion heads made by Clemons, Cragar, Frontenac, Gemsa, Hal, Hunt, Rajo, Roof, Winfield, and others. The Frontenac, or "Fronty," DOHC sixteen-valve conversion, manufactured by Arthur and Louis Chevrolet (yes, that Chevrolet) was extremely popular with racers and hot rodders searching for maximum performance. It was not unusual for highly modified Fronty Fords to produce more than 125 horsepower and redline at over 5,000 rpm. There was also a rare "Peugeot-type" OHV, sixteen-valve head-conversion kit for Model T fours manufactured by Laurel Motors Corporation in Anderson, Illinois.

In the 1920s in California, the Model T Ford gave birth to the exclusively American hot rod movement. When Ford introduced its new and improved 40-horsepower Model A in 1928, the car took over where the T left off. Modified early Ford four-cylinders delivered V-8 performance, powering roadsters, coupes, and belly tankers (lakesters or streamliners). They could be found on weekends at both the dry lakes in the Mojave high desert (El Mirage, Muroc, and Rosamond) and the wood-board and dirt racetracks in California. Racing on the dry lakes was sanctioned by the Russetta Timing Association (RTA)

and Southern California Timing Association (SCTA). When the 65-horsepower flathead V-8 debuted in 1932, it assured Ford's domination of the hot rod field until the advent of OHV V-8s in 1949.

Ford's Model B four-cylinder was, and still is, the engine of choice for builders of race cars, regardless of body styles. The later-model fours had fuel pumps instead of gravity feed, pressurized main and camshaft bearings, higher compression, and improved carburetion. Late in the production cycle, a new counterbalanced crankshaft was introduced. By virtue of replacing the heavier body of the stock Model T with a featherweight, race car–like body, it became faster simply by shedding a couple of hundred pounds. Once engines were modified, these "speedster"-bodied cars were ready for wood-board and dirt-track racing.

Many Ford speedsters being road raced today were built in the 1930s and 1940s utilizing Model A chassis with Model B engines and single- or two-seat bodies. Styles range from customized, stock-appearing Model A roadsters to one-off, streamlined boattails. Most are powered by Model B fours, either L-head or OHV; the more exotic examples sport double-overhead-cam conversions and are capable of over 100 miles per hour. In addition to road racing, speedsters also compete in both quarter-mile drags and land speed racing during Speed Week at the Bonneville Salt Flats.

A number of original Model T speedsters are still being raced today. Ed and Karen Archer of Hayward, California, own *Old No. 4*, a restored 1915 Ford powered by an original engine fitted with a Rajo OHV conversion, now pumping out 50 horsepower. A throwback to the early days of racing, the Archers' speedster engine has dual carbs fed by a hand-operated pump and a vintage German Bosch magneto.

Ed Archer retained the speedster's single drum brakes inside the transmission and twelve forward speeds, made possible by a stock Ford two-speed transmission, original three-speed Muncie auxiliary transmission, and a Ruckstell two-speed rear axle. The 99-inch wheelbase track car rides on vintage 23-inch, wood-spoke Artillery wheels and has a top speed of 100 miles per hour!

The Archers were inducted into the Speedster and Racer Hall of Fame in 2005. In 1968, they worked with Vic Sala to restore *Old No. 4* to its former racing glory. Ed is founder of the Calistoga Classics dirt-track races. He and Karen regularly compete in hill climbs, drag races, and cross-country tours in their vintage speedster.

Speedster enthusiast Bill Stelcher of Sarasota, Florida, has been road racing British sports cars, including his favorite 1965 Elva MK, since the 1960s, and is well known on the prewar historic racing circuit. His No. 29 Riley Special, a 1929 Ford chassis with a two-place Rootlieb boattail speedster body, has been lowered four inches for road racing. Under its fiberglass hood is a 100 horsepower, 1932 Model B four-cylinder with a 1933 Riley four-port OHV head and a pair of Stromberg 81 carburetors.

"Built specifically for vintage racing, I installed hydraulic brakes, custom Blockley tires, five-point seatbelts, and a roll bar," says Stelcher, who competes in prewar classes at Indianapolis Speedway, Road America, Pittsburgh Vintage Grand Prix, Darlington Historic Racing Festival, Blackhawk Farms, Roebling Road, and Mid-Ohio Raceway. He also competes in FAST hill climbs and has run "on the sand" at the Ormond Beach Festival of Speed.

Powered by a mild-mannered Model B Ford, L-head four with a single Stromberg 94 carburetor, Ford Heacock's custom-bodied 1929 Ford is one of the most striking Model A speedsters on the road racing circuit. Vintage racer, collector, and moving force behind the Lake Mirror Classic Concours in Lakeland, Florida, Heacock's speedster was found in Sweden in 2008 by its previous owner/racer Ray Morgan. It was competing in historic racing events in Europe, including the prestigious Vintage Grand Prix Series.

"Since it's right-hand drive and features extensive louvers and streamlining, Ray Morgan and I are pretty sure it was built in Europe," says Heacock.

Over the past few years, interest in running Ford speedsters in Historic and Vintage racing and rallying events has been a growth segment of the hobby both here and abroad. Cars are being imported from the United States as well as being constructed by craftsmen throughout Europe specifically for competitive events.

Racer Claus Mueller, manager of Munich, Germany's, Café Racers, is active in classic car rallies and historic races in a handcrafted 1929 Ford Model A race car. It was originally built in Argentina with a one-off aluminum speedster body and right-hand drive. It weighs 1,600 pounds and is powered by a 70-horsepower Model B four built to H&H Model A Super Touring specifications. The blueprinted Super Touring four has a custom long-block, H-beam rods, counterweighted crank, 1.75-inch intake and 1.60-inch exhaust valves, milled 5.5-to-1 Snyder head, and H&H cam. It functions well both on the road or track.

According to Mueller, "I converted to left-hand drive and installed a Mitchell overdrive for a 26 percent reduction in rpm at cruising speeds. I plan on racing at the Rossfeldrennen in Germany and will participate in qualifying for the 2015 Mille Miglia (Brescia-Rome-Brescia). It's only a four, but it runs like a V-8."

Both then and today, Ford Model T and A speedsters continue to deliver more bang for the buck than any other cars on the track. They have proven to be timeless and affordable, just like the originals.

$45 BUYS THIS SNAPPY SPEEDSTER

Just the graceful, racy sport car you want and you save big freight rates and one-half original cost through buying it knocked-down.

All parts cut to exact fit and accompanied by such complete, simple instructions that anyone can assemble it.

Complete with hood, Fiat radiator shell, instrument board, upholstering, metal and wood parts, bolts, screws, etc.

Car owners and dealers: Send today for complete details.

CENTRAL AUTO SUPPLY CO.
Eng. Dept. 123, Louisville, Ky.

PACO SPEEDSTER BODY FOR FORD CARS

The highest quality of material and workmanship, coupled with years of experience in building and designing racing bodies, have made the Paco Racing Body for Fords popular with drivers who want the snappiest car on the road. Especially designed for hard usage. All possible details of equipment. Very quickly and easily installed.

A FEW GOOD FEATURES

Fits any Model T Ford. Full streamline, with long cowl and bullet rear end. Very comfortable seats. Removable upholstering. Extremely large carrying space in rear. Fifteen gallon gas tank.

Pressure pump and guage installed. Specially bent foot pedals. Cast iron wedges for dropping steering post. All wood work is of clear oak, reinforced with angle iron braces.

The above cuts show special equipment for track work.

The PACO gives the Ford all the class of the famous foreign racers.

Write for illustrated literature and prices.

PEORIA ACCESSORY COMPANY, Peoria, Illinois

Original advertisements for "speedster" bodies for Model T Fords, ranging from toylike featherweight racing bodies to more sophisticated conversions for road cars.

FLATHEADS FOREVER!

Until the advent of modern OHV V-8 engines in 1949, Ford's flathead V-8, introduced in 1932, was the enthusiast's engine of choice. It still is for traditional old-school hot rodders and competitors in prewar-class road racing.

As early as the 1930s, Ford was capitalizing on what would become known in the 1960s as "Win on Sunday, Sell on Monday" marketing. It all started with the 1932 Ford side-valve, flathead V-8, the first engine of its kind to be mass produced and available in popular-price vehicles. The 221-inch V-8 was rated at 65 horsepower at 3,400 rpm and, in 1933 and 1934, increased to 75 and 85 horsepower, respectively.

A major win at the 1933 National Road Race in Elgin, Illinois, established Ford as a feared competitor in road racing. Savvy dealers wasted no time bragging about Ford's win in local advertising. This drove customer traffic and V-8 model sales. Almost instantly, new V-8 Ford roadsters could be found, less mufflers and fenders, tearing up racetracks.

While modified Model T and Model A Fords gave birth to hot rodding in the 1920s, it was the flathead V-8 that took it to the next level in the 1930s. Displacing 221 cubic inches and weighing just 585 pounds, the first V-8 was only 20 percent larger than the Model A four yet produced 62 percent more power. It didn't take long for stripped-down Fords with modified V-8s to become the cars to beat at Southern California's dry lakes.

Racing engineer Henry Miller and partner Preston Tucker of Miller and Tucker Inc. had been trying for years to get Henry Ford's son, Edsel, to commit to racing programs. They finally succeeded in the early 1930s when Edsel signed off on building a team for the 1935 Indy 500. Miller and Tucker built ten front-wheel-drive Miller-Ford Specials, powered by flatheads, for the race. They were the first front-drive, four-wheel, independent suspension cars seen at Indy. Unfortunately, it was not a successful venture; none of the cars finished. Years later, in 1948, Preston Tucker would develop and build the highly advanced and controversial Tucker 48 sedan.

After World War II, hot-rodding, racing, and the speed equipment industry experienced incredible growth. As the dry lakes became less and less available for racing, the popularity of quarter-mile drags surged. It would not be until 1950 that the first organized track, Santa Ana Drag Strip, would open on a Southern California airfield. In 1951, Wally Parks, then editor of *Hot Rod* magazine and founder of the National Hot Rod Association, produced the first official NHRA race at the Los Angeles Fairgrounds in Pomona, California. The flathead also distinguished itself in NASCAR competition. Jim Roper, driving a Lincoln, won the first NASCAR race on June 19, 1949, at Charlotte Speedway.

Over the Ford flathead's more than two-decade lifecycle, V-8 engine displacement grew from 221 to 255 cubic inches and 65 to 112 horsepower.

One of the ten flathead-powered front-drive *Miller-Ford Special* open-wheel racers built for the 1935 Indy 500. Photo taken during practice, prior to paint and racing livery. *Ford Motor Company*

Teenager Fran Hernandez with the flathead-powered '32 Ford roadster that he built and raced at El Mirage in a photo taken in 1939. Years later, Fran would start his thirty-year career at Ford, most spent managing drag, Trans-Am, and NASCAR racing programs and the building of Boss 429 Mustangs. *Fran Hernandez Collection*

The 1935 *Miller-Ford Special*, chassis No. 5, has been restored and is owned and vintage raced by Tom Malloy. The engine is a modified four-carburetor, aluminum-head flathead. *Wesley Allison*

This is what a typical Southern California '32 Ford hot rod looked like back in the day. This one was photographed in 1962 at fifth-mile drags in Virginia Beach, Virginia, running 79.53 miles per hour in the 14s. Owned by Joe Montgomery, its power came from a 100-horsepower, 292-inch flathead with a single carb.

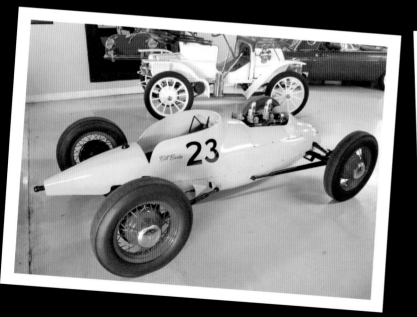

Bill Burke built the first "belly tank" race car in 1946, creating a new class now known as lakesters. He started with a $35 World War II surplus P-51 "drop tank," added a dual-carb flathead, and competed at El Mirage. With the original long gone, Burke oversaw the building of this "tribute" using original surplus parts and Flathead.

A beautifully detailed Ardun-Merc with four-carbs in a '32 Ford rod. The Ardun conversion, originally produced by Zora and Yura Arkus-Duntov for truck applications, turns a flathead into a higher-revving, more powerful OHV engine with Hemi combustion chambers. Output is increased more than 60 percent over stock.

In 1937, Ford introduced a smaller, lighter version, displacing 136 cubic inches and rated at 60 horsepower. It had first been produced in Europe in 1935 for use in small British, French, and German Fords.

In the late 1940s, Ford had a substantial contract to export garbage trucks to England, primarily for use in London. The problem was that the available flathead engines were grossly underpowered for the job, which put the contract in jeopardy. They brought in Zora Arkus-Duntov, an engineer with racing experience, to consult on the project. Working with his brother, Yura, they conceived a sophisticated OHV conversion for the 239-cubic-inch V-8 that would solve the typical overheating and hill climbing problems associated with heavily loaded trucks. With overhead valves, they could extend the flathead's usable rpm range and substantially increase horsepower and torque. Dubbed the Ardun (ARkus-DUNtov), the projected output was 160 horsepower at 3,600 rpm, peaking at 175 horsepower at 5,200 rpm. At 3,600 rpm, the flathead delivered only 100 horsepower. This increase in horsepower was just what Ford was looking for.

In 1947, the Ardun Mechanical Corporation, with an office in Manhattan and the shop in Queens, was primarily working on high-security military programs. Being a racer, Arkus-Duntov welcomed the Ford engine program. While the brothers conceived the OHV conversion concept, credit for the final design of the cast Alcoa 355-T6, heat-treated Ardun heads with hemi combustion chambers goes to a staff engineer, George Kudasch. His next project was designing OHV heads for Ford's V-8-60 used in midget race cars.

After Ardun supplied a couple of hundred kits to Ford, the carmaker decided they needed a larger displacement engine and opted to go with the 337-cubic-inch Lincoln in 1948. Since the extremely wide Ardun engine was too big to fit in passenger cars, the Ford project was over. There were a few hundred kits left in inventory; they ended up in hot rod and race shops and at Allard in England. Four years later, Arkus-Duntov went to work for General Motors, where he would later become internationally known and respected as the Godfather of the Corvette.

Ford's V-8-60 was embraced by dirt-track racers as well as builders of sports car specials. It was also very popular with imported sports car owners in search of alternative powerplants for both road and track. There was no shortage of speed equipment for the small V-8, including OHV conversion kits.

Legendary hot rodders and racers wasted little time developing speed equipment for the flathead. The list included cam-grinder Ed Iskenderian, aluminum intake manifold and head pioneer Vic Edelbrock, Ansen's Lou Senter, Bell Auto's Roy Richter, So-Cal Speed Shop's Alex Xydias, and speed merchants Barney Navarro and Meyer Kong, among others. Racing venues increased thanks to George Wight and George Riley; Muroc Racing Association (MRA); Lou Baney, Russetta Timing Association (RTA); Bill Burke, Southern California Timing Association (SCTA); Art Benjamin, Valley Timing Association (VTA); and, of course, NHRA's Wally Parks.

Bill Burke, in addition to his involvement with SCTA and Bonneville Speed Week, is best known as the originator of the belly-tank race car, a mainstay of land speed record racing on the Salt Flats. Now known as lakesters, the cigar-like cars were originally built with bodies crafted from war surplus aircraft drop tanks. Burke was the first to build one, using a $35 P-51 Mustang fuel tank and a flathead V-8. After one season racing at El Mirage in 1946, it was sold, never to be seen again. He built his next belly tanker in 1949, honored as "the World's Fastest Hot Rod" in the August issue of *Hot Rod*.

To re-create Burke's original race car, Geoff Hacker and Rick D'Louhy put together a team in Tampa, Florida, in 2008 headed by Ted Kempgens and Tom Bambard of Creative Motion Concepts. The mission was to use a period-correct

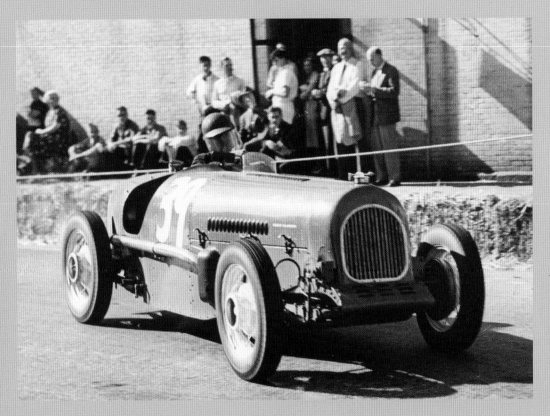

Miles Collier, at the bottom of the hill and turning right in his flathead-powered Riley *Ardent Alligator* onto the main drag to win the 1949 Watkins Glen Grand Prix. He beat some of the most prestigious marques—Ferrari, Bugatti, Delahaye, Mercedes-Benz 540K—to win the second annual GP. *Revs Institute for Automotive Research*

Collier turns right off the Watkins Glen main street and then left and up the Old Corning Hill. *Eric Davison*

surplus military drop tank and a vintage flathead. Ninety-year-old Bill Burke agreed to serve as project consultant to the team to ensure its authenticity. Burke's participation was critical as period parts and techniques authentic to the original build would be used. It was completed in 2009 and Burke's grandson drove it at Bonneville Speed Week, followed by a cross-country tour of shows and a six-month display at the NHRA Museum. It is currently at Sarasota, Florida's Classic Car Museum.

At the first SCTA-sanctioned Bonneville Speed Week in 1949, Dean Batchelor drove the Xydias and Batchelor So-Cal Speed Shop Special. It was powered by a single flathead V-8, running 193.54 miles per hour and setting an E/Streamliner record. Later driven by Bill Dailey, the streamliner averaged 208 miles per hour on the salt.

Powerful and versatile, flatheads excelled in a wide variety of racing activities in the 1930s through 1950s. One of the last places you would have expected to see a winning flathead was at the Watkins Glen Grand Prix in 1949. Those were the early days of American road racing, a hobby/sport dominated by wealthy men driving rather sophisticated sports and touring cars. Frank Griswold won the first race in 1948 in a brand-new Alfa Romeo 8C 2900B Touring Berlinetta.

Many participants started racing as members of the Automobile Racing Club of America (ARCA), the premier road racing sanctioning organization founded by Miles and Sam Collier in 1933. At the outbreak of World War II, ARCA was dissolved and replaced by the Sports Car Club of America (SCCA) in 1944.

Organized by Cameron Argetsinger, the father of Grand Prix (Formula One) racing in America, the length of the 1949 GP was doubled to 100 miles on a 6.6-mile course on public roads in and around the village of Watkins Glen. The starting grid in 1949 was a veritable who's who of sports car racing and exotic

marques. Briggs Cunningham entered three cars, one of which was a Ferrari V-12 166 Inter, a car seen racing in the United States only once before. There were a bunch of Bugattis, a Duesenberg J, George Weaver's Maserati, James Melton's Mercedes-Benz 540K, Dave Garroway's SS-100, and a few hot-rodded, Ford-powered Anglo-American race cars.

Briggs Cunningham was the odds-on favorite and, until the fourteenth lap, had a healthy lead on the field. The spoiler was the flathead-powered *Ardent Alligator*, a 1929 Riley Brooklands that was rebodied and repowered in 1939, owned and driven by Miles Collier. The modified Mercury V-8 was rated at

Zora Arkus-Duntov racing his Ardun-Allard at Watkins Glen, 1949. He successfully raced Allards in Europe and appointed Allard to handle distribution of his Ardun OHV conversion kit for the flathead after the Ford contract was over. *Harold Lance*

175 horsepower—more than three times the output of the Riley's original 55-horsepower four.

Miles Collier started in twelfth place and, by the thirteenth lap, had set a lap record at 5.39 minutes, lowering it again on the fourteenth lap by clocking a 5.24. And that was just for starters. He later freight-trained Cunningham's Ferrari, winning the GP with an eight-second lead. Miles Collier's hot-rodded No. 39 Riley-Mercury Special embarrassed some of the most prestigious names in racing. It broke the previous year's track record by nearly 7 miles per hour with an average speed of 75.38 miles per hour.

The *Ardent Alligator* has a long racing heritage that continues today. Owners Joanne and Pete McManus of Thornton, Pennsylvania, compete in historic racing events. And it's still powered by a flathead fitted with Edelbrock aluminum heads and three carburetors.

Ford's flathead lived on long after being replaced by the Y-block OHV V-8 in 1954. Today, you can buy new, much-improved aftermarket flathead blocks and heads as well as Ardun OHV conversions. There's no end in sight for Henry's first V-8.

An engine dynamometer cell at Edelbrock Equipment in 1950s, with the three-carb flathead used in Hernandez-Meeks '32 Ford roadster. Bobby Meeks, left, was Vic Edelbrock's top engine builder; Fran Hernandez, right, ran the machine shop from 1950 to 1956. *Fran Hernandez Collection*

The Start of Something Big!

It was the best of times when we saw overhead-valve V-8s, dual quads, and superchargers; it was the worst of times when we experienced the AMA racing ban. It was the prelude to Total Performance.

The 1950s ushered in an era of aggressive competition, both on the street and racetracks. Ford, Chrysler, and General Motors did whatever it took to lure buyers into showrooms. Detroit's competitive spirit during the mid- to late 1950s set the stage for some of the most exciting years in automotive performance history. Ford's weapon of choice was an all-new, short-stroke, overhead-valve Y-block V-8, first released in 1952 for Lincoln and then in 1954 by Ford and Mercury.

The overhead-valve V-8 was introduced in popular-priced 1954 Fords a full model year before Chevrolet revealed its vaunted small-block V-8. The 239-cubic-inch Y-block was rated at 130 horsepower. The midpriced Mercury received a 161-horsepower, 256-inch version. Weighing 610 to 630 pounds including accessories, Ford's Y-blocks represented a new generation of lighter, modern V-8 engines. The Y-block designation came from its deeply skirted block, giving it a "Y" profile.

It was the 160-horsepower, 317-cubic-inch Lincoln V-8 that gave Ford its first OHV engine bragging rights. Lincolns prepared by Bill Stroppe & Associates in Signal Hill, California, were winners of the grueling road race across Mexico,

Bill Stroppe–prepared Lincolns powered by Y-block V-8s won the Mexican Road Race (Carrera Panamericana), taking class wins in the 1952, 1953, and 1954 races. This Lincoln Capri is one of two that took firsts in 1954, the last year of the road race. *Ford Motor Company*

One of the many DePaolo-built '56 T-Birds that ran at Daytona Beach Speed Weeks on the sand in 1956 and 1957. Note the Moon discs, streamlined headlight covers, and small Plexi screen replacing the full windshield. *Ford Motor Company*

This radical single-seat *Battlebird* is the only survivor of two built for the 1957 Daytona Speed Week. Race-car conversion was executed by Jim Travers and Frank Coons (TRACO), under contract to Pete DePaolo. The lightweight T-Bird has aluminum body panels and fairings, magnesium wheels, and Halibrand aluminum quick-change and ran 200 miles per hour. *M. M. "Mike" Matune Jr.*

the Carrera Panamericana. First run in 1950, the race crowned a single winner. It was then expanded in 1952 to multiple classes: Sports Cars and Stock Cars with large and small-displacement engines. The nine-stage, six-day race over approximately 2,100 miles lasted just five years and was cancelled in 1955 for safety reasons.

In 1952, a Lincoln Capri driven by Chuck Stevenson won the race and he led a one-two-three Lincoln finish in 1953. Stroppe Lincolns took the first two spots in the last race in 1954, with Ray Crawford taking the gold. Stroppe also prepared and managed Mercurys in NASCAR-USAC competition. John Holman was on the Stroppe-Lincoln team and, in 1957 with Ralph Moody, created Holman & Moody. In 1965, Holman & Moody acquired Stroppe & Associates.

On January 17, 1953, in New York City, GM revealed a Concept Corvette sports car at its Motorama extravaganza, which triggered Ford, one month later, to start working on its Thunderbird. Unlike the six-cylinder Corvette with its unique fiberglass body, Ford's sporty two-seater reflected the styling cues and V-8 power of the future 1955 Ford Victoria. The T-Bird went from concept to prototype in just one year and was revealed at the 1954 Detroit Auto Show.

Whereas Chevrolet positioned the Corvette as a sports car with an optional 195-horsepower, 265-cubic-inch V-8, Ford tagged the T-Bird as a "personal luxury car" with a standard 292-cubic-inch Y-block V-8 rated at 193 or 198 horsepower, depending on transmission. In 1955, Ford sold more than sixteen thousand T-Birds while Chevrolet sold just seven hundred Corvettes.

In 1956 and 1957, Ford raised the T-Bird's performance profile with larger, more powerful engines. The 1956 T-Bird had a standard 292-inch engine and optional 312-inch single- and dual-quad engines (dealer installed) with up to 225 horsepower. For 1957, the T-Bird was available with the widest range of engine options in the industry. Beyond the standard 292, you could order from a menu of four 312 engines, from 245 to 300 horsepower. Included were a D-code, single four-barrel engine; two E-code dual four-barrel engines with different camshafts; and an F-code supercharged engine.

Working with DePaolo Engineering in 1956 and 1957, Ford fielded dozens of blueprinted-stock as well as heavily-modified new Fords and T-Birds for standing- and flying-mile competition at the Pure Oil Trials and Speed Weeks on the old Daytona Beach course. In 1957 alone, fifteen supercharged T-Birds (part of a hundred-car NASCAR homologation program) "ran on the sand" during Speed Weeks.

One of the most interesting cars in 1957 was a heavily modified No. 98 T-Bird, chassis C7FH170266. No. 98 was one of two single-seat Experimental Class race cars, dubbed *Battlebirds* by the media. One was Lincoln-powered, while No. 98 was fitted with a magneto-sparked, Hilborn fuel-injected, 400-plus-horsepower 312-inch engine. The *Battlebird* engines were relocated 6 inches rearward for better weight distribution and mated to Jaguar four-speed transmissions. Riding on Halibrand knock-off magnesium wheels shod with Firestone Super Sports, the lightweight *Battlebirds*, with Halibrand aluminum quick-change rears, were full-on race cars.

Credit for converting T-Birds into *Battlebirds* goes to legendary race-car engine builders and constructors Jim Travers and Frank Coons (TRACO), who were retained by DePaolo. The aluminum bodywork—doors, hood, trunk lid skins,

and streamlining fairings—was executed by famed body builder Dick Troutman (Troutman & Barnes) and Dwight Clayton.

Driven by Chuck Daigh and Marvin Panch at Daytona in 1957, the No. 98 *Battlebird* lost its engine while making a two-way flying-mile pass. A new engine was installed and Chuck Daigh ran 93.312 miles per hour in standing-mile competition, earning a third place. Danny Eames took a first in the Experimental Class standing mile, running 98.065 in a modified T-Bird. Marvin Panch entered the No. 98 *Battlebird* in a road race at a nearby airport, finishing second to Carroll Shelby's 4.9 Ferrari.

Ford sold the *Battlebirds* and other company-owned race cars in 1957. The Lincoln-engined car was destroyed in an accident, leaving No. 98, now in the 3Dog Garage collection, as the only survivor.

Between 1955 and 1957, Ford OHV V-8 displacement grew from 239 and 256 cubic inches in 1954, and 272 and 292 cubic inches in 1955. Ford increased displacement to 312 cubic inches in 1956. Also in 1956, Ford offered a dual-quad, 225-horsepower engine and a dealer-installed M-260 Performance Kit consisting of a hotter camshaft, new cylinder heads, and dual four-barrel carbs, upping horsepower to 260. Large displacement 368-inch Y-block engines were available for Lincoln in 1956 and in 1957 for Mercury.

Winning races proved to be key in the success of Ford's new V-8-engined cars. In NASCAR's 1956 Grand National Series, run on dirt and paved tracks as well as road courses, Fords (including five Mercurys) won nineteen races. Fords racing at the Bonneville Salt Flats also delivered impressive performances. Texan Karol Miller, a popular Gas Coupe/Sedan racer at Bonneville Speed Week, was clocked in his new street-driven 1956 Ford Victoria at 153 miles per hour, averaging 150 miles per hour in C/Gas Sedan. It was powered by a 302-cubic-inch Y-block with

Pete DePaolo with one of the two '67 Fairlanes DePaolo Engineering built for Ford that set 458 USAC and FIA speed and endurance records at the Bonneville Salt Flats in September 1956.
Fran Hernandez Collection

Stroppe Mercurys won the 1956 and 1957 USAC races at Paramount Ranch in Agoura, California: Sam Hanks in 1956 and Troy Ruttman in 1957. This shot is from 1956, on the track that was seen in the 1957 film *The Devil's Hairpin*, which was open for sports car and stock car racing both years. *Fran Hernandez Collection*

dual four-barrel carburetors. He drove the same car, retrofitted with a Latham-supercharged 259-inch engine, to Bonneville in 1958, clocking 153.32 miles per hour, and then to Florida to run at Daytona Beach.

In 1957, Ford offered high-output engines in passenger cars as well as T-Birds. You could order the hottest dual-quad and supercharged 312-inch engines with three-speed manual (with or without overdrive) or Ford-O-Matic transmissions in *any* model, from base two-door sedan and station wagon to T-Bird! The lineup consisted of a single four-barrel 312/245, dual-quad 312/270, and a Paxton-McCulloch supercharged 312/300. Law enforcement agencies favored Police Interceptor two-door sedans with E-code 270-horsepower engines. A 300-horsepower F-code T-Bird could accelerate to 60 miles per hour in the 6-second range with a top speed of 125 miles per hour.

Supercharging was Ford's answer to Chevrolet's fuel injection in 1957. Chevrolet was racking up wins in NASCAR and USAC until Ford countered with supercharged 312 engines with six-plus pounds of boost and horsepower ratings in excess of 340. Prior to 1957 when NASCAR's Bill France banned supercharging, multiple carburetion, and fuel-injection, Ford's racing accomplishments were spectacular, with twenty-seven Grand National wins plus twelve USAC firsts. Top Ford drivers included Tim Flock, Fireball Roberts, Curtis Turner, Joe Weatherly, and Glen Wood.

In addition to drag and stock car racing, Ford's participation in competitive events in 1957 was broad-based and countrywide. DePaolo Engineering, Ford's captive race shop, prepped sedans and T-Birds that raced at Bonneville, set flying- and standing-mile records on the sand at Daytona Beach, and built the Ford that averaged 117 miles per hour for twenty-two days in the Stephen Trophy Trials at Indianapolis Motor Speedway.

Ford was aware that, while winning races unquestionably helps sell cars, setting durability/reliability records would give dealers even more to brag about. In 1956, Ford signed off on a program to build "stock" 1957 Fords to run at Bonneville for USAC and FIA National and International records.

Pete DePaolo built two Fairlane 500s powered by blueprinted, stock-spec, 270-horsepower dual four-barrel engines. In September 1956, the 1957 Fairlane 500s, driven by Johnny Mantz, Chuck Stevenson, and Jerry Unser Jr.,

averaged 130.94 miles per hour for 100 hours, 120.62 miles per hour for 24 hours, 109.39 miles per hour for fourteen days, and 108.16 miles per hour for 50,000 miles. On September 28, 1956, USAC and FIA officials certified that Fairlanes set an incredible 458 records! One car set an International Class B speed record at 106.55 miles per hour over fourteen days and 35,800.30 miles; the other set a National Class B speed record at 107.09 miles per hour over twenty days and 51,403.99 miles, along with six American Class B Closed Car Standing-Start speed records.

Ford celebrated by having its advertising agency, J. Walter Thompson, create a three-page advertorial hyping the record-setting event as "The Longest Left Turn in History." It was placed in a variety of mass audience publications, including the October 29, 1956, issue of *Life* magazine.

Just about all brands had been involved in racing, and cars were getting quicker and faster each year. Pressured by dealers to advertise wins and performance options to increase showroom traffic, carmakers responded with print and electronic advertising that supported racing. However, in the mid-1950s, the Automobile Manufacturers Association voiced disapproval, focusing on liabilities of racing and potential Congressional interference.

Driving AMA fears were two fatal accidents at major tracks in 1955. First was Bill Vukovich's death at the Indy 500, followed by Pierre Levegh's catastrophic crash at Le Mans. A Mercedes-Benz 300SLR driven by Levegh exploded on impact at 125 miles per hour. It careened into the crowd, killing eighty-three spectators and injuring dozens more. GM President Harlow Curtis was the first to champion the proposed ban.

In 1957, the AMA banned direct factory participation in organized racing and motorsports while encouraging carmakers to play down performance and racing and play up safety in advertising and marketing. All members initially observed the ban, but it turned out to be a short-lived victory for the trade association. Not long after agreeing to the ban and closing their front doors to racers and racing, carmakers' back doors started opening up!

Ford divested itself of race cars as well as the contents of DePaolo Engineering. DePaolo was not interested in continuing without a Ford contract. John Holman and Ralph Moody purchased the inventory, including the *Battlebirds*. It was the end of one era and start of a new one.

CHAPTER 2

1961

FORD BUILDS A SHOWROOM SUPERCAR!

Ford's back on track—the street, the drag strips, and the high-speed ovals—with a slick, new Galaxie Starliner and the most powerful big-block yet. It's a full frontal assault.

By 1961, Henry Ford II was coming under pressure internally as well as from dealers to pull out of the restrictive 1957 Automobile Manufacturers Association's racing ban. Most of Ford's racing activities, like those at Chrysler and General Motors, were being run out of Dearborn's back door, and successes on the racetrack were not being used to bolster new car sales. That would change in June of 1962 when Henry Ford announced that he was no longer supporting what had come to be a "wink-wink" ban.

However, high-performance powertrain development and racing support were alive and well at Ford in 1961. A champion of the cause was Dave Evans, who headed up covert racing efforts and worked with engineers Charlie Gray, John Cowley, Don Sullivan, and Don Wahrman. They interfaced with NASCAR/USAC teams, drag racers, and dealers who supported racing.

New for 1961 was a stunning Starliner fastback coupe that could be ordered with an optional $109 performance package. This included an FE-series big-block engine displacing 390 cubic inches and rated at 375 horsepower at 6,000 rpm. With single four-barrel carburetion, high-compression, solid lifters, and three-speed stick, it delivered outstanding performance. Four-speed transmissions came later in the model year and were often dealer-installed on earlier cars along with factory tri-power induction.

Tri-power packages were available at Ford dealers for $260 plus installation. This addition of three Holley two-barrel carburetors could increase quarter-mile speeds by 3 to 4 miles per hour and lower elapsed times by up to .05 second, with horsepower increasing to 401 at 6,000 rpm.

Ford offered the same performance options on base-model, two- and four-door Fairlane and Galaxie sedans, which traded the Starliner's slippery aerodynamics for an inconspicuous boxy look. Stock-car racers ordered Starliner coupes for obvious reasons but, surprisingly, the general public never warmed up to its thin, roof-pillar fastback styling. In 1961, sales of the traditional Galaxie Victoria coupes hit 75,437 units, while Starliner sales languished at under 30,000. The Starliner was not back in the lineup in 1962, causing grief for NASCAR and USAC racers who relied on its aerodynamic benefits for the superspeedways.

Nick Smith owns this beautifully restored Starliner coupe with 390/375 power, three-speed stick with overdrive, and dog-dish hubcaps. Donald Allen restored it. *Factory Lightweight Collection*

Ford was determined that the high-performance 390 engine would be ordered *only* by serious enthusiasts. You could not get the 390/375 engine in a station wagon or with automatic transmission, power steering, or power brakes. What you *did* get was heavy-duty everything: larger brakes, special driveshaft, stout rear end, beefy suspension, and a wide choice of final drive ratios.

All HP 390 engines came with special blocks with beefed lower ends; larger oiling passages; magnafluxed cranks, pistons, and rods; and high-rpm valvetrains. Heads were factory machined for 10.6 to 11.0:1 compression. Stock exhaust manifolds were cast iron, tuned like custom tube headers and similar to those used on the 300-horsepower 352 Special engines that Ford released for racing in 1960. Dealers with a high-performance customer base stocked rear end gear sets ranging from 3.10 to 5.83:1, tri-power manifolds, Holley carburetors, and Borg-Warner four-speeds.

There was one special-order 390 four-barrel engine that did not appear in the salesman's customer order book. It was called the 330-horsepower

While 1961 models were being manufactured, Ford was still building 352 Special engines rated at 300 horsepower for racers. With its high-flow exhaust manifolds, high-compression, solid lifters and HD blocks, it influenced the engineering of the 390/375 engine for 1961. *Ford Motor Company*

Interceptor and, like the 375-horsepower engine, had the "good" block, solid-lifter valvetrain, high-lift camshaft, and header-style exhaust manifolds. You could even order it with automatic transmission in any style body, including station wagon, and ordering was restricted to law enforcement agencies

Midyear, Ford announced factory installation of four-speed transmissions and received NHRA-approval for running in A/Stock and Super/Stock classes at the

1961 NHRA Nationals in Indianapolis over the Labor Day weekend. Prepared NHRA S/S 401-horsepower Starliners consistently ran trap speeds of 103 to 105 miles per hour in the mid-13s.

Ford test driver Len Richter was very competitive with a 1961 Galaxie two-door, base-model 302 sedan fitted with a dealer-installed Borg-Warner T-10 four-speed. He ordered his car with radio delete and light rubber mats in place of carpeting.

While Richter preferred the "plain pipe rack" sedan, popular drag racers like Phil Bonner, Dick Brannan, Les Ritchey, and others with dealership-sponsor contracts went the high-profile Starliner route. John Vermeersch and Bill Pearson campaigned an A/Stock Starliner well into the 1962 season.

Starliners made a great showing on the NASCAR and USAC high-speed ovals and the Daytona Beach Speed Trials. Jim Rathman successfully raced a Zecol-Lubaid-sponsored No. 43 Starliner. Zecol-Lubaid Racing Team's Don White, in a stock 375-horsepower Starliner passenger car with a blueprinted engine and roll bar prepped for running top end, clocked 159.32 miles per hour to set a new flying-mile record.

Ford's official representation in stock car racing was Holman & Moody, owned by John Holman and Ralph Moody. They had bought out the old DePaolo Engineering operation that fronted for Ford from 1955 to the signing of the 1957 AMA ban. Fred Lorenzen, running a Holman & Moody Ford, won Martinsville on April 19, Darlington on May 6, and Atlanta on July 9. Fords won seven Grand National races in 1961, including three of the eight superspeedway events. Holman & Moody was also building engines for the Woods Brothers No. 21 car and grinding camshafts for many other teams.

Ford was well on its way to cementing its reputation as a winner on high-speed ovals and quarter-mile drag strips, and in the marketing of high-performance passenger cars. Bragging about it had to wait until 1962 when Henry Ford announced that Ford would no longer abide by the AMA ban.

This sedan still has its column-mounted Sun tach, original floor shifter for the dealer-installed four-speed, light rubber mats in place of carpeting, radio delete, and bench seat. *Factory Lightweight Collection*

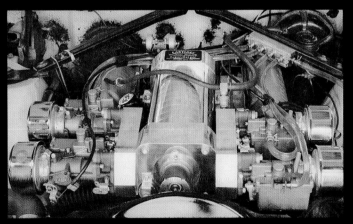

After Latham Manufacturing's successful years of supercharging Fords and Thunderbirds at Daytona Speed Week (1956–1959), its Axial-Flow superchargers with four side-draft carburetors became very popular with owners of FE-engined Fords. This is a typical setup on a 1961 Thunderbird installed by a Ford dealer. It cost well under $1,000 installed.

CHAPTER 3

1962

A Year of Change!

More displacement, more horsepower, more racing, and a sports car called Mustang I confirmed that the only constant at Ford in 1962 was change.

Henry Ford was fed up with the ineffective AMA racing ban and had no qualms letting the public know about it: "The AMA ban on auto racing is null and void within Ford Motor Company in 1962." On June 11, 1962, Ford's board chairman—who, ironically, was president of the AMA—sent a letter to the trade association stating, "The [racing ban] resolution adopted in the past by the AMA no longer has either purpose or effect. Accordingly, we are withdrawing from it."

Ford, like Chrysler and General Motors, had signed the original AMA agreement but never really stopped developing high-performance engines and heavy-duty chassis and drivetrain components. Much of this equipment had been cataloged for police, fleet, and export applications. Now they were ready to come out of the closet to go racing and advertise high-performance options and accomplishments

The new 406-cubic-inch engine came in two flavors: 385 horsepower with a single four-barrel and 405 horsepower with tri-power. With 11.4:1 compression, these engines generated tree-stump-pulling torque: 444 pounds-feet at 3,400 rpm with a single carb and 448 pounds-feet at 3,500 rpm with tri-power. Both 406 engines featured special heavy-duty blocks, .500-inch lift camshafts, 1.76:1 ratio rocker arms, and dual-point ignition.

When you ordered a full-size 406 Galaxie, the engine was part of a bumper-to-bumper, heavy-duty package. Standard equipment included a Borg-Warner four-speed, four-pinion differential with no-cost options up to 4.11:1 gears, large wheel bearing rear axles, oversize fuel lines, 15-inch wheels, police brakes, heavy-duty radiator, and special springs and shocks. Tuned cast-iron headers with low-restriction dual mufflers were great for the street and marginal—compared with tube headers—for track use.

Ford confirmed its commitment to drag racing in 1962 by giving the Experimental Vehicles Garage (X-Garage) at the Dearborn Proving Grounds the go-ahead to develop lightweight Galaxies specifically for the 1962 NHRA Nationals. At the same time, Ford hired Dick Brannan, a drag racing salesman

The engine in the Alderman Lightweight is a 406 Thunderbird (though not available in a Thunderbird) fitted with dual Holleys, original air cleaner, and "tin" valve covers. *Factory Lightweight Collection*

at Romy-Hammes Ford in South Bend, Indiana, to work on the 406 lightweight project. Brannan had just cleaned house at a big Super/Stock race over the weekend at Detroit Dragway in his 405-horsepower 1962 Galaxie.

"The track was packed with top competitors, including two Ford test drivers, Bill Humphrey and Len Richter, in factory cars," said Brannan. "In the final eliminations, I beat Dave Strickler in his 'Old Reliable' 409 Chevy to take the

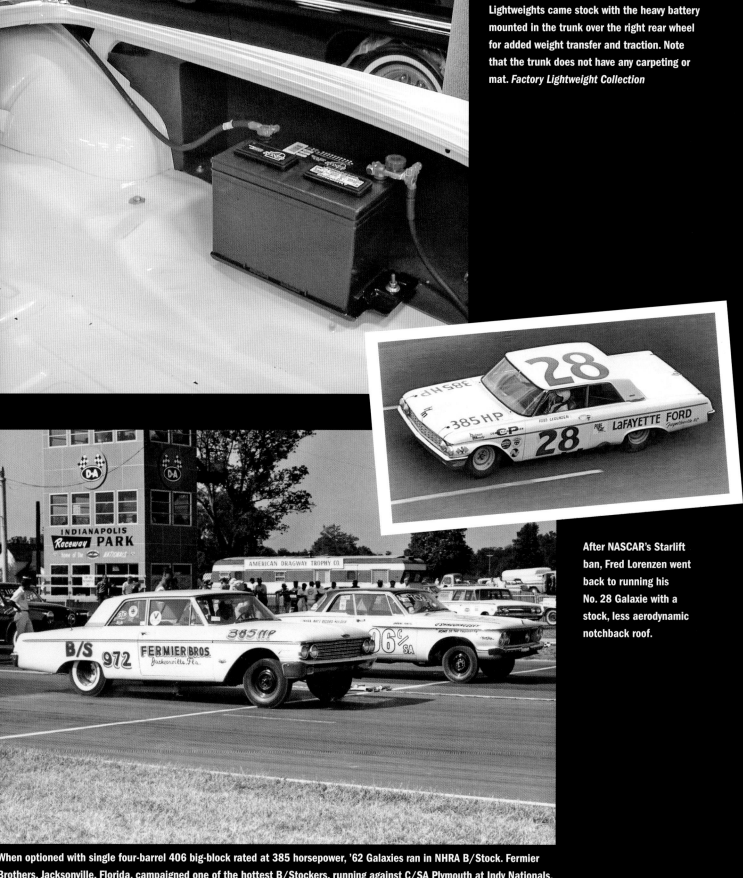

Lightweights came stock with the heavy battery mounted in the trunk over the right rear wheel for added weight transfer and traction. Note that the trunk does not have any carpeting or mat. *Factory Lightweight Collection*

After NASCAR's Starlift ban, Fred Lorenzen went back to running his No. 28 Galaxie with a stock, less aerodynamic notchback roof.

When optioned with single four-barrel 406 big-block rated at 385 horsepower, '62 Galaxies ran in NHRA B/Stock. Fermier Brothers, Jacksonville, Florida, campaigned one of the hottest B/Stockers, running against C/SA Plymouth at Indy Nationals.

Dick Brannan, right, with Jerry Hammes and two Romy-Hammes sponsored '62 Fords with 406 engines. One car was for Super/Stock, the other for Factory Experimental. *Dick Brannan*

Super/Stock win. The track had never seen a Ford win Super/Stock before and track owner Gil Cohn was so sure we were cheating that he offered us double the win money if our car was found legal. It was—and he did!"

Brannan added, "The following Wednesday I received a call from Dave Evans, a manager in Ford's Special Vehicles Department, inviting me to Dearborn to learn more about their drag racing plans. He later offered me a position in his group. My first assignment was working in Engineering Building One on the 406 Galaxie lightweights that went on to beat the Chrysler and GM factory cars."

Tasca Ford campaigned a new midsize Fairlane, *Challenger II*, in 1962, powered by a 406 engine that was not available in the car. The biggest engine Fairlane came with was the new 221-inch small-block, forcing Tasca to run in A/Factory Experimental. *Tasca Family Archives*

Brannan had majored in engineering and business in college, and was a Ford employee from 1962 to 1969. He was then rehired as a consultant until 1972, when all factory-sponsored racing activities came to an end. Over the years, he worked on NASCAR/USAC stock car, drag, GT40 Le Mans, and Indy racing programs. He also served as captain of Ford's Drag Racing Team and competed in everything from lightweight Super/Stock Galaxies and Thunderbolts to A/FX Mustangs. In July 1963, Brannan set the NHRA National E.T. record at 12.42 seconds in the first 1963½ 427 lightweight Galaxie, which had been hand-built in in the X-Garage.

In 1962, Dearborn Steel Tubing built approximately a dozen 406 Galaxie lightweights for high-profile Ford dealers, including Jerry Alderman Ford and Ed Martin Ford, and drivers like Tasca Ford's Bill Lawton, Len Richter, Dick Brannan, Phil "Daddy Warbucks" Bonner, Les Ritchey, Gas Ronda, Mickey Thompson, and others. The conversion from stock to lightweight netted an approximate 4 percent weight reduction, with special parts created to fit both sedans (C2AZ-6200012-A) and convertibles (C2AZ-7600012-A). By mid-1962, Ford released a new, beefier 406-inch FE engine block with cross-bolted mains.

Vehicles tagged for lightweight conversions were ordered as six-cylinder models without radio, heater, clock, or carpeting. Proprietary parts included fiberglass front fenders, hood, deck lid, and doors, along with aluminum bumpers and inner fender panels, Lincoln aluminum brake drums, and "thin" side glass. Not all lightweights received all the special parts and some were built expressly for A/FX competition running 406 engines fitted with dual Holley quads instead of tri-power. The majority of the originals were rebodied in 1963.

In early June 1962, famed sports car constructors Troutman and Barnes in Culver City, California, received body molds from Ford for an experimental sports car—the Mustang I. Known internally as Project W-301, the Mustang I was a concept for a serious sports car. Championed by Ford general manager Lee Iacocca and styling chief Gene Bordinat, the Mustang I was conceived to give Ford a sporty, hip image while also testing the waters for a future sports car. It

The radical Mustang I Experimental Sports Car, with body by Troutman & Barnes and a 109-horsepower German Ford V-4, was built in just a few months and shown to the public with Dan Gurney driving at the US Grand Prix, Watkins Glen. *Ford Motor Company*

did everything it was supposed to do and, more importantly, Mustang I laid the groundwork for what would become the game-changing GT40.

Troutman and Barnes created the Mustang I's tubular steel space frame, stressed aluminum body, and full-length belly pan per specifications supplied by Ford Design and lead engineer Roy Lunn.

With its aerodynamic body and full belly pan, the Mustang I benefitted from extensive wind-tunnel time and Computer Aided Design (CAD), a first at Ford. Its belly pan eliminated wind resistance typically caused by crossmembers, springs, steering components, and suspension brackets. Four adjustable coil-

over-spring shocks finished off the four-wheel fully independent suspension. Chassis rigidity was further enhanced by a built-in roll bar and fixed-mount bucket seats. An adjustable steering column and pedals with 4 inches of travel insured a comfortable driving position.

One of Lunn's goals was to set the standard for a 1.5-liter sports car that could be raced in SCCA and FIA events. He chose the compact German Ford Taunus 12M, 60-degree V-4, midship mounted with a four-speed transaxle. Ford Engineering built two 11:1 compression, 91-cubic-inch engines, one with a single carburetor for the road, rated at 89 horsepower at 6,500 rpm, and a

This stunning, aerodynamic stressed-aluminum body with full belly pan-mounts to tubular steel chassis was developed in the wind tunnel using Ford's first application of computer-aided design. The GT40's Roy Lunn was lead engineer. *Ford Motor Company*

track version with a pair of Weber two-barrel carbs, rated at 109 horsepower at 6,500. At 1,544 pounds, the track-engined Mustang I could sprint from 0 to 60 miles per hour in under 10 seconds with a top speed in excess of 100 miles per hour.

Constructed in approximately one hundred days, the Mustang I debuted on October 7, 1962, at the United States Grand Prix at Watkins Glen. Dan Gurney hot-shoed the Mustang I around the track and spectators went wild. Ford followed with successful reveals at Laguna Seca and Daytona, then in Europe.

Ford's streamlined two-door 1961 Starliner was not only beautiful, it was also incredibly successful in NASCAR/USAC competition. Its aerodynamic qualities proved unbeatable on superspeedways. Unfortunately, it was not popular where it counted—in dealer showrooms. The public was not impressed and Ford reluctantly restyled the 1962 Galaxie with a traditional notchback roofline. That did not sit well with Holman & Moody and other racing teams. They had lost their aerodynamic advantage!

Dearborn came up with a streamlining solution to the notchback roofline, albeit a very short-lived one. It was a detachable hardtop called "Starlift" and could be used to convert a 1962 Ford convertible into a Starliner-like coupe. Holman & Moody produced a handful of Starlift conversion kits and

Ford gave the kit a part number for their parts catalog. H&M built only three Starlift convertibles.

Fred Lorenzen won the Atlanta 500 on June 10, 1962, averaging 101.98 miles per hour in H&M's No. 28 Starlift Galaxie. Bill France was not happy and NASCAR pulled the plug on the controversial Starlift hardtop. In 1962, Fords won ten races and Mercury one on the USAC circuit, while there were just six wins in NASCAR's Grand National division.

Two of the three H&M Starlift convertibles were parted out, while the third was returned to Ford where it was repowered with a bored and stroked 483-inch, 11.8:1 compression big-block that generated 455 horsepower and 600 pounds-feet of torque at 4,000 rpm. Fitted with a unique crankshaft with hollow rod throws, it was used for severe-duty testing of new lubricating techniques and low-end durability.

Working with Holman & Moody and Fred Lorenzen, in October 1962 Ford took the 483-inch No. 28 Starlift convertible to Bonneville to run for USAC Class B and Unlimited Class records. Lorenzen set forty-six national and international USAC and FIA records in the same car that he had driven to victory in the Atlanta 500. After a setback in NASCAR, Ford now had a lot to brag about—and they did!

Ed Martin Ford was a major sponsor of Fords in NHRA and AHRA competition. This shot of their E/Stock Automatic Thunderbird, powered by a 390 big-block, was taken at the NHRA Nationals.

The Wood Brothers pit crew in action, servicing Marvin Panch's 385-horsepower No. 21 NASCAR '62 Galaxie. The engine was a single four-barrel 406. *Fran Hernandez Collection*

SHELBY COBRA: THE YEAR OF THE SNAKE!

It was an engine swap that would turn a quintessential British sports car into an icon and Carroll Shelby into a legend.

When it came to sports car racing, Carroll Shelby was a late bloomer. He had drag raced a 1932 Ford while growing up in Dallas, Texas, but it wasn't until 1952, at age twenty-nine, that he raced his first sports car—a borrowed MG-TC—in Norman, Oklahoma. Shelby won that race and, between 1952 and 1960 when he retired due to a serious heart condition, he accomplished what few amateur or professional racers achieve in a multidecade lifetime of competition.

Over a period of nine years on the SCCA circuit, Shelby distinguished himself, primarily driving sports cars owned by sponsors and friends. In August 1954, Shelby was on the team that set seventy international Class D land speed records in two Austin-Healeys (stock-body and streamliner) on the Bonneville Salt Flats. He was the SCCA National Champion in 1956–1957, and was named Sports Car Driver of the Year by *Sports Illustrated* in 1956 and 1957. In 1958. the *New York Times* named him Sports Car Driver of the Year.

Shelby was equally successful racing in Europe and in 1958 was hired as a team driver by John Wyer, Aston Martin Racing manager. In his first race at Aintree in the United Kingdom, Shelby placed second, then climaxed his European career by teaming with Roy Salvadori in 1959 to win the 24 Hours of Le Mans in an Aston Martin DBR1.

During 1960, Shelby gradually withdrew from racing activities and spent more time with his newly acquired Goodyear racing tire distributorship and his Carroll Shelby School of High-Performance Driving, along with pursuing his dream of building an American-engined sports car. The tire operation was located in a small section of Dean Moon's speed emporium in Santa Fe Springs, California, where the prototype Shelby Cobra, CSX2000, would be built. Shelby's driving school was based at Riverside Raceway with Shelby American employee Peter Brock producing (with Ken Miles) the school's curriculum.

Shelby's dream to build a sports car with an American powerplant was paramount in his plans to move forward. While racing for Aston Martin, Shelby

Decades after Shelby Cobra production ended, owners of small- and big-block Cobras, street and race variants, are still racing and enjoying Cobras at major vintage racing venues like the Laguna Seca Historics.
M. M. "Mike" Matune Jr.

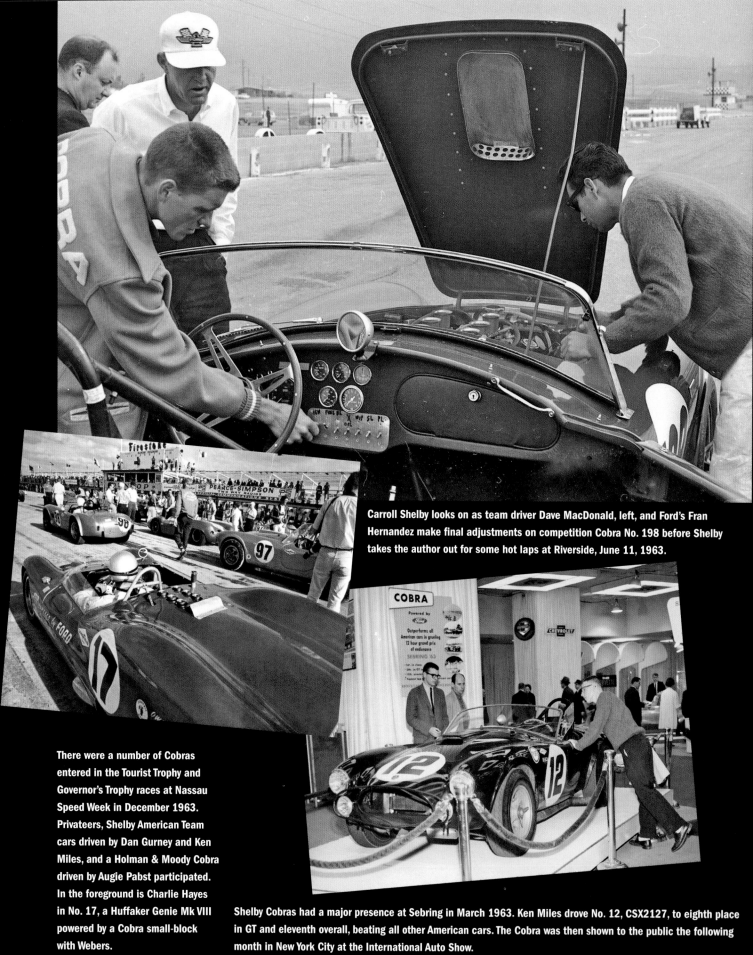

Carroll Shelby looks on as team driver Dave MacDonald, left, and Ford's Fran Hernandez make final adjustments on competition Cobra No. 198 before Shelby takes the author out for some hot laps at Riverside, June 11, 1963.

There were a number of Cobras entered in the Tourist Trophy and Governor's Trophy races at Nassau Speed Week in December 1963. Privateers, Shelby American Team cars driven by Dan Gurney and Ken Miles, and a Holman & Moody Cobra driven by Augie Pabst participated. In the foreground is Charlie Hayes in No. 17, a Huffaker Genie Mk VIII powered by a Cobra small-block with Webers.

Shelby Cobras had a major presence at Sebring in March 1963. Ken Miles drove No. 12, CSX2127, to eighth place in GT and eleventh overall, beating all other American cars. The Cobra was then shown to the public the following month in New York City at the International Auto Show.

CSX3002, the first 427 big-block Cobra built, is shown here at Shelby American in Venice, California, prior to finishing and paint. *Ford Motor Company*

became familiar with the AC Ace, a popular British sports car powered by a 2-liter straight six. AC was buying prewar, BMW-patent OHC six engines from Bristol, but they were switching to Chrysler engines and stopping production of the old six. AC began acquiring 2.6-liter straight-six engines from Ford of Britain, as used in its Zephyr. While the Zephyr engine, with optional Ruddspeed three-carb intake and twelve-port head, generated up to 170 horsepower, only thirty-seven Ford six-powered Aces were sold.

In 1961 when Carroll Shelby first approached Derek Hurlock, president of AC Cars, about building an American V-8-engined sports car, he had neither the funds needed for the project nor access to an engine. All he had was a dream.

While Ford did not have a proven high-performance, small-displacement V-8 in 1961, they were in the process of developing a compact and lightweight 221-cubic-inch V-8 with a thin wall-cast block for the Fairlane. Shelby contacted Dave Evans at Ford in mid-1961, proposing that a Ford engine be used in his sports car. Evans was receptive and forwarded Shelby's pitch to his boss. It eventually made its way to Lee Iacocca, Ford Motor Company vice president and general manager of Ford Division. Iacocca embraced the idea of a Ford-powered, two-seat sports car, later meeting with Shelby to start what would become a lifelong relationship.

When Ford agreed to supply engines and, equally important, funds to start the venture, Shelby had what he needed. Evans agreed to ship two 221-inch engines to Shelby in late 1961. One complete engine with four-speed transmission was forwarded to AC Cars for installation in the prototype Cobra. Ford's 221-inch engine would grow to 260 cubic inches for the 1963 model year and 289 cubic inches in mid-1963.

Built at AC Cars with input from Carroll Shelby, the prototype CSX2000 Cobra went through a number of engineering changes after three months of road and track testing. As part of the transformation from AC Ace to Cobra, the prototype was fitted with a limited-slip Salisbury rear with inboard disc brakes; beefier chassis, front spindles, bearings, and A-arms; and lengthened leaf springs. It was airfreighted to Los Angeles in late February 1962—minus paint, engine, and transmission— and then trucked to Shelby American in Santa Fe Springs.

By the time the prototype arrived, Ford had increased the Fairlane small-block's displacement to 260 cubic inches so a very early production 260 engine (#XHP-260-1) was shipped to Shelby for the first Cobra. Fitted with a single four-barrel carburetor, 9.2:1 compression pistons, and a solid-lifter cam and valvetrain, it was rated at 260 horsepower.

Shelby American was incorporated in March 1962 and, later in the year, moved to a facility in Venice, California. In March 1965, Shelby American moved into an incredible 96,000-square-foot property on 12.5 acres adjacent to the Los Angeles airport. Shelby's new two-building facility housed Cobra and GT350 Mustang manufacturing, race car and engine assembly, painting, and a dynamometer cell. In just three short years, Carroll Shelby made a quantum leap from a small space in a friend's shop to a facility capable of building hundreds of vehicles a month!

On April 21 to 29, 1962, Shelby introduced his first and, at the time, only Cobra, painted Pearl Yellow by California customizer Dean Jeffries, at the sixth annual International Automobile Show at the New York City Coliseum. Owned by Carroll Shelby since new, CSX2000 is currently on display in the Shelby Museum in Las Vegas, Nevada. It's still powered by its original four-barrel,

260-cubic-inch engine and, except for a variety of paint jobs over the years, is pretty much in "survivor" condition.

It would be hard to find an automotive journalist or magazine editor working during the 1960s who didn't have a favorite Carroll Shelby story—and I'm no exception. From June 10 to 12, 1963, I attended the 1964 Ford Technical Press Conference at Riverside Raceway. The host hotel was the Mission Inn. Both it and the racetrack are long gone. The night before the first track day, a few of us were invited to Carroll's suite for after-dinner drinks. Both he and the party were going strong when I left around 1:00 a.m. The next morning I found out that the party had wrapped up just a couple of hours ago!

I headed to the track and at 8:00 a.m. was queued up to experience the Cobra in real life. My driver? Carroll Shelby! He couldn't have had more than a couple of hours sleep. They strapped me in, we exchanged pleasantries, and my knuckles were starting to turn white as we roared into the first corner.

It remains one of my most exhilarating rides in a race car—pure adrenaline. Riverside was his home track; he knew the line and could've probably driven it blindfolded! He joked with me as he flawlessly straightened corners, keeping the Weber-carbed 289 screaming at just a tick under redline. We pulled into the pits and all I wanted to do was go back for another lap!

From February 1962 to December 1966, Shelby American produced Ford small- and big-block Cobras using two chassis and body configurations. Between February 1962 and October 1964, total production of narrow-body Cobras with modified original AC Ace chassis totaled 655. The first seventy-five Cobras—sixty-two street models, four factory team race cars,

The most desirable street 427 Cobra is the rare S/C, or Semi-Competition, which could be street-driven and raced. CSX3042, owned by Steve Juliano, represents exactly what you may have seen if you had shopped for an S/C at a Shelby dealership in 1965 or 1966. It came stock with rear fender flares, front oil cooler scoop, side exhausts, Le Mans gas filler, roll bar, hood scoop, differential cooler, Halibrand mags, and a Rebat battery mounted behind the passenger's seat. Most had medium-riser dual-quad 427 engines, although some were shipped with single-quad versions. *Steve Juliano*

During big-block production, Shelby American produced twenty-five full Competition Cobras (including two prototypes) powered by 480-horsepower, medium-riser 427 engines with 12.4 compression ratio. They came standard with all the S/C 427 features plus suspension upgrades, a 13-quart oil sump, tuned headers, front and rear sway bars, racing seats, and a windscreen. CSX3017 was originally sold by Shelby to Ford of Canada. Then it went to Comstock Racing Team. *Miller Motorsports Park/Jeremy Henrie*

one Dragonsnake, seven privateer competition cars, and one special factory-prepared race car—were powered by the single four-barrel 260-cubic-inch engine. By the time some of the race cars hit the track, engines had been swapped out for 289s.

Of the 580 Cobras powered by 271-horsepower 289 High Performance engines, 453 were street models, 6 were Daytona Coupes, and 1 was a bare chassis. The balance were competition cars, including 4 Dragonsnakes. The total production number for small-block Cobras also includes 61 COB/COX AC 289 Sports, built at AC Cars under Shelby American license for domestic use (CObra Britain) and export (CObra eXport). Competition cars were built for specific sanctioning bodies and events, including Daytona, FIA, Le Mans, Nassau, Sebring, and USRRC.

In 1965, Shelby's new Cobra Daytona Coupe did what no other American carmaker had ever done—win the FIA Group 3 World Manufacturers Championship. Ferrari had dominated international road racing for more than a decade; the Daytona Coupe proved to European carmakers that American automobile manufacturers were competitors to be reckoned with.

The first major change in Shelby Cobra production came in the 1965 model year with the introduction of the big-block 427 Cobra, built on a new, large-diameter tube chassis with fully independent coil-spring suspension. With a gross weight of approximately 2,150 pounds and powered by a 425-horsepower big-block, the new street Cobra boasted an approximate 6:1 power-to-weight ratio. A longer, wider, more aggressively styled body complemented the 427 Cobra's ground-shaking performance—0 to 60 miles per hour in under 4 seconds and 0 to 100 miles per hour in under 8 seconds!

While the first 427 Cobra chassis (CSX3001) arrived in October 1964 and the first production 427 Cobra (CSX3002) was built in November, the actual first 427 Cobra was a one-off 289 Cobra (CSX2196) that was repowered and built for Shelby Competition director and legendary racer Ken Miles. Built to upstage Chevrolet's lightweight Corvette Grand Sport, it came to be known as the Shelby 427 Flip-Top Cobra. Weighing some 500 pounds less than a production small-block Cobra and fitted with a 427, Miles' one-off lightweight proved to be a handful on the track. The 427 was later replaced with a lighter, experimental 500-horsepower, NASCAR 390-inch aluminum big-block, courtesy of Ford Engineering. Unlike a traditional Cobra, the big-block prototype was fitted with tilt-up front and rear body clamshell sections fashioned from ultra-thin aluminum and flip-down doors.

The Flip-Top Cobra had a less than stellar racing history. After testing and sorting out at Riverside Raceway in 1963, Miles entered it in its first public race at Sebring in March 1964. It was involved in a crash and did not finish. In December 1964, Miles brought the Cobra to Nassau for Speed Week to run against some of the world's hottest sports racers, including Grand Sport Corvettes. While it ran away from the Grand Sports early in the race and kept an impressive lead, an oil line malfunction caused the Cobra's engine to fail; add one more Did Not Finish to its racing log. The Flip-Top Cobra had a few more outings before it was retired and used as a development vehicle at Shelby American.

Between November 1964 and December 1966 when the last big-block Cobra (CSX3360) was built, Shelby American produced 343 second-generation Cobras. Included in that number were 260 street models, three bare chassis, 27 S/C (Semi-Competition) cars, 1 Daytona Super Coupe, 25 Competition Roadsters, and 27 AC COB/COX models.

During the 1965 to 1967 model years, there were minimal cosmetic running changes, including wheels, taillights, wide and narrow fender flare options, and oil cooler scoops. The really big news was the selection of big-block engines with approximately the first one hundred cars receiving 427/425 low riser center-oiler engines with dual quads. Other powerplants included the 427 medium-riser side oiler rated at 425 horsepower with a single four-barrel and the 428 Police Interceptor single four-barrel rated at 385 horsepower. In addition to polished chrome valve covers, engines were also fitted with finned cast aluminum Cobra Le Mans valve covers.

Carroll Shelby passed away in 2012 at age eighty-nine, but he and his work will never be forgotten.

CHAPTER 4

1963

The Birth of Total Performance

"With Eight Pipes In The Organ, What Noble Music It Makes," read the headline of Ford's midyear advertising campaign spotlighting the new, dual-quad, 425-horsepower 427 Galaxie.

I was a newbie magazine editor in 1962 when Ford revealed details of its 1963 model lineup to the press. Little did I know that, as far as Ford was concerned, 1963 would come in like a lamb and go out like a lion! Ford's new lineup would change less than six months after the public introduction of the new 1963 Ford and Mercury models. That's when Ford worked its midyear magic, spearheaded by hot and hotter versions of a new 427-cubic-inch big-block engine along with Galaxie and Mercury Marauder two-door hardtops with lower, fastback-style rooflines. Also new, for what would be 1963½, was a sporty 164-horsepower 260 V-8 Falcon Sprint and a Fairlane powered by a solid-lifter 289 V-8 rated at 271 horsepower.

My invitation came for Ford's 1963½ press event and I didn't hesitate to respond seconds after opening the envelope. It would be my first time attending an industry event. I not only posted the reply, but also called Ford's New York public relations office to insure being on the guest list.

In those days, typical press ride-and-drive programs for new cars were securely held under wraps at automakers' test tracks. However, this one was an invitation to participate in Ford's International Press Road Rallye in Monaco from January 2 to 5, 1963: "Won't you please join us to drive 427 Galaxies, and other midyear models, in and around Monte Carlo and on Monte Carlo Rally routes in the Maritime Alps?" Also mentioned was a reception hosted at the Palace by Prince Rainier III and Princess Grace.

It was all a bit overwhelming, as I had never traveled further from New York City than Newport News, Virginia. The next morning I applied for an expedited

Another 427 Galaxie at Check Point 3 in Col de Braus. Journalists on the Rallye, right, check times with the Ford of Europe PR guy. I had just gone through in my Galaxie.

Darel Dieringer won the NASCAR Grand National race at Riverside Raceway on November 3, 1963, in a new Mercury Marauder built by Bill Stroppe & Associates. *Fran Hernandez Collection*

This photo of the first and second place winners at Daytona 500 was shot after cars qualified. Marvin Panch's name is visible on the door of No. 21, a Wood Brothers Galaxie; Fred Lorenzen finished second in the Holman & Moody No. 28 Galaxie. *Ford Motor Company*

Left: Bob Tasca, left, and driver Bill Lawton, setting up a 427 engine built by John Healey. Even when dressed for the office, Tasca was a totally hands-on car guy, and loved to work in the shop on race cars at his East Providence, Rhode Island, dealership.

Above: Ford dealer Bob Tasca, left, with '63½ Lightweight Galaxie driver Bill Lawton, right, in 1963 after being presented with the trophy for their Super/Stock Eliminator win. Engine builder and mechanic John Healey holds the class-win trophy. *Tasca Family Archives*

Left: Holman & Moody built '63½ 427 Galaxies with disc brakes for export to racing teams in the United Kingdom. This is Bill Shepherd's Touring Class H&M racer, originally driven by Jochen Mass, Jack Sears, and Jim Clark. Sears won the British Touring Championship in 1963 and is shown here driving No. 63 at Goodwood. *Stuart Schorr*

Right: Al Joniec was a top Ford racer in NHRA Division 1 and in 1963 ran a 427 Lightweight for Al Swenson Ford, where he worked as a mechanic. At the NHRA Points Meet at York US 30, he beat Super/Stocks driven by Bill Lawton and Dave Strickler and was one of the fastest and quickest Super/Stocks at the NHRA Nationals. In 1964 he joined the Ford Drag Team. *Al Joniec Collection*

passport. The "royals" held little interest to me, but I immediately started fantasizing about driving a new 427 Galaxie in the Alps! On New Year's Day 1963, I boarded a Ford-chartered Pan Am flight for Nice, France, with a fuel stop at Shannon Airport in Ireland.

It was an incredible trip. More than fifty years later, I can still remember the exhilaration and terror of driving a four-speed, 425-horsepower Galaxie behemoth with drum brakes on some of the world's most beautiful and dangerous roads. With a 119-inch wheelbase, the new Galaxie tipped the scales at over 3,700 pounds. The four-speed, 260 V-8 Falcon Sprint proved to be right at home on the twisty roads with almost endless switchbacks and sheer, unprotected dropoffs.

The new Galaxie Sports hardtop and Mercury Marauder looked better than the carryover notchback, or "boxtop," roof models, and they had special appeal to stock car racers. Street performance enthusiasts didn't much care about the aerodynamic advantages of the new slick Sports Hardtop. They liked the way it looked, but it was the 427 under its hood that turned them on.

The 406 single four-barrel and tri-power big-blocks were discontinued when the 427s were announced with Q-code 410 horsepower at 5,600 rpm with a single Holley 780-cfm four-barrel and R-code 425 horsepower at 6,000 rpm with dual Holley 650-cfm four-barrels. The new 427, essentially a bored-out (4.13-inch to 4.23-inch) 406, came stock with cross-bolted mains, reinforced forged steel rods, 11.5:1 pistons, solid-lifter valvetrain, and choice of single- or dual-quad intake. Like previous Ford big-block performance engines, tuned header-type exhaust manifolds were utilized with full, low back-pressure dual exhaust systems.

Welcome to 1963½—the automotive industry's first official "½"-year model introduction and Ford's first strike in its quest for world motorsports domination.

Before the year was out, Ford seriously impacted stock car, drag, and Indy 500 racing, as well as world rally competition. That's what Total Performance was all about.

Premier stock car constructors Holman & Moody, Bill Stroppe and Associates, Bud Moore Engineering, the Wood Brothers, and others welcomed Ford's switch to a Sports roof Galaxie. They had been racing 406 two-door sedans in 1962 and still mourned the loss of the 1960–1961 Starliner fastbacks.

Ford's wind tunnel and instrumented high-speed track testing revealed that the new Sports Hardtop model had an approximate 25 percent aerodynamic advantage over the previous notchback model. Working with a complex formula, Ford engineers calculated the amount of "aero horsepower" required to attain certain speeds. At 140 miles per hour, a car with a notchback roofline required approximately 200 aero horsepower while the new Sports Hardtop needed approximately 125. At 160 miles per hour, a modified 1963½ Galaxie still offered a 75 Aero Horsepower (350 vs. 425) advantage.

Fords distinguished themselves on February 24, 1963, at the Daytona 500, the first major race Ford contested after Henry Ford II withdrew from the AMA racing ban in 1962. On the NASCAR Grand National circuit, Fords won twenty-three events and Mercury one. It was at the Daytona 500 that Ford dominated the field. New 1963½ Galaxies finished one-two-three-four-five! Tiny Lund crossed the line first in the No. 21 Wood Brothers car, originally prepared for and qualified by Marvin Panch.

Panch was in the hospital recovering from burns sustained at the track a few days earlier and was unable to drive. He crashed while attempting to set a closed-course speed record in Briggs Cunningham's Ford 427-powered Birdcage Maserati. Tiny Lund saved his life by pulling him from the burning sports car to safety. Panch wanted Lund to drive in his place.

Ford engineer Dave Farell makes a pass in a mule that's fitted with a modified Ford 9-inch rear with 3.89 gears, B-W T-10 four-speed with 2.36 first gear and a special 3-inch-diameter driveshaft. Top end was 114.7 miles per hour, with quarter-mile ETs in the high 14s.

Lund was followed by Fred Lorenzen driving the No. 28 Holman & Moody car, Ned Jarrett in the No. 11 Burton-Robinson race car, and Nelson Stacy in the No. 29, and Dan Gurney in the No. 0 Holman & Moody Galaxies. A month earlier on January 20, 1963, Gurney had won the Riverside Raceway 500 in a Holman & Moody Galaxie. On November 3, 1963, Darrel Dieringer won the Grand National race at Riverside Raceway in the Stroppe-prepped No. 16 Marauder.

Fords and Mercurys from Holman & Moody and Stroppe also had successes in USAC competition with five wins going to Fords driven by Curtis Turner and A. J. Foyt and four wins for Mercury. Indy 500 winner Parnelli Jones scored three firsts, including a win at Pikes Peak, in Mercurys.

Holman & Moody built a number of NASCAR-prepared 1963½ Galaxies with 427 engines and stocklike interiors for export to England. Some even had lightweight body panels. Alan Mann Racing and John Wilment Automobiles raced them successfully in Appendix J/Touring events at Silverstone, Brands Hatch, and Nürburgring, and at tracks in South Africa and Australia.

Above: Dan Gurney tests the new all-aluminum Fairlane Indy engine in a Lotus, running 150 miles per hour, in March 1963 in this photo taken at Ford's Desert Proving Ground in Kingman, Arizona. Tests showed that Weber 48IDA carburetors had to be replaced by larger 58IDAs.

Right: Dan Gurney in Lotus-Ford No. 93, testing at Indianapolis Motor Speedway. Looking on are Jim Clark, Colin Chapman, and Ford Special Vehicles executives. Gurney qualified to start in twelfth position at 149.019 miles per hour. He finished seventh.
Ford Motor Company

Jim Clark finishes second in Lotus-Ford No. 92, behind winner Parnelli Jones in a traditional Offy roadster. Many thought he should have won because Jones' Offy was leaking oil on the track and he wasn't black flagged. This was the start of a revolution at the Brickyard, and two years later Clark would return to win the 500. *Ford Motor Company*

Ford's success in NASCAR impacted retail sales of Galaxies, with Ford ending 1963 by setting a new sales record—almost 650,000 units—that would never be broken. The Galaxies with maximum appeal to enthusiasts were the two-door hardtops with either Q-code 427/410 or R-code 427/425 engines and four-speeds. Because of the enormous torque of the 427 engines (480 pounds-feet at 3,700 rpm), you could not order the popular Equal-Lock limited slip differential. There was an optional Gleaseman Dual-Drive limited slip assembly available from Ford dealers for $110 plus installation. One other dealer-installed option was an exhaust cutout package for $45, plus installation, that allowed exhaust to bypass the mufflers.

From the midyear introduction of the 1963½ models to the end of the calendar year, Ford sold 3,857 R-code, 425-horsepower and 1,038 Q-code, 410-horsepower Galaxies. As delivered with skinny tires and stock tuning, an R-code Galaxie could go from 0 to 60 miles per hour in 7.5 seconds and run through the quarter-mile at 95 to 96 miles per hour in the low 15s. With typical Day Two tuning—headers with open exhausts and "cheater" slicks—R-code cars could run 105 to 108 miles per hour in the mid-12s.

Prior to the Lightweight program, Fords had not done well in Super/Stock drag racing, often falling prey to Chevys, Dodges, and Plymouths with aluminum body panels. Working for Ford, drag racer Dick Brannan took the lead on the 1963½ Lightweight initiative. In 1963, Brannan won between sixty-five and seventy races and set twenty-two track records in his lightweight Galaxie. He set

the first National record for a Ford in NHRA Super/Stock competition, 12.42 seconds, in early July in his No. 823 Galaxie sponsored by Romy-Hammes Ford. Later in the season, elapsed times dropped into the 12.10s and as low as 12.03 seconds at York US 30 drag strip. Brannan's Super/Stock 427 Galaxie was the first Lightweight, hand-built in late 1962 at Ford's X-Garage.

"After assembling the Ford Drag Team, which included Phil Bonner, Bill Lawton, Ed Martin, Les Ritchey, Gas Ronda, and Mickey Thompson, we worked on putting the big Ford on a diet," said Brannan. "Starting with a stock Galaxie 500 two-door with a shipping weight of 3,615 pounds, we got Ritchey's car down to 3,510 pounds and Ronda's down to 3,425 pounds."

Brannan's first car, built with help from Ford engineer Homer Perry, was even lighter since it was built on his carryover 1962 Lightweight chassis from a six-cylinder car.

"Perry worked with me and helped get a painted 1963½ Galaxie body shipped from the plant to the X Garage. My 1962 chassis weighed 26 pounds less than a comparable 1963 chassis used for the bulk of the approximate 214 Lightweights produced. A number of the early 1963½ Lightweights were actually rebodied 1962 Fords, like my first car. All were Corinthian White with red interiors except my No. 823, which was tan."

All *production* 1963½ Lightweight 427 cars were built around Ford 300 Series six-cylinder or 260-289 V-8 chassis (lighter-gauge steel) and ordered without any sealers, seam fillers, or sound-deadening materials. They were then fitted with fiberglass doors, trunk lids, hoods, and front fenders. Interior deletes included carpets, front bench seats, radio, heater, clock, and, in some cases, dome lights. The suspension was heavy-duty and the 427 dual-quad engine was mated to a Borg-Warner T-10 four-speed with light alloy case, hardened gears, and a 2.20 first gear. Light side glass, aluminum front bumpers, lightweight bucket seats, RC Industries 34-pound cast bell housings, and trunk-mounted batteries were added after the cars were received from assembly plants in San Jose, California; Atlanta, Georgia; and Norfolk, Virginia.

In addition to the turnkey Galaxie Lightweights, Ford also offered dealers Lightweight Conversion Kits so they could build their own, as well as customer cars, for local competition. The kit could be ordered under DSO #AS-225-39D for $1,099. Approximately 2,100 kits were processed for dealers.

In late 1962 and early 1963, Ford Project and Development engineers in Dearborn massaged the midsize Fairlane as part of the 1963½ Total Performance initiative. Since installing a big-block engine in the midsize coupe would require extensive chassis and suspension modifications, the 1963½ Fairlane was made available with the company's highest performance small-block, the new, high-revving, 11.0:1 compression 289 rated at 271 horsepower at 6,000 rpm and generating 312 pounds-feet of torque at 3,400 rpm. The lightweight, small displacement engine showcased Ford Engine & Foundry's expertise in thinwall block casting.

Ford engineer and drag racer Dave Farell was charged with building a small fleet of stock and modified 289/271 small-block Fairlane mules. One had an overhead cam V-8 that had little chance of ever reaching production.

From the outside, Farell's Fairlane looked like any other Sport Coupe—right down to its single exhaust pipe, 260 fender emblems, hubcaps, and whitewalls. It didn't sound stock and the 289 under the hood, according to its valve covers, had 40 more horsepower than the production 289/271. It sounded good and ran even better.

Under the hood looked mostly stock with the 289 equipped with tuned cast-iron exhaust manifolds and topped off with an aluminum intake manifold and a Ford/Holley four-barrel. However, the solid-lifter, high-compression 289 had spent a lot of tuning time on a dynamometer. The distributor had its vacuum advance plugged and was running on 6 degrees of initial timing at 700 rpm and full centrifugal advance of 26 degrees at 7,000 rpm. Thanks to a tankful of Sunoco 260, there were no traces of detonation. Small changes included the addition of a 427 Galaxie heat stove for the choke and an aluminum fan.

Performance was impressive considering the Fairlane mule weighed in at approximately 3,300 pounds and the engine was putting out between 300 and 312 horsepower. Its drivetrain consisted of a steel-cased Borg-Warner four-speed (2.36 First gear); 10.4-inch, 10,000-rpm clutch; special 3-inch-diameter driveshaft; and modified 9-inch rear with 3.89 gears.

Farell had documentation from the Desert Proving Ground where he ran a top end of 114.7 miles per hour. On the drag strip, he was able to run 0 to 60 miles per hour sprints in 8.40 seconds and quarter-mile times in the high 14s at 92.69 miles per hour and low 15s on skinny 7.00x13-inch street tires. Runs were made with a stock exhaust system and shifts were thrown at 6,500 rpm. Farell claimed that tests showed little to no power increases when a full dual exhaust system was installed. The Fairlane felt quick and strong, delivering performance commensurate with its over-300-horsepower engine. Ford decided to stick with the stock 289/271 for 1963½.

It was Don Frey who influenced Ford senior management to consider challenging the status quo at the Indy 500, America's most prestigious race. Ford hadn't contested the 500 since its rather dismal failure to finish the race in 1935. For decades, it would be variations of the original Harry Miller engineered multi-cam, multi-valve four-cylinder Offenhauser engine that ruled the roost at the Indy Brickyard.

In June 1962, Frey pitched Iacocca on building an engine based on Ford's new, successful, high-revving 260-289 small-block for the 1963 500-mile classic. Approximately one month later, Dan Gurney and Lotus' Colin Chapman, unaware that Ford had been discussing an Indy 500 project, approached Iacocca and Frey with a pitch for a Ford-powered, rear-engined, open-wheel

Transmission wizard Doug Nash campaigned a Ford F-100 in NHRA B/FX competition. He ran 108 miles per hour in the 12.7s in his factory sponsored F-100XL, built by Dearborn Steel Tubing and powered by a 427 engine.

Another potent NHRA B/FX Ford, a 289-powered Falcon, ran out of George May Ford. There were a number of 289 B/FX Falcons, many with blueprinted 289s with Weber 48IDA carburetors. Similar engines were run in competition Cobras.

Lotus race car for Indy. Chapman was internationally respected for his "lighter is better" expertise, which was showcased on Lotus sports and race cars. Their proposed Lotus Indy racer looked like a small cigar compared with the big, flashy front-engine Offy roadsters that had been dominating the race for decades.

Could a featherweight British car, powered by a variant of a production pushrod Ford V-8, unseat the reigning all-American cars with sophisticated four-cam, four-valve engines? Obviously, enough people at Ford thought so and the project received approval by the end of July 1962. By September 1, Ford Engineering started collecting dyno testing and durability data on a special 260-cubic-inch V-8. Iacocca appointed Leo Beebe as Special Vehicles Manager and the Indy program was given top priority.

By January 1963, Bill Gay's group at Engineering had built an all-aluminum, 256-cubic-inch pushrod engine with a forged steel crank, forged aluminum pistons, and four Weber 48IDA two-barrel carbs. In order to get the required horsepower, the Webers, which were used on 260-289 Cobra race cars, had to be replaced by larger 58IDAs. By the end of March, Indy engine specs were locked in and the prototype turned over to Colin Chapman for testing at Indianapolis. Prior to this, Dan Gurney tested an unmarked prototype at speeds up to 150 miles per hour at Ford's Desert Proving Ground.

Built in-house at Ford Engineering, the all-aluminum, race-ready Indy engine, code AX230-2, weighed approximately 375 pounds fitted with Weber 58IDA carburetors, tuned headers, a magnesium oil pan, and gear-drive camshaft. It was dynoed at 376 horsepower at 7,200 rpm. At the time, an engine producing 1 horsepower per pound of weight on commercial gasoline was quite an achievement.

Two Lotus-Ford race cars, prepared by Lotus Cars Ltd. in England, were flown to Indianapolis for the start of the 1963 Indy 500. Jim Clark and Dan Gurney were chosen to debut the new cars. Unlike any other car run at Indy, the new Lotus-Ford racer was of monocoque construction with a 28-inch-wide stressed-skin body, 96-inch wheelbase, and an overall length of just 150 inches. Wet weight was just 1,130 pounds.

Clark qualified at 149.750 miles per hour for fifth position and Gurney, at 149.019 miles per hour, for twelfth for the starting lineup at the forty-seventh running of the Indy 500. At the end of 500 miles, Parnelli Jones took the win in his Offy roadster that had been leaking oil on the track. Many felt it should have been black flagged. That would have given the win to Clark, who finished second. Clark was also named Rookie of the Year. Dan Gurney, who started twelfth, finished seventh. Both Ford-powered Lotus race cars were running at the end of 500 miles, proving the worth of Ford's small-block engine and Colin Chapman's lightweight racer.

Ford would be back in 1964 with a sophisticated engine of its own. In 1965, Jim Clark would return to win the Indy 500, setting the course thereafter for Ford engine wins each year through 1971.

Falcons Flock to Monte Carlo!

The 1963½ Falcon Sprint and Monte Carlo Rallye Falcons were revealed in the shadow of the Maritime Alps.

Monte Carlo is magical—the fairy tale centerpiece of the Principality of Monaco that, in 1963, was governed by Prince Rainier III and Princess Grace. Monte Carlo is where the rich and famous docked their super-yachts, partied, gambled in the fabled Place du Casino, and dined at one of the world's finest restaurants, Le Louis XV Alain Ducasse. Each January, it becomes the epicenter of world championship rally competition.

Since its inception in 1911 by Monaco's Prince Albert I, the Automobile Club De Monaco organizes the Rallye Automobile Monte-Carlo, or Monte Carlo Rallye. It's the same club that presents the Monaco Grand Prix. In January 1963, Ford entered three V-8 Falcons built by Holman & Moody in the ultra-high-profile, grueling endurance competition. Participation in the Rallye was timed to the introduction of the V-8-engined 1963½ Falcon Sprint, where it was revealed to select media in Monte Carlo the first week of January.

Unlike most corporate sanctioned competition programs at Ford, the idea of participating in the Monte Carlo Rallye did not come from the usual suspects. Ford's advertising agency, J. Walter Thompson, had been searching for new marketing ideas to boost sales and enhance their client's image. It was the agency's creative director, Barney Clark, who pitched the idea of entering Falcons in the "Monte" and shooting a series of ads. Clark had come from Campbell-Ewald, Chevrolet's agency, where he had been responsible for iconic Corvette advertising. Ford Division bought the concept.

Introduction of the Falcon Sprint and three rally Falcons was incorporated into Ford Division's 1963½ Monaco Press Preview that I attended. The highlight of the program for me was driving in the Press Road Rallye (Team 21). In addition to the 427/425 Galaxie, I also drove a Falcon Sprint on a 53-mile section of the official Monte Carlo Rallye route. It was powered by a 260-cubic-inch V-8 and fitted with a four-speed Borg-Warner T-10 transmission and 3.50 rear gears. Even though it had drum brakes, I found the Sprint to outperform smaller, disc-braked British Ford Zodiacs and Zephyrs that I also sampled. The drive route took us on tight paved and unpaved two-lane roads and 180-degree switchbacks in the Maritime Alps in Italy and France.

My teammate and navigator was Jim Steinfirst, then senior editor of *Automotive International* and the first president of the International Motor Press Association (IMPA). When we came back to Monte Carlo, we found a paved lot, ideal for running "stopwatch" 0-to-60-mile-per-hour sprints. Without the benefit of a limited-slip differential, the best we could manage was mid-to-high nines, dipping into the tens. Not too impressive after driving a 425-horsepower 427 Galaxie!

Ford was not really prepared to go head-to-head with experienced European teams with veteran racers and professionally prepared smaller cars, many with front-wheel drive. As soon as the program was approved, Ford Special Vehicles Activity's Jacque Passino worked with Ford's US PR director Tom Tierney, Ford Europe PR director Walter Hayes, and Holman & Moody to put together a team worthy of flying the Ford USA banner. George Merwin was named Competition Manager.

Since Holman & Moody had experience preparing V-8-engined Falcon Challengers for endurance road racing in 1962, they built three Monte Carlo Falcons. They knew how to build bulletproof 260 V-8 engines and powertrains that could survive more than 2,000 miles of severe use. Engines were rated at between 250 and 300 horsepower.

Skid plates were strategically placed between the chassis rails, suspension components were either pirated from larger cars or handcrafted for the project,

Three Ford Monte Carlo Rallye teams with Falcon No. 221, prior to start of the event. From left to right: Trant Jarman, Gunnar Haggbom, Margaret McKenzie, Anne Hall, Peter Jopp, and Bo Ljungfeldt. The Jarman & Jopp Falcon finished first in class and thirty-fifth overall.

and the interior was fitted with race car bucket seats and full engine and rally instrumentation, including a Sun tach and Halda Speedpilot.

George Merwin and Jeff Uren assembled an eclectic international racing team. Anne Hall (UK) was paired up with Margaret McKenzie (UK), Trant Jarman (US) drove with Peter Jopp (UK), and Bo Ljungfeldt (Sweden) partnered with Gunnar Haggbom (Sweden). While in Monte Carlo, I became friendly with Jopp and Jarman and wrangled an invitation to drive their Falcon (providing it survived) a couple of months later at Ford's Dearborn Proving Ground.

Ford's Monte Carlo effort represented the first serious American involvement in a legendary European road rally. Since 1911, the Monte Carlo Rallye had been dominated by European and British marques. However, the trio of 1963½ Falcons did not represent Ford's first appearance at the Monte. In 1936, Lonel Zamfirescu and Petre G. Cristea won the rally in a homebuilt, highly modified, lightweight 1935 Ford roadster that started life as a coupe donated by Ford of Romania. It was powered by a flathead V-8 with British low-compression heads for reliability, a Weber two-barrel carburetor, and a Vertex magneto.

However, Ford Falcons did not win the 1963 Monte Carlo Rallye. Jopp and Jarman finished thirty-fifth overall but won Class 8 (cars with engines over 3,000cc), while Ljungfeldt and Haggbom in Falcon No. 223 finished forty-third overall and second in Class 8. They also set an incredible record that established Ford as a serious contender. For the first time in the event's history, one driver, Bo Ljungfeldt, a road racer with little rally driving experience, posted the fastest times on all six special speed stages of the rally. Anne Hall and Margaret McKenzie did not finish due to a technicality.

Even under the best of conditions, the Monte Carlo Rallye is a torturous test of physical and mental endurance. Of the 296 cars starting in 1963, only 102 cars, including 2 of the 3 Falcons, finished. The Falcons were unquestionably the fastest cars entered and proved to also be reliable. The last 500 of the route's approximately 2,500 miles were in the French Alps, leading to the finish in Monte Carlo. Those roads included serpentine curves and high-mountain passes, like Col de Braus that connects Sospel and L'Escarène.

Kenneth Rudeen summed up Ford's first serious Monte effort best in "The Awful Auto Ride," an article he wrote for the February 4, 1963, *Sports Illustrated*: "The new kings of the mountains, in fact, are the Ford Falcon Sprints and a sort of superman named Bo Ljungfeldt. Le Grand Bo, as forty-year-old Bo Tage Georg Ljungfeldt came to be known, stormed through the mountains with

Hank Carlini, Ford Competition technician, right, goes over the engine specs of the Holman & Moody 260-inch V-8 in the Monte Carlo Falcon. He warmed up the tires before I made acceleration runs. The blueprinted and balanced engine uses a combination of 260 and 289/271 parts plus H&M race parts to get approximately 300 horsepower. *Ford Motor Company*

such ferocious zeal that he would have won the rally outright but for penalties received elsewhere on the journey."

Unfortunately, I did not get an opportunity to either drive or ride in one of the competition Falcons in Monte Carlo. But two months later, thanks to Peter Jopp and Ford's Tom Tierney, I was tossing the Jopp & Jarman No. 221 Falcon around at the Dearborn Proving Ground. After Jopp showed me the line around the road course, still capped with spots of snow and ice, I made a few laps plus a couple of runs on the high-speed section of the track. Because of weather conditions, the posted top speed was 105 miles per hour and that's as fast as I drove. Considering the engine's 6,500 rpm redline and 4.11 posi gears in the Falcon's narrowed 9-inch Galaxie rear, I wasn't sure how much faster I could have gone without hand-grenading the small-block.

At full throttle on the road course, the Falcon behaved more like a well-sorted-out competition sports car than a beefed-up big sedan. It pretty much went wherever I pointed it without much fuss. Holman & Moody had reworked the stock steering using a custom Pitman-idler arm combination to achieve quick 2.25 turns lock to lock. Everything from the Falcon's tie rods and lower control arms to extra leaf rear springs were either custom H&M components or pirated from a Galaxie. Koni and Gabriel supplied the adjustable shocks.

What really surprised me was the rally car's impressive braking on the twisty road course. Unlike a production Falcon with drum brakes, the rally car was fitted with custom Bendix-Dunlop 11.5-inch front discs and 11-inch rear drums with special fade-resistant linings. Stopping at high speeds on the oval and repeated use of the brakes on the road course did little to reduce the effectiveness of the proprietary brake conversion.

Senior Ford competition technician, Hank Carlini, spent a lot of time with me going over the Falcon's engine specs. Holman & Moody blueprinted and balanced the 260 engines using a combination of 260 and 289 components, plus special race parts. Rated at approximately 300 horsepower at 6,500 to 7,000 rpm, the engine featured an H&M camshaft with solid-lifter valvetrain and ported and polished 289/271 big-valve heads with chambers cc'd for 11.5:1 compression. Other modifications included a big Holley four-barrel mounted on a 289/271 Fairlane intake manifold, 289/271 exhaust manifolds with a single low-restriction exhaust system, and a dual-point distributor with full centrifugal advance.

Carlini made a couple of passes on Ford's drag strip to warm up the 15-inch Dunlop SP tires before turning the Falcon over to me. Shifting the T-10 four-speed with 2.20 first gear at 6,200 rpm, my best quarter-mile time was 90.6 miles per hour in 15.2 seconds. The sprint from 0 to 60 miles per hour took 8.1 seconds. I felt it was an impressive performance for a car that was built for endurance under the worst possible weather conditions and not for racing.

Ford's Falcon Monte Carlo rally program proved to be an overwhelming marketing success. It created a halo for the brand and Ford Motor Company, even though the best Falcon overall finish was thirty-fifth. Tom Tierney spun the story, focusing on Falcons taking first and second in class so that it looked like Ford took home all the marbles. Monte Carlo Falcon media coverage exceeded that of all three of the combined makes that finished in the top three spots—Saab, Citroën, and Mini Cooper. Ford advertising sung the praises of the fast and durable Falcon Sprints. To the average compact car shopper in 1963, it appeared that Falcons had outperformed and outlasted the best Europe had to offer!

For me, it was a never-to-be-forgotten experience. I drove Ford's hottest 1963½ performance cars in the Alps, met Princess Grace and Prince Rainier at a champagne reception at the palace, gambled in the fabled casino, and dined with Mr. and Mrs. Benson Ford and the top international media at the Hotel de Paris Monte-Carlo. For a young car guy who wrote about hot rods and customs, it was Nirvana!

"Now remember, Marty, you can't really slip that clutch—it's either in or out." Sage advice from veteran rally driver Peter Jopp before taking the No. 221 Monte Carlo Falcon out on the drag strip at Ford's Dearborn Proving Ground in March 1963. He was right! *Ford Motor Company*

At speed on the road course at Ford Proving Ground. Even with patches of snow and ice, I found the Falcon handled more like a well-sorted-out competition sports car than a beefed-up sedan. Quick steering with 2.25 turns lock to lock was really appreciated. *Ford Motor Company*

1963 FALCON CAYUSE

A sporty Falcon Cayuse, followed by a two-seat Coyote, preceded the Mustang. The Mustang team was not happy!

While Dearborn Steel Tubing (DST) would become best known for production of the Super/Stock 1964 Fairlane 427 Thunderbolt, in 1963 it created the Falcon Cayuse convertible. It joined other concepts and customized production models in Ford Special Projects Manager Jacque Passino's Custom Car Caravan.

A study in asymmetrical creativity, the Cayuse had an off-center grille, hood scoop, and rear license plate mount. Credit for the design goes to stylist Vince Gardner, contracted by Ford in 1962 to create three special Falcon convertibles. At the time, Vince headed up the Experimental Styling and Design section at Dearborn Steel Tubing.

By the time Gardner landed at DST in the early 1960s, he had already been involved in the design of some impressive cars and garnered accolades as a top-flight stylist. He was a clay modeler at Auburn and had worked alongside Gordon Buehrig on the legendary Cord 810. He later worked for Raymond Lowery at Studebaker and created the two-seat Gardner Special, a winner at the 1950 National Roadster Show in Oakland, California.

The Cayuse with modified 260-inch V-8 was the first delivered to Ford and used for PR photos. When Gardner invited me to his studio, the car I photographed was the No. 2 Cayuse. The white one in his studio being modified at the time was the No. 3 car, later shortened by 18 inches and badged Coyote. Gardner invested approximately 750 hours designing the Cayuse, working on the prototype and creating the molds. There was talk of marketing a Cayuse-conversion kit, but that never happened.

The first step in the Cayuse conversion was making clay molds for the fiberglass grille surround and the peaked hood with offset scoop. French Cibie quartz-iodine headlamps were incorporated into the front end. Chromed steel mesh was installed to finish off the hood scoop and the grille section was fitted with a 1963½ Sprint emblem. The balance of the grille treatment made use of simple, clean 0.125x0.5-inch chromed steel bars.

After the Cayuse's wheel wells were radiused, all stock rear end trim, including the taillights and fuel filler, were removed. A full-width rear grille was fabricated and an offset license plate mount fitted into the grille. The trunk lid was shaved and the bumper filled for a smooth finish. Gardner relocated

The first of three customized Falcons was photographed with a model by Ford for PR for Falcon as part of the 1963 traveling Custom Car Caravan.

Stylist Vince Gardner with renderings for two- and four-seat custom Falcon convertibles submitted to Ford for approval of the Cayuse project. The third customized Cayuse was shortened 18 inches and badged Coyote.

The asymmetrical styling theme was carried over for the rear with the offset license-plate mount. The trunk lid was dechromed and the fuel filler relocated to the trunk.

This mildly customized interior has a Falcon Sprint steering wheel, a Ford tach, and wood-grained trim. A hidden switch controls the electric solenoid for the trunk-lid release.

The Cayuse tends to look longer and lower thanks to all trim being removed and the wheel wells opened and neatly flared.

the fuel filler to the trunk. A dash-mounted switch controlled the solenoid for deck lid operation, making gassing up a little easier.

Gardner modified the rear fenders to accept 1962 Ford taillights fitted with chrome tube centers. Before being repainted, the Cayuse was fitted with hand-polished alloy wheels, wood dash trim, Ford tach, and a Falcon Sprint steering wheel. Blue Pearl lacquer was then applied, and the next day it was loaded into a Custom Car Caravan display truck for its debut at the Daytona 500. Ford couldn't have chosen a better venue to unveil its latest specialty cars, as Ford 427 Galaxies driven by Tiny Lund, Fred Lorenzen, Ned Jarrett, Nelson Stacy, and Dan Gurney took the first five spots!

The Cayuse and Coyote were very well received, but production was not in the cards. At the end of the tour, the three Gardner-designed Falcons were tagged for the crusher and, at the last minute, saved by an appeal from DST. However, all the Cayuse tooling was destroyed. The three Falcons are still alive and well in the hands of enthusiasts.

The second Falcon Cayuse was the subject of the cover story in the July 1963 issue of *Custom Rodder* magazine.

2 FORD S/S ROAD TESTS! 427 GALAXIE
MONTE CARLO 'SPECIAL'

CUSTOM RODDER

JULY/35 CENTS/PDC

SCOOP! VINCE GARDNER'S LATEST, A LOW-COST KIT TO CONVERT ANY FALCON INTO A CAYUSE!

GARY REVIEWS BASIC CUSTOMIZING; PART 1 OF A NEW SERIES; BRAZING

1963 427 Fairlane: Anatomy of a Mule!

Before there was a Super/Stock 427 Thunderbolt, there was *ZIMMY-1*, the A/FX factory prototype for the 1964 Super Stocker.

Most Ford fans were confused when Tasca Ford's Bill Lawton first staged the Ming Green A/FX 1963 Fairlane coupe at the 1963 NHRA Nationals. They were used to seeing 1963 Fairlanes running in D/Stock, like *Ill Lord Fotus*, the Fairlane Milo Coleman drove for the class win at 13.75 seconds at 99.88 miles per hour. What was a stock-looking Fairlane doing in A/FX? After Lawton made a 12.21-second/118.42-mile-per-hour pass during time trials, it was obvious that *ZIMMY-1* was not just a modified stocker.

Driven by Bill Lawton, *ZIMMY-1* fell prey to Don Kimball's 1963 Z11 Chevy during eliminations. Before shipping the car back to Ford, Lawton did manage to set the NHRA A/FX National Record at 121.29 miles per hour at the Division 1 Points Meet at Connecticut Dragway.

ZIMMY-1 was powered by a blueprinted 427 big-block, which, at the time, was only available in 1963½ Galaxies. This unique Fairlane was the result of a joint venture between Ford Engineering (Dan Jones), Ford Special Vehicles (Charlie Gray), Ford Engine & Foundry (Bill Gay), Dearborn Steel Tubing (Andy Hotten), and Tasca Ford (Bob Tasca). The car was named after Frank Zimmerman, the

Tasca Ford's Bill Lawton on his way to a new A/FX NHRA National Record at the Division 1 Points Meet, 121.29 miles per hour, running a flat fiberglass hood with air intakes in the grille.

Even though *ZIMMY-1* was constructed at Dearborn Steel Tubing, Tasca Ford's techs made a number of suspension and chassis modifications, which ended up being incorporated into the engineering of the Super/Stock Thunderbolt.

Ford sales manager who also headed up the Special Vehicles Group. *ZIMMY-1* was Ford's mule, or prototype, for the 1964 Fairlane 427 Thunderbolt.

Over its short lifetime, *ZIMMY-1* was powered by three different big-blocks—406 and two 427s—and fitted with a variety of fiberglass hoods. While at DST, it was built with fiberglass front fenders, hood, and deck lid and aluminum inner fender panels and bumpers. Ready to race, weight was 3,320 pounds.

After being sorted out, *ZIMMY-1* was raced at the Nationals with a 427 high-riser with ram-air induction built by Ford Engineering. They used the latest 427 NASCAR short-block, which utilized a steel crank, 12.7:1 forged pistons, and machined and polished heads with 2.197-inch intake and 1.735-inch exhaust valves. They topped off the engine with Holley dual-quads.

Ford engineers crafted tubular steel headers for the 427. As with 427 Galaxie Lightweights, the Fairlane's engine was bolted to a Hurst-shifted Ford four-speed (2.36 first gear). To aid clutch cooling during repeated runs, the scattershield's mounting bolts were shimmed for 0.125-inch spacing. A heavy-duty 427 Galaxie driveshaft, shortened to 54 inches, hooked up the powertrain to a big Ford rear with thirty-one-spline axles and a Detroit Locker differential with 4.44 gears.

When transplanting a 500-horsepower engine into an under-3,300-pound car engineered for 271 horsepower, much attention had to be paid to the chassis and suspension. To effectively and safely transfer weight at launch, the chassis was preloaded using a special left front coil spring and shock assembly, and two-leaf (right) rear spring. The stock right front spring and shock and left rear three-leaf spring and shock were retained.

Increasing horsepower is relatively easy compared with getting power to the pavement. Completing the chassis loading was the fabrication of a pair of boxed steel traction bars, similar in design to the ones used on 427 Galaxie Lightweights and later on Thunderbolts. The traction bars measured 31 inches long and ran from the axle housing forward to chassis mounting points that added structural rigidity and aided in weight transfer. A trunk-mounted 95-pound battery sat over the right rear wheel.

ZIMMY-1 was actually a work in progress while at Tasca Ford. Many small changes initiated by Bob Tasca, John Healey, and Bill Lawton were incorporated into the final engineering of the 1964 Thunderbolt. They experimented with a variety of fresh air induction packages, the best being a sealed-air box with 8-inch-diameter hoses ducting through grille inlets.

In 1964, *ZIMMY-1* provided the blueprint for the creation of the Super/Stock 427 Thunderbolt. Totally illegal for the street, the mule most likely went directly to the crusher after being returned to Dearborn. Its legacy lives on in surviving Thunderbolts.

Cobra in a Birdcage!

Three American racing legends—Carroll Shelby, Briggs Cunningham, and Al Momo—joined forces in 1963, resulting in an exotic Maserati sports racer powered by Ford.

Transplanting American V-8 engines into imported sports racers gained popularity in the early to mid-1960s. American V-8s were often inexpensive, simple to modify and maintain, and in many cases lighter than imports. Most importantly, they produced maximum horsepower and torque at considerably lower and more usable rpm for improved performance and durability.

Ford's lightweight 260-289 V-8, which was elevated to International status by Carroll Shelby's Cobras, caught the attention of Alfred Momo and Briggs Cunningham in 1963. Momo managed Briggs Cunningham's racing team and operated a racing services facility in New York City. Cunningham built sports cars and race cars from 1951 to 1955, took Corvettes to Le Mans in 1960, and was the highest-profile racing team owner-driver in the United States in the late 1950s and early 1960s.

In 1963, Cunningham spent a lot of time racing Momo-prepared Maserati Tipos, also known as Birdcages because of their unique triangulated, small-diameter tubular chassis construction. The original Tipo chassis weighed just 66 pounds and resembled a large birdcage. It was originally fitted with a 3-liter

DOHC V-12 engine. While considered state of the art because of unique space-frame construction, they were plagued with suspension failures leading to serious handling and reliability issues. At the time, Maserati was cash-starved, negatively affecting race car development.

Both Cunningham and Momo were aware of Shelby's success with Ford-powered Cobras and decided to bring him in while Momo was rebuilding one of two Maserati Tipo 64 Birdcages (#64.002). It had been built in 1962 as a Tipo 63 and later returned to Italy for chassis updates, rear suspension change, weight reduction, and relocation of the engine for better weight distribution. Its fully independent rear suspension was replaced with a De Dion setup located with its own tubular framework. Power came from a 60-degree, 183-cubic-inch V-12 with four cams and six Weber 35-DCV carburetors. Output was 320 horsepower at 8,200 rpm.

Shelby suggested a 289-cubic-inch Cobra competition engine that would develop more usable horsepower and torque at more than 1,000 rpm *less* than the V-12. I spent a day in August 1963 at Momo Competition after the Shelby 289, fitted by Al Momo with four Weber 4610-M1 carburetors, was installed and fired up. The 289's headers were plumbed into rear exit quad megaphones. It had an incredible bark—much more raucous than a competition Cobra. Rated at

Briggs Cunningham's Shelby-powered, aluminum-body Birdcage Tipo 64.002 being prepared for new American racing livery (white paint with blue stripes). The weight was just 1,400 pounds.

340 horsepower at 7,000 rpm, the engine was fitted with ported and polished heads, like the ones used on FIA Cobras, and Spalding Flamethrower ignition.

Unlike previous Birdcages that Cunningham had raced, this was the first to utilize a De Dion rear suspension with a five-speed gearbox and an interchangeable fifth gear. To adapt the Cobra engine, Momo chopped the Ford bell housing and utilized a Maserati flywheel and clutch. Clutch and throttle linkage were converted to hydraulic-assist utilizing slave cylinders.

To compensate for the new powerplant, adjustable Armstrong shocks and beefier 42-millimeter knock-off hubs were added. An aluminum cross-flow radiator, aided by small vents in the aluminum rear body panels, cooled the fanless engine. Ready to race, the Ford-engined Maserati Birdcage weighed 1,400 pounds, exactly 1 pound less than with the V-12!

With the help of Willem Oosthoek, author of *Birdcage to Supercage*, and Larry Berman, Cunningham historian, we were able to track the Ford-powered Birdcage's racing history. The first time out with Walt Hansgen driving, #64.002 took a third overall at the Watkins Glen SCCA Nationals on August 24, 1963. Primary drivers were Cunningham, Augie Pabst, and Paul Richards. Dr. Dick Thompson also spent some seat time in Tipo #64.002.

Over the years, ownership of #64.002 passed from Cunningham to Pabst and then to Ham Vose. It competed at the Bridgehampton Double 500, the Los Angeles Times GP at Riverside, and many regional events in 1963. The last big race it ran was the USRRC event at Augusta. In later years, still fitted with the Shelby Cobra engine, it was on display at the Blackhawk Collection.

Master tuner, race-car builder, and Cunningham Racing Team manager Al Momo makes final adjustments to a Ford engine's #4610-M1 Webers (from a 4-liter Maserati) before firing it up for the first time. Note how the Spalding distributor looks like a magneto.

The chassis on the Tipo 64 #64.002 has smaller chassis tubes than the Tipo 63 that had been sent back to Italy to be updated and converted to latest Tipo 64 specs—"toothpicks." The shocks are adjustable Armstrongs. Borrani wire wheels with Dunlop racing tires are fitted on larger 42-millimeter knock-off hubs.

CHAPTER 5

1964

Win on Sunday, Sell on Monday!

Ford continues its winning ways with new engines, race-only cars you can buy, a game-changing Mustang, and aggressive dealer marketing and advertising programs.

"It is the full intent of the Ford Division to continue its total commitment to open competition during the 1964 model year, said Ford Special Vehicles Manager Frank E. Zimmerman to dealers. "For only under the conditions existent in competitive events can we assure ourselves that we bring to you and the public a product of durability and reliability, totally tested . . . a total performance Ford. Let your total dealership reflect total performance!"

Zimmerman presented Ford dealers with sales and marketing programs tied to Ford's racing activities in North America and Europe—NHRA, NASCAR,

SCCA, FIA, USAC—that would bring young performance enthusiasts into their dealerships. These programs supplied details about sponsoring race cars, campaigning drag racing cars, and starting and hosting Falcon and Mustang owners clubs. In addition, Special Vehicles produced publications outlining specs and details for ordering NHRA A and B/Stock 427 Galaxies and 427 Fairlane Thunderbolts, along with part numbers and descriptions of 1964 and 1964½ engine, rear axle, transmission, and body parts.

For 1964, Ford and Mercury offered a full line of high-performance models ranging from 260 V-8 Falcon Sprints and 289/271 Comets, Mustangs, and Fairlanes to 427 (410- and 425-horsepower) Galaxies and Marauders. The all-new 1964½ Mustang, available with the 289/271 engine, was in a class by itself

The author with a 427/425 Galaxie road test car in 1964, supplied by Ford with bare steel wheels, exhaust cutouts, and a dash-mounted tach. This photo, taken after running the car at Westhampton Drag Strip, was used for a *CARS* magazine distributor promotion. No helmet was needed at the track!

Checking out the 289/271 Fairlane Riverside Raceway road course in June 1963. Even with HD suspension, the Fairlane was best suited for the street. Optional engine package was one of the best small-displacement engines available in 1964.

Bob Tasca with the trophy collection displayed at Tasca Ford, East Providence, Rhode Island. Tasca was one of the earliest dealers to embrace the Win on Sunday, Sell on Monday concept, often displaying its race cars on showroom floors. *Tasca Family Archives*

Ford offered a special B/Stock 427 Galaxie package that could be ordered at any dealership. This special model came with a low-riser 427 engine and either four-speed manual or automatic and a choice of rear-end ratio. Barrie Poole was Canadian National Record Holder in the B/Stock Galaxie, photographed here at the 1964 NHRA Indy Nationals.

and first-year Mustang sales skyrocketed. Full-size Galaxie and Marauder models had the horsepower and image, but were also saddled with size and weight.

As much as I enjoyed driving the new Mustang, I found the sculpted and face-lifted Galaxie hardtop with dual-quad 427/425 power and four-speed to have the most appeal. Galaxies could also be ordered with a single four-barrel, 410 horsepower 427. Even with its manual steering, lack of factory limited-slip rear option, and voracious appetite for Sunoco 260, I loved cruising in an R-code Galaxie!

My introduction to the 1964 Galaxie was in the summer of 1963 at the 1964 Ford Technical Press Conference at Riverside Raceway. I had the opportunity to drive a prototype 500XL Galaxie with the R-code 425-horsepower engine, B-W T-10 four-speed, 3.50:1 gears, and skinny 6.70x15-inch tires. Spanning 210 inches and weighing in at close to 4,000 pounds, I didn't expect it to handle well on the Riverside track and it did not disappoint. It was solid feeling and, even with its standard heavy-duty suspension and brakes, was not at home on a twisty sports car track. We did manage to run some 0-to-60-mile-per-hour sprints with most runs in the mid- to high sevens.

Essentially carryover for 1964, the R-code 427/425 engine was equipped with dual Holley quads on a low-rise manifold; .500-inch lift, 306-degree duration camshaft; forged 11.5:1 pistons; steel crank; improved big-valve heads; dual-point ignition; and free-flow, long-branch exhaust manifolds. You could order rear gears from 3.00 to 4.11:1, but until mid-1964 production, you could not get the big 9-inch rear with thirty-one-spline axles. The only way you could get a limited-slip differential was to buy a Detroit Locker and have it installed at a speed shop or Ford dealer. In mid-1964, Ford replaced the T-10 four-speed in 427 Galaxies with its own, beefier top loader four-speed.

In addition to driving later-production 427 Galaxies on the high-speed oval at the Dearborn Proving Ground in the spring, I also spent a week with a Wimbledon White R-code 427 Galaxie 500 in New York. The Galaxie had

Tasca Ford received one of the first batch of eleven Vintage Burgundy Thunderbolts built by DST as well as the two prototypes. It was a very competitive car, setting both ends of the NHRA National record—126.05 miles per hour in 11.69 seconds—at the Division 1 Points Meet at Connecticut Dragway. John Healey, right, built the T-Bolt's engine; driver Bill Lawton and Tasca Ford racing tech are pictured at left.

Ford built fifty Lightweight 427 Galaxies in 1964, twenty-five with four-speeds and twenty-five with beefed automatics, for running in NHRA in AA/Stock and AA/SA. Lightweights had 427 High-Riser engines with fresh-air induction as used in Thunderbolts. Osborn Trucking Lightweight was an NHRA Record Holder in AA/SA. *Factory Lightweight Collection*

manufacturer's license plates, not unusual for a media test car, but it also had paperwork in the glove compartment indicating that the car had been shipped to New York from Charlotte, North Carolina, home of Holman & Moody. It also didn't look stock. There was a tach mounted on top of the dash, whitewall tires on bare 15x15.5-inch steel wheels, and side-exit exhaust outlets. Designed like lakes pipes with caps that could be removed, these looked more like NASCAR exhausts. In 1963½, Ford listed an optional, dealer-installed Exhaust Cutout option, but this was the first I had seen.

After running the Galaxie in A/Stock at Westhampton Drag Strip on Long Island, my best time was 15.4 seconds at 95 miles per hour—not good enough to win anything. On the way home, we stopped at a shopping mall that was pretty much empty to clock some 0-to-60 times. The best we could do was 7.4 seconds. The Galaxie didn't have the right tires or a limited-slip differential, but it sounded great with those straight exhausts!

In February 1964, Ford Division sent its district offices a Distribution Bulletin outlining limited availability of a 427 Galaxie two-door hardtop powered by the updated 427 high-riser engine, lightened and engineered specifically for NHRA A and B/Stock competition:

This car should be ordered under DSO #84-0018 for four-speed and DSO #84-0007 for automatic transmission. This car is a maximum performance vehicle and should only be sold to the knowing customer who understands the warranty implications if the car is used in competitive events. Wholesale pricing to dealers is $3,950 for a four-speed car and $4,150 for an automatic, plus normal delivery charges.

—N. M. Bergen, Manager, Ford Distribution Department

Stock 1964 Galaxies with 427 engines were already approximately 40 pounds lighter than 1963 models, so a minimum of fiberglass body panels were utilized on the 1964 Lightweights. A unique fiberglass hood was standard and fresh air was ducted to the carburetors via hoses connected to intakes in the grille. All sound deadening materials, insulation, and carpets were deleted and lightweight Bostrom bucket seats installed.

Unlike the B/Stock Lightweight and production R-code 427/425 Galaxies, the hottest Lightweight was powered by the latest high-rise 427 with valvetrain developed for NASCAR racing. Output with open headers was approximately 500 horsepower. Updates included new pistons, larger-port heads with reconfigured combustion chambers and lightened 2.19-inch intake and 1.73-inch exhaust valves, dual 780 cfm Holleys on a tall aluminum manifold, and 7,000-rpm valvetrain.

The only options available on Lightweights were transmissions—either the top loader four-speed with 2.36 first gear or modified Lincoln C6 automatic—and

Joe Orlando drove the Al Maroone 427 Lightweight Galaxie to a class win at the 1964 NHRA Indy Nationals. He was later disqualified for running illegal valvetrain components. Mike Schmitt got the win in the Desert Motors Lightweight and went on to win NHRA Little Stock Eliminator World Championship.

Below: Holman & Moody's star driver Fred Lorenzen won eight of eleven starts in spite of Plymouth and Dodge Hemi-engine cars. Ford still managed to take thirty wins in NASCAR Grand National competition and won the 1964 NASCAR Manufacturer's award. The Ford 427 NASCAR engines were updated with 7,000-rpm valvetrain components and new heads, valves, and pistons. *Ford Motor Company*

Skip Hudson in Holman & Moody '64 Galaxie during a pit stop at the 1964 Motor Trend 500 at Riverside Raceway with Ford's Fran Hernandez, in sweater and with clipboard, right, in the pits with the H&M team. The Galaxie has a rich racing heritage, having also been driven by Augie Pabst, winner of the 1964 FIA International Sedan Race at Sebring and by Ned Jarett in 1965. Now restored, this car is owned and raced by John Craft. *Ford Motor Company*

Mercury's top driver in USAC competition was Parnelli Jones. On July 4, 1964, he won his second straight Stock Car Class win at Pikes Peak in a 427 Mercury Marauder. Bill Stroppe prepared the big Mercury for stock-car racing. *Fran Hernandez Collection*

final drive ratios. Stick cars came with 4.57:1 while automatics were fitted with 4.71:1. Rears were 9-inch Galaxie with thirty-one-spline axles and Detroit Locker differential. Battery was factory mounted in the trunk over the right rear wheel.

To be legal in NHRA Stock classes, Ford built a total of 50 Lightweights, twenty-five sticks and twenty five automatics. The Galaxie Lightweight was prototyped at Ford's X-Garage along with a one-off, all-fiberglass 1964 Galaxie, VIN #4W66R100023, as a joint venture between Ford and Plaza Fiberglass in Toronto, Canada. Since heavy fiberglass had to be used in the support structure, the car ended up weighing approximately 50 pounds more than a steel-bodied Lightweight. Since it could not be used in NHRA Stock classes, the fiberglass Galaxie was crushed.

Galaxie Lightweights made a great showing at tracks around the country. In June 1964 at the *Hot Rod* Magazine Championships at Riverside Raceway, Larry Dacini ran 113.44 miles per hour in 12.60 seconds to win B/FX and Jesse Mendez took the C/FX win with a 94.83 mile-per-hour, 15.06-second run. Mike Schmitt, driving the Desert Motors AA/SA Lightweight, won class honors (111.80 miles per hour in 12.18 seconds) at the 1964 NHRA Indy Nationals and went on to win the NHRA Little Stock Eliminator World Championship.

A Distribution Bulletin sent to all Ford dealers on March 16, 1964, announced availability of a special, limited-production 427 Fairlane. It would later be dubbed Thunderbolt. Available with only one option—four-speed or automatic—it was a race-only Fairlane powered by the 427 high-riser and equipped with tubular headers, lightweight body parts, Plexiglas side windows and backlight, and drag tires.

According to the Bulletin, "This Super/Stock car—as furnished—is capable of running the quarter-mile in less than 12 seconds, the present NHRA record. Wholesale dealer pricing is $3,780 with four-speed and $3,980 with automatic, plus delivery charges. They are not for operation on the street."

Ford Thunderbolts, built for Ford by Dearborn Steel Tubing, dominated Super/Stock competition at major NHRA events in 1964, winning class

and elimination honors while setting new records. DST built one hundred Thunderbolts for NHRA homologation for Super/Stock, then filled orders for twenty-seven additional cars. Thunderbolts were joined by a small number of 427 Comets, built for Mercury to run in NHRA A/FX competition. They, too, were incredibly successful.

Bolstered by Gas Ronda's Super/Stock win in his Thunderbolt over Butch Leal in Mickey Thompson's T-Bolt at the Winternationals and Leal's Super/Stock win at 122.78 miles per hour in 11.76 seconds at the Indy Nationals, Ford won the 1964 NHRA Manufacturer's Cup.

Even though thwarted by Hemi-powered Dodges and Plymouths and Bill France's refusal to accept Ford's 427 SOHC engine, Ford still won NASCAR's 1964 Manufacturer's Award of Excellence. It was awarded to Ford because of the thirty wins in the Grand National Division, more than twice that of its nearest rival. Fred Lorenzen, in his Holman & Moody Galaxie, won eight of eleven starts and finished in the top ten five times. Dan Gurney, driving a Wood Brothers 427 Galaxie, won his second straight Motor Trend 500 at Riverside Raceway.

At the time, Holman & Moody was building NASCAR race cars using production Galaxies shipped from the Norfolk, Virginia, assembly plant without engines. They developed the first boxed steel chassis that became the standard for all cars running in NASCAR.

While Fords won two races in USAC's Stock Car Division in 1964, Mercury posted eight wins, including Pikes Peak. Parnelli Jones, driving Bill Stroppe 427 Marauders, won seven races and, for the second year in a row, finished first in the Stock Car Class at Pikes Peak. Jones was named USAC Stock Car Champion, Stroppe won the Team Owner's title, and Mercury took the Manufacturer's Award.

Prior to the availability of the yet-to-be-announced 1965 Mustang fastback, Ford contracted with Dearborn Steel Tubing to build a Falcon for Dick Brannan. It was powered by the same 427 high-riser engine installed in the DST Thunderbolt. Engineered for A/FX competition, the Falcon was equipped with a four-speed and 9-inch Galaxie rear with thirty-one-spline axles, 4.57:1 gears, and a Detroit Locker. Initially fitted with a B-W T-10 transmission, it was replaced with a beefier Ford top loader four-speed and the final drive ratio was changed to 4.86:1.

According to Brannan, "I was preparing to use the stronger top loader in the 427 Mustangs scheduled for 1965, so we yanked out the Falcon's T-10 and made the swap. We were also experimenting with final drive ratios."

A second Skylight Blue 427 Falcon was completed at DST for Phil Bonner. Both Brannan and Bonner had Thunderbolt Super/Stocks and ran the 427 Falcons with 10-inch slicks in A/FX. Body modifications included fiberglass front fenders, hood, and front bumper. In order to run the big slicks, the rear fenders and wheel wells had to be modified.

Like the previous year, Ford saved some of the biggest news—the all-new Mustang and DOHC Indy engine—for midyear introductions. On April 17, 1964, I attended the Mustang launch at the 1964 New York World's Fair and witnessed the birth of a legend. The new long-hood, short-deck Mustang, available as a notchback coupe or convertible, started production a few weeks earlier. It was one of the most successful new car launches in history. Just eighteen months later, on March 2, 1966, the one millionth Mustang was built!

Right from the start of production, the Mustang was available with a choice of eight engine/transmission combinations. The most interesting enthusiast powertrains were the four-speed 260 and 289-cubic-inch V-8s, especially the solid-lifter 289/271 introduced a few months after the initial Mustang launch.

Just three months after its introduction, the FIA granted the Mustang status as a "Touring Car" for competition worldwide. Thanks to Holman & Moody and Alan Mann Racing in the UK, Mustang rally cars started competing in International road rallies as early as August 1964.

Holman & Moody had prepared 260 Falcon Challengers in 1962 and the three Falcons that competed in the 1963 Monte Carlo Rallye, giving them a head start when the Mustang was introduced. H&M developed 260–289 engine modifications and chassis, brake, and suspension components and tuning specs for Falcons. They quickly applied them to the new Mustang in the summer of 1964. Holman & Moody supplied engines, parts, and specifications to Alan Mann Racing and they prepared three Ford-supplied Mustangs for International rally competition. A total of four 1964½ Mustangs, three from Alan Mann and one from Ford of France, made the starting grid of the 1964 Tour de France Automobile.

Peter Procter and Andrew Cowan, driving No. 83, license plate DPK7B, won the TdF in an Alan Mann/Holman & Moody Mustang with teammates in another Mustang finishing second in the Touring Class. The ten-day, 4,000-mile road rally—won by a Ferrari GTO—required seventeen speed trials at several racetracks, including Le Mans and Monza. Powered by blueprinted and balanced 289 engines that dynoed at 285 horsepower, the lowered and beefed Mustangs were fitted with close-ratio four-speeds, front disc brakes, narrowed Galaxie 9-inch limited-slip rear ends, and quick steering. They rode on 15-inch wheels with Goodyear Stock Car Special tires. During some of the timed speed events, the Mustangs proved to be capable of 150 miles per hour with 0-to-60 mile-per-hour times of 6.8 seconds.

After surprising the international rally community in 1963 with Falcon class wins and speed records at the Rallye Automobile Monte-Carlo, Ford returned for an encore performance in 1964. Ford's George Merwin worked with Alan Mann Racing to put together a team of eight 289 V-8 Falcons built to Holman & Moody specs. All eight Falcons finished and, once again, Bo Ljungfeldt delivered an outstanding performance. Together with Sager Fergus, the No. 49 Falcon, powered by a 305-horsepower engine, finished second overall, edging out the Saab that was favored to win. They also won the over-3,000cc class and set the fastest time of the event on the Monaco Grand Prix course. After the 1964 Monte Carlo Rallye, Ford, Alan Mann, and Holman & Moody concentrated on running Falcons, Fairlanes, and Mustangs in road racing competition in the UK and Europe.

Just a month after the 1963 Indy 500 and debut of the Lotus-Ford "lightweights," Ford Advanced Engine Development, headed by Executive Engineer Bill Gay, assembled a team to design a new and improved Indy racing engine. Unlike the Fairlane-based pushrod V-8 used in 1963, the new engine

Hard-charging Dick Brannan worked for Ford and campaigned the first of two 427 Falcons, built by Dearborn Steel Tubing for NHRA A/FX competition. It was an interim car for Brannan until fastback '65 Mustangs became available. The front fenders, hood, and front bumper were fiberglass. This photo was taken during the 1964 *CARS* Magazine Super/Stock Invitational at Cecil County Dragway.

would be state-of-the-art with four overhead camshafts and fuel injection. Approved in April 1964 and displacing 255.3 cubic inches with a 3.76-inch bore and short 2.87 stroke, the fuel-injected, all-aluminum, and magnesium race engine delivered 425 horsepower at 8,000 rpm with a maximum torque of 295 pounds-feet coming in at 5,000 rpm on 103 octane race gas. The compression ratio was 12.0:1.

The new Indy engine featured four overhead camshafts driven by fourteen straight-cut spur gears, noisier but far more efficient than a single or multiple chains. Aluminum four-valve heads spark plugs mounted in the center of the pent-roof design combustion chambers. Weighing in with tuned 180-degree headers at 395 pounds, it was the most modern engine at the Brickyard in 1964.

Lotus built three race cars powered by DOHC engines for the 500, with two assigned to Jim Clark and Dan Gurney and one reserved as a spare. Chassis #1 went to Clark, who clocked 158.828 miles per hour—seven miles per hour faster than the existing lap record—during qualifying to win the pole. Chassis #3 went to Dan Gurney.

Prior to the start on race day, Indianapolis Motor Speedway looked like a Ford festival with Mustangs and other Ford vehicles blanketing the pit lanes. The official pace car was a Mustang. Henry Ford's grandson, Benson Ford, drove the Indy Pace Car—a Holman & Moody modified Mustang convertible—to start the 500-mile race. It was built on the Mustang assembly line during the first hour of production and rushed to Holman & Moody for engine and chassis/suspension upgrades. The engine was a 450-horsepower 289 mated to a top loader four-speed. In place of the stock Mustang rear was a narrowed Galaxie assembly with limited-slip differential and 3.25:1 gears.

The race was marred by a fiery seven-car accident—the most horrendous in Indy 500 history—that took the lives of veteran drivers Dave MacDonald and Peter Sachs.

A. J. Foyt won the race in a traditional Offy-powered roadster, but it would be the last year that a front-engined roadster would win the American classic.

In 1964, Ford and Mercury drivers and racing teams took home prestigious motorsports honors and awards from NASCAR, NHRA, USAC, IMCA, and ARCA.

Dick Brannan wrenches the Falcon's 427 High-Riser engine, similar to what he ran in his Super/Stock Thunderbolt. Brannan was a key player in the Lightweight drag-racing cars program and went on to run the Ford Drag Racing Team.

Because of Carroll Shelby's Cobra racing accomplishments in the United States and Europe, Ford was presented with the Alec Ulmann Cup "for best performance of a US engine manufacturer in the world's classic endurance road races and GT class wins at Le Mans and Sebring." Alec Ulmann was a pioneer of sports-car road racing in North America and the founder of the Sebring 12-Hour Grand Prix of Endurance in Florida.

Ford did a lot of winning on Sunday in 1964; Ford dealers did a lot of selling on Monday!

Falcons did very well in SCCA Sedan Class road racing and Mike Eddy still owns this Falcon, one of the pioneering SCCA racers in So-Cal Region, first A/Sedan in region. Originally a '63 model, it was rebodied in 1964. Today, Eddy competes in Historic Trans-Am group competition and won the Spirit of Monterey Award at Mazda Laguna Seca Raceway in 2014.
M. M. "Mike" Matune Jr.

1964 Mustang 427 Prototype:
Hemi-Haunter!

The 427 Fairlane Thunderbolt was still a hot Super/Stock contender when Ford laid out its plans for building an A/FX Mustang to replace it.

Back in the day, factory-sponsored drag cars running in NHRA Stock, Super/Stock, and later A/FX had relatively short lifespans. Everything was happening so quickly in 1964 that Ford's Experimental Garage barely finished one prototype race car before they started on the next. Before Ford switched to altered wheelbase A/FX Mustangs (and Comets) with 427 SOHC engines in 1965, they built a prototype 1964 Mustang coupe.

The prototype 427 Mustang (VIN #5F07F100028) was a Wimbledon White hardtop and was campaigned by Bob Ford Inc. from Dearborn. While the conversion from stock to 427 race car was handled internally, the Mustang was shipped directly from the assembly plant to Dearborn Steel Tubing to have its shock towers modified to accept the 427. Then it was trailered to Ford's X-Garage where Bill Holbrook and his team completed the transformation.

The dual-quad, 500-horsepower engine was Ford's latest 427 high-riser, known internally as "Series 7,000," with lighter-weight valvetrain and steel crankshaft and rods. Bob Ford Racing Team's Kenny Salter blueprinted the engine at the dealership that was home to seven sponsored drag cars. A local fabricator, Bob Conner, crafted the 1.625-inch headers hooked up to a single-muffler exhaust system. Holbrook had backed up the engine with a steel-cased, four-speed top loader with a 2.36:1 first gear, 427 Thunderbolt driveshaft, and Ford 9-inch rear with thirty-one-spline axles and 4.86-geared Detroit Locker. Its first runs were at Detroit Dragway where Ford test driver Len Richter ran 123 miles per hour in 11.50 seconds.

This prototype for the 427 Mustang was built in Ford's Experimental Garage with help from Dearborn Steel Tubing. It was sold to Bob Ford Inc. for $1.00 as part of Ford's drag-racing program.

I caught up with Richter and Salter at the 1964 NHRA Nationals and was able to check out exactly what the transformation from stock to FX involved. After the shock towers were cut and spaced, the 427 engine dropped into the stock engine position using Thunderbolt mounts. The Mustang's A-frames, sway bar, and steering were K-code (289/271) components.

For structural rigidity and improved weight transfer, 66-inch boxed steel bars ran from pivot mounts on the rear subframe to the front end. Suspension modifications include K-code shocks, clipped rear leaf springs, and adjustable Air Lifts with 200-psi preload on the right side. Stopping this 3,236-pound, 500-horsepower 427 Mustang was a major concern, so Holbrook's techs installed K-code front and 427 Galaxie rear brakes. All undercoating and body sealers were removed and fiberglass front fenders, Thunderbolt-style hood, and Plexiglas windows were installed. The goal was not to weigh under the NHRA class minimum of 3,200 pounds and they made it by 36 pounds.

Finished in Bob Ford Racing Red trimmed with gold, the A/FX Mustang attracted a lot of attention at Indy. It was a tough A/FX field and the prototype retired early. Later, Kenny Salter had an accident with the prototype and Ford most likely crushed it.

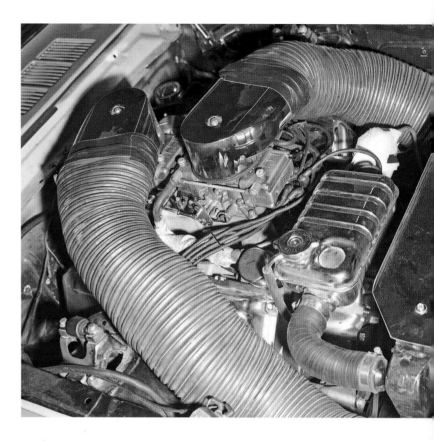

This engine was built by Kenny Salter using the latest 1964 7,000-rpm 427 with dual quads, fresh air induction, and dynode at over 500 horsepower. It's fed by a rear-mounted Stewart Warner electric fuel pump with 0.375-inch lines, set at 6 to 7 psi.

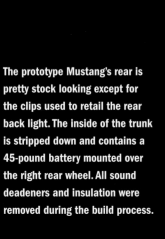

The prototype Mustang's rear is pretty stock looking except for the clips used to retail the rear back light. The inside of the trunk is stripped down and contains a 45-pound battery mounted over the right rear wheel. All sound deadeners and insulation were removed during the build process.

427 Comet and Fairlane:
Thunder, Lightning, and Chaos!

Ford and Mercury make a quantum leap from Stock to Super/Stock and FX in 1964, supported by Thunderbolts, Cyclones, and a blown fuel Super Cyclone.

Even though Ford selected the full-size 427 Galaxie as its quarter-mile halo car, Ford racing czar Jacque Passino and engineers Frank Zimmerman, Charlie Gray, and Dick Brannan knew that it would not be enough to get the job done.

Winning and even setting records in A and B/Stock with prepped 427/425 Galaxies, and in AA/Stock with higher-power, lightweight variants, was not really newsworthy. Ford needed a purpose-built race car and representation in NHRA's top-tier, high-profile Super/Stock category. Members of the recently formed Ford Drag Council agreed unanimously. For Super/Stock, they would need a smaller, lighter car powered by the potent 427 high-riser engine. Enter the 427 Fairlane, later dubbed Thunderbolt.

Responsibility for the program that would conceptualize, engineer, and produce a 427 Fairlane Super/Stock Ford was in the hands of Special Vehicles Activities Group managers Jacque Passino and Frank Zimmerman, along with engineers and in-house drag racers Dick Brannan and Charlie Gray.

Dearborn Steel Tubing received the contract to build one hundred 427 Fairlanes, with production split between four-speed and modified Lincoln C6 automatic, to comply with 1964 NHRA Super/Stock and Super/Stock Automatic rules. The division of stick and automatic cars varies depending upon whom you ask. I've seen 50/50 and 51/49 in favor of sticks in books and magazines, while statistics supplied by a Drag Council member reveals fifty-nine automatics and forty-one four-speeds.

Since the NHRA had refactored its Super/Stock class weight break to 7.5 pounds per cubic inch, the 427 Fairlane had to come in at 3,202 pounds to be competitive. DST was supplied with Fairlane 500 two-door sedans that had been ordered by Special Vehicle's Vern Tinsler. He designed and engineered the famous traction bars that would be installed on all Thunderbolts. A Fairlane designated for Thunderbolt conversion was shipped from the assembly plant without insulation, sound deadeners, seam sealers, carpeting, radio, heater, wheel covers, passenger-side windshield wiper, sun visors, trunk mat, jack, spare tire, arm rests, rear window cranks, and mirrors.

Record-setting drag racer, Ford engineer, and member of the Ford Drag Council Dick Brannan was instrumental in the Super/Stock Thunderbolt program. He received the first Thunderbolt, shown here with Dick at the Fiftieth Anniversary Thunderbolt Reunion in 2014. It's in the Don Snyder Museum in New Springfield, Ohio. *Joe Curley*

Right: Gas Ronda puts some light between his front tires and the tarmac at Cecil County Dragway during the 1964 *CARS* Magazine Super/Stock Invitational. Ronda won the Super/Stock class at the NHRA Winternationals and went on to win the NHRA Super/Stock World Championship.

Left (top): Bill Lawton, right, drove the Tasca Ford Thunderbolt, one of the first eleven built for Drag Council members. This photo of Lawton and John Healey was taken at a special *CARS* Magazine Match race with Bud Faubel's Super/Stock Dodge. In this car, set up and maintained by Healey, Lawton set both ends of S/S record—126.05 miles per hour in 11.69 seconds—at the NHRA Division 1 Points Meet at Connecticut Dragway.

Left (bottom): Dick Brannan testing the first production Thunderbolt in October 1963. Note that the fiberglass hood is fitted with a clover-leaf scoop, which just about all the first eleven recipients thought was extremely ugly. All cars were fitted with teardrop scoops before they left Ford's Dearborn Proving Ground. *Dick Brannan Collection*

Right: Hubie "Georgia Shaker" Platt, one of the most popular Thunderbolt drivers, had a long career driving Fords. His T-Bolt sponsored by Frank Vego Ford, Atlanta, Georgia, is shown here waiting for the green at the 1964 NHRA Indy Nationals.

Joe Curley's Thunderbolt was ordered on a Ford DSO submitted directly to Dearborn Steel Tubing in June 1964. Raced locally in Chicago when new, it's spent most of its life in private collections. It's never been caged or tubbed and still has its the 427 High-Riser engine it was born with. Curley shows, tracks, and drives his T-Bolt on the street. *Peter Tromboni Photography*

"I had a leading role in the final development of the 427 Fairlane, along with Vern Tinsler and Danny Jones," said Dick Brannan. "Danny had previously worked on Ford's Indy engine program and was a valued asset. Together we worked with DST's James "Hammer" Mason, the Thunderbolt's Project Manager. Mason was a tremendous help as we tested and improved the early cars going to our team."

In order to get the Fairlane light enough to be competitive, DST installed fiberglass front fenders, hood, and front bumpers. Aluminum bumpers were later installed after Chrysler complained to NHRA. While the glass windshield was retained, the backlight and side windows were changed to plexiglass. Safety clips, as used on NASCAR race cars, were installed to keep the plexiglass backlight from blowing out at high speeds. Front plexiglass side windows were functional but rears were fixed. A pair of lightweight Bostrom Econoline van bucket seats was installed in place of the front seat.

The largest engine available in a Fairlane was the 289 small-block. In order to shoehorn a 427 into the engine compartment, the inner fender panels and upper control arms and brackets had to be modified. Large 6-inch-diameter hoses, connected to screened grille inlets, directed fresh air to the aluminum air box atop dual Holley #4150 four-barrel carbs mounted on a tall aluminum manifold. The battery was moved from the engine compartment to make room for one of the air induction hoses; a 95-pound battery was mounted in the right side of the trunk to increase traction.

Dearborn Steel Tubing turned out almost turnkey Super/Stock race cars for Ford. Suspensions were beefed with two-leaf rear springs on the left side and three on the right to help offset the 427's incredible torque. Vern Tinsler's traction bars, crafted from square tubing, linked the 9-inch Galaxie rear to a crossmember containing a driveshaft safety loop. Thunderbolts were delivered

Don Nicholson, like Ronnie Sox, switched from Chevy to Mercury for the 1964 season. He started off with the single 427 Comet station wagon built, then switched to a coupe when one was available. He was runner-up for Eliminator honors at the 1964 NHRA Winternationals, losing out to Ronnie Sox in a 427 Comet coupe. Nicolson set the NHRA A/FX record at 11.05 seconds at Cecil County Dragway. He is shown here at the 1964 *CARS* Magazine S/S Invitational.

Les Ritchey and Pete Petre campaigned this Thunderbolt, one of the first eleven built. Ritchey, a member of the Ford Drag Council, prepared it and Gas Ronda's T-Bolts at his shop, Performance Associates, in Covina, California. Ritchey, a top West Coast racer and tuner, moved on to a factory 427 Mustang A/FX racer in 1964.

with NHRA-spec, 7-inch cheater slicks, but it was up to owners to tweak engines and add roll bars.

Engines selected for installation in Thunderbolts were identical to the ones used in the 1964 Galaxie Lightweights—427 high-riser big-blocks with the latest heads and high-rpm, solid-lifter valvetrain and headers. This was a pure and simple racing engine with cross-bolted mains, steel crank, forged high compression pistons, and heads with fully machined combustion chambers. Originally developed for NASCAR competition, the 7,000-rpm, solid-lifter valvetrain utilized lightweight, tuliped valves—2.19-inch intakes and 1.73-inch exhausts. Thunderbolts were fitted with tubular headers but retained a single pipe and muffler exhaust system to meet NHRA rules.

The cars to beat in early 1964 NHRA Super/Stock competition were Dodges and Plymouths powered by 426-inch Max Wedge engines. Many of the most successful Mopars—including the Ramcharger Dodges—were those equipped with TorqueFlite automatic transmissions. Unfortunately, the automatic Thunderbolts with modified Lincoln C6 transmissions and without high-stall-speed converters were no match for the S/SA Mopars. Many automatic T-Bolt owners swapped to top loader four-speeds and ran in S/S.

After the first eleven 427 Fairlanes were built for Drag Council members, DST built additional cars in batches of one to five at a time based on DSOs from Ford dealers. The first eleven Vintage Burgundy Fairlanes—ten four-speeds and one automatic—were released at the Dearborn Proving Ground in October 1963. DST followed up with thirty-nine Wimbledon White Fairlanes—thirty automatics

and nine four-speeds—delivered between December 1963 and February 1964. The third batch consisted of five groups of ten Wimbledon White cars—twenty-two four-speeds and twenty-eight automatics—delivered between February and May 1964. Over time, an additional twenty-seven T-Bolts were built for dealers, with approximately twenty to twenty-five submitting DSOs directly to Dearborn Steel Tubing. Total production was 127 427 Fairlanes.

"In late November or early December, we made the decision to call the 427 Fairlane Super/Stock 'Thunderbolt' and Frank Zimmerman got it approved," said Brannan. "Since I was a pilot, I loved the idea of naming the new race car after a World War II fighter plane. We agreed on 'Thunderbolt,' the legendary World War II P-47 fighter."

He added, "The Thunderbolt was one of the most successful Super/Stock cars ever built. In 1964, we won the NHRA Winternationals with Gas Ronda running 120.16 miles per hour in 12.05 seconds to win the Super/Stock class. Butch Leal won Super/Stock class in his Thunderbolt at the NHRA Indy (Summer) Nationals turning 11.76 at 122.78 miles per hour. Gas Ronda eventually won the NHRA Super/Stock World Championship. Bill Lawton, in the Tasca Ford Thunderbolt, set both ends of the S/S record—126.05 miles per hour in 11.69 seconds—at the NHRA Division 1 Points Meet at Connecticut Dragway."

Lincoln-Mercury committed to a drag racing program for the first time in 1964. While they did not have an in-house racing operation comparable to Ford's large and well-funded Special Vehicles Group, they did have a secret weapon—Fran Hernandez. He was a hands-on racer and already interacting with Stroppe so he became Mercury's point man when they decided to enter vehicles in NHRA competition. He worked on the project with Mercury's Al Turner.

Hernandez and Turner targeted NHRA's FX class with 427 Comets, so as not to compete with 427 Fairlanes in Super/Stock. GM was pulling back on drag racing activities, leaving top drivers like Ronnie Sox, "Dyno Don" Nicholson, Tom Sturm, and others looking for rides for 1964. A number of them signed on to drive A/FX Comets.

Mercury's A/FX Comets were a little more complicated to build, so Hernandez worked with the Logghe Brothers in Detroit to reengineer the Comet's chassis and also with Plaza Fiberglass in Toronto to produce fiberglass front ends from the doors forward, including the bumper. Plans called for building approximately twenty red-and-white 427 Comets, including two prototypes, a coupe and station wagon. Interestingly, the Comet station wagon was built on a 109.5-inch wheelbase chassis, shorter than the 114-inch wheelbase coupe and weighing approximately 250 pounds more. The wagon's advantage was more weight over the rear wheels for improved traction. Dearborn Steel Tubing was given the contract for 427 Comet assembly.

Don Nicolson and "Fast Eddie" Schartman were contracted to test and evaluate the prototypes. They were quite crude and the coupe had to be crushed after R&D, but the wagon survived. The station wagon was given to Nicholson to race until a production coupe was available. Then the wagon went to Schartman.

Like the 427 Super/Stock Fairlane, the 427 Comet received a 427 high-riser engine, four-speed transmission, 9-inch rear with thirty-one-spline axles and a Detroit Locker, plexiglass side windows and backlight, lightweight bucket seats, and proprietary traction bars. Chassis work included modified front A-arms, coils, and shock towers. The 427 station wagon, unlike the coupe, retained its side glass and utilized a fiberglass hood with a Thunderbolt-style teardrop scoop. A unique, dual-scooped fresh air induction hood was used on the coupes.

Mercury's new 427 Comets distinguished themselves in A/FX competition on both coasts. At the *Hot Rod* Magazine Championships at Riverside Raceway, Bill Shrewsberry, in Jack Chrisman's Comet, took home the A/FX class win, running 122.11 miles per hour in 11.70 seconds. Jack Chrisman thrilled the crowds,

running his supercharged and nitro-fueled 427 Super Cyclone Comet at over 150 miles per hour in the quarter! At the NHRA Winternationals, Shrewsberry won the A/FX class while Ronnie Sox, in the Sox & Martin Comet, beat Don Nicholson to take Eliminator honors.

Nicholson campaigned the 427 Comet station wagon until his coupe was ready. Then Eddie Schartman used it primarily for match racing and on the NASCAR drag racing circuit. He won Top Stock Eliminator in the wagon (updated with a 1965 front end) at the 1965 NASCAR Winternationals.

Nicholson had an incredible win record with his coupe—almost eighty wins and a single loss—and set a new NHRA National A/FX record at Cecil County Dragway. Comet racers got their cars into the 10s and Nicholson was undefeated in more than seventy match races in 1964.

Jack Chrisman also campaigned the most outrageous 427 Comet to carry factory and dealer sponsorship—the 1,000-horsepower, blown-fuel Super Cyclone. Primarily an exhibition racer, it also ran in NHRA B/Fuel Dragster class at major NHRA meets. Chrisman built the dragster-in-disguise at his race car shop in Long Beach, California.

I watched Chrisman smoke the Comet's M&H slicks halfway down the quarter at the 1964 NHRA Indy Nationals and blow off a couple of real dragsters. Win or lose, Chrisman never failed to thrill the crowds. At its first public appearance at the Fremont, California, drag strip on July 12, 1964, the *Super Cyclone* laid down an impressive 148.27 miles per hour run in 10.38 seconds.

Because the Super Cyclone had a big 427 engine with a GMC 6-71 supercharger with Hilborn four-port injection, extensive tubular frame construction, and safety equipment, it weighed more than you would think. At Indy in 1964, it tipped the scales at over 2,800 pounds. The engine transmitted its torque to a 3.90 rear via a direct-drive dragster hookup. Running on a healthy mix of nitro and alcohol, Chrisman got his Super Cyclone into the high 6s at over 155 miles per hour during the 1964 season. He came back in 1965 with an updated 1964 Comet A/FX car with Woody Gilmore tube chassis and blown/injected 427 SOHC cammer.

Both Ford and Mercury left their marks in the 1964 NHRA Super/Stock and FX record books. This would continue in 1965 with A and B/FX entries—Mercury with its Comets and Ford switching to 427 wedge and SOHC Mustangs.

Nobody sat down at the 1964 NHRA Indy Nationals when Jack Chrisman staged his B/FD 427 Comet. They knew there was going to be plenty of smoke when Chrisman launched his 1,000-horsepower, supercharged, fuel-burning Comet. The only class it fit into in NHRA was for fuel dragsters! Best runs were in the high 6s at over 155 miles per hour.

289 Mercury Comets:
Total Performance and Durability!

Dearborn Steel Tubing's 1964 Comets set more than one hundred FIA speed and endurance records at Daytona and Bill Stroppe Comets were still running at the end of the grueling 3,188-mile East African Safari Rally.

On October 23, 1964, four specially-prepared 1964 Comets, powered by 289/271 K-code small-blocks, crossed the finish line at Daytona after averaging more than 100 miles per hour for 100,000 miles. The lead car, driven by Iggy Katona, averaged in excess of 108 miles per hour, while the others averaged approximately 105 miles per hour. In order to average 105 miles per hour for 100,000 miles, Comets had to circle Daytona's steeply banked, 2.5-mile oval with 31-degree corners at speeds of up to 112 miles per hour for forty days.

Because the event was run at Daytona and included challenging both national and international speed and endurance records, a number of race

Durability Run Comets, powered by solid-lifter 289/271 small-blocks, ran for forty-two days at average speeds in excess of 105 miles per hour, stopping only for fuel, tires, and driver changes. The Comets were prepared by Dearborn Steel Tubing.
Ford Motor Company

Above: The author, wearing a Flintstone Flyer helmet borrowed from lead driver Iggy Katona, chats with Roger Ward prior to doing some hot laps in specially prepared fifth Comet. The bright red Caliente was driven at an average of 124.42 miles per hour for 10,000 miles.

Durability Run Comets, powered by solid-lifter 289/271 small-blocks, ran for forty-two days at average speeds that exceeded 105 miles per hour, stopping only for fuel, tire, and driver changes. The Comets were prepared by Dearborn Steel Tubing. *Ford Motor Company*

All Mercury team cars in the East African Rally were built by Bill Stroppe and trimmed in red-white-and-blue livery. This photo was taken during the rally and shows one of two Comets to finish the grueling, nearly 3,200-mile off-road adventure. *Ford Motor Company*

sanctioning organizations were involved. NASCAR enforced safety standards while licensing of drivers and the verification of records was handled by the Automobile Competition Committee of the United States (ACCUS), representing the FIA. In addition to proving the performance, reliability, and durability of its newly introduced 289 Comets, Mercury came away with a treasure trove of national and international records.

Like Ford's Monte Carlo Rallye promotion, the idea for the Comet Durability Run came from Mercury's advertising agency, Kenyon & Eckhardt. Mercury's Fran Hernandez contracted with Dearborn Steel Tubing to build four 289/271 Comets for high-speed durability. Hernandez already had an FIA Competitor's license, No. 442, and put together a roster of professional stock car racers including Buddy Baker, Iggy Katona, and Benny Parsons, plus test drivers and amateur racers. DST's Andy Hotten managed the team and was a driver. Katona, the MARC stock car racing champion from 1955 to 1957 and in 1962, was named chief driver and assigned to the lead Comet.

DST prepared five Comet 289 Caliente hardtop coupes for the program, with much of the work focused on safety equipment. The Comets were factory equipped with optional heavy-duty driveshafts and rear ends, and DST installed variable-rate Autolite shocks, HD steel wheels, approved roll bars, shielded fuel tanks, extra instruments, and NASCAR hood, door, and deck lid tie-downs. Four cars were slated for the program with an extra car provided for special track use.

On September 20, Hernandez received a letter from G. William Fleming, Business Manager for ACCUS, giving the Lincoln-Mercury Division and Ford Motor Company the green light for the Comet Durability Run:

> You are hereby granted official permit, Number R-1-63, to conduct attempts for FIA World's Unlimited and International Class C records at the Daytona International Speedway, Daytona Beach, Florida, during the months of September, October, and November, 1963. You are permitted to assault all records for Standing Start and Flying Start in International Class C and World's Unlimited Class up to and including 125,000 and 200,000 Kilometers for a duration of 45 days.

Stopping only for gas and tires, Comets had to survive 100,000 miles at speeds over 100 miles per hour—and they did. However, Hernandez wanted more. He saw an opportunity to also break national and international FIA speed and endurance records while at the track. The Comet's 289 engine put it in FIA Class C and Hernandez calculated that Mercury could pick up some serious bragging rights. He was right.

In addition to four cars averaging more than 100 miles per hour for 100,000 miles, the leading team car averaged in excess of 108 miles per hour for 100,000 miles, setting a new world's Unlimited Class record. The previous world record

Fran Hernandez managed the East African Rally program from inception to car construction. *Ford Motor Company*

Chief Driver Iggy "Flintstone Flyer" Katona with Mercury's Fran Hernandez prior to going out in the lead Comet. Katona was MARC stock-car racing champion from 1955 through 1957 and in 1962. *Fran Hernandez Collection*

Comet No. 74 on one of the better roads, after sustaining some right front fender damage. At least one of the bridges that rally cars had to cross was only about as wide as the Comet! *Ford Motor Company*

Fran Hernandez managed the East African Rally program at Stroppe & Associates, from inception to car construction and during prerally testing and the actual running. In order to be able to drive the rally cars, he had to get a separate FIA Competitor license issued by the Automobile Association of East Africa. *Fran Hernandez Collection*

had been 65.93 miles per hour set in 1960. Mercury picked up more than one hundred US and international FIA records during the course of the event.

One Comet completed a shorter 10,000-mile run at an average of 124.421 miles per hour, shattering the International and US Class C record for closed cars. Homer Newland was at the wheel when the bright red Comet got the checkered flag on October 16 for the 10,000-mile run. Andy Hotten's pit crew knocked off pit stops, including tire changes, in approximately 35 seconds!

Based on Ford's success at the Monte Carlo Rallye in 1963, Mercury had Hernandez put together a Comet team to compete in the 1964 East African Safari Rally. Just a decade old at the time, this rally was considered to be the most brutal ever. Comet drivers would have to deal with washed-out mud roads, bridges as wide as a small car, and wild animals, including menacing water buffalos, on the four-day, 3,188-mile Safari. In 1953, only seven of the eighty-four starters survived.

Bill Stroppe was given the contract to build Comet Calientes with the same powertrain used in the Durability Run cars for the East African Safari Rally. In addition to building six team cars, Stroppe built two, No. 0 and No. 00, to check out the course prior to the start of the rally. They were fully prepared rally cars but did not compete.

Rally Comets started life as 289/271 V-8 Caliente hardtop coupes with four-speed Ford top loader transmissions and limited-slip, 4.57-geared HD rear ends. The solid-lifter small-block came with 10.5:1 pistons and four-barrel carburetor to generate 312 pounds-feet of torque at 3,400 rpm.

Included in the rally preparation was installation of special Autolite shocks; beefed front spindles, radius rods, and spring tower supports; 40-amp alternators; and undercarriage skid plates. Each team Comet was fitted with a roll bar, fiberglass shielding for the stock gas tank, an additional trunk-mounted

COMET
EAST AFRICAN SAFARI Rally
MARCH 26-30, 1964

This is the medallion attached to the base of the 13.5-inch-high ebony statue from the Mercury East African Rally team. Crafted in Kenya, it has the rally logo and livery on its base and was shipped from Nairobi. It's one of many prized possessions from Ford's golden era of high-performance still in the author's collection.

22-gallon gas tank with transfer valves, and a 3-gallon Moon dragster tank filled with windshield washer fluid. Interiors received racing bucket seats, complete instrumentation (including Sun tach), and a Halda Speedpilot.

On March 26, 1964, Mercury's Comet team started on an incredible 3,188-mile, figure-eight adventure through Kenya, Tanganyika, and Uganda. Mercury was the first US factory team not only to compete in the rally but to actually finish. A total of ninety-four cars started and on March 30, twenty-one finished, including two Comets in eighteenth and twenty-first. All the Stroppe Comets—even the ones sidelined by accidents—were still running. The winning car was a Ford Cortina GT driven by Kenyans Peter Hughes and Bill Young.

In advertisements and dealership display materials, Kenyon & Eckhardt celebrated Comet speed and endurance accomplishments on the high-banked Daytona track and incredible reliability over more than 3,000 miles off-road in East Africa.

BOB TASCA'S THUNDERING 427 T-BIRD

The "one of none" 427 Thunderbird was built by Ford and customized by the Alexander Brothers for super-dealer Bob Tasca.

Officially, Ford never offered a 427 T-Bird option in 1964, nor did they build any. However one car, optioned with a rarely seen Export Suspension, drove out of the Wixom, Michigan, assembly plant with a single four-barrel 427 under its hood and 390 emblems on the fenders. Tasca Ford of East Providence, Rhode Island, ordered it for owner Robert Tasca.

Tasca Ford was one of the country's top performance car dealerships in the 1960s and early 1970s, actively campaigning 427 Galaxie Lightweights, a 427

Thunderbolt, and Mustangs. Bob Tasca's personal relationships with Ford senior management and Special Vehicles engineers made it possible for a 1964 Thunderbird to be built with a 427 engine.

When I drove the 427 Thunderbird for a story I was doing for *CARS* magazine in October 1964, Bob explained, "Friends at Ford Engineering prepared a stock, hydraulic-lifter, single-four-barrel 427 engine so that it would pass inspection as just another 390. Then it was delivered to the Wixom plant and tagged for a Thunderbird coupe ordered by Tasca Ford. The 427 installation did not go smoothly, causing glitches that actually shut down the line. But it was driven off the line!"

When I drove the car, it had been already customized by Larry and Mike Alexander in Detroit and modified by Tasca Ford's John Healey. He blueprinted the T-Bird's engine, retaining the C2SE camshaft and dialing it in at 0.454-inch lift and 288 degrees duration. Heads were machined for 71.3cc chambers, resulting in 10.88:1 compression.

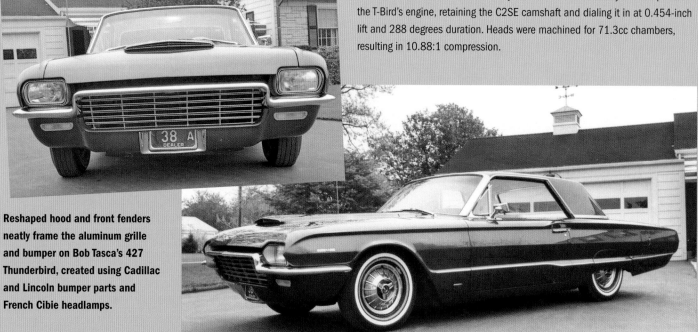

Reshaped hood and front fenders neatly frame the aluminum grille and bumper on Bob Tasca's 427 Thunderbird, created using Cadillac and Lincoln bumper parts and French Cibie headlamps.

Stock trim moldings and emblems were deleted and the car sits 3 inches lower than stock. The Alexander Brothers customized the car and applied more than twenty coats of Candy Apple Red over a Candy Gold underbase.

The lavish interior was updated with chrome trim, TASCA 427 emblems, and a Ford Rotunda tach mounted in the dash just above the console.

The Alexander Brothers flush-mounted the Rotunda tach in the brushed-aluminum dash panel. The tach usually mounts in a cup, fitted to the steering column or screwed into the top of the dash. Not visible is the trick electronic speedometer.

Stock moldings and emblems were removed, and the Alexander Brothers handcrafted TASCA 427 interior and exterior emblems for the car.

The mounting angle of a 390 engine in a Thunderbird differs from that of a 427 engine in a Galaxie, causing problems with fuel delivery. Healey machined a tapered aluminum plate to fit between the 780 cfm Holley and the stock aluminum intake manifold. It leveled the carb and also reduced fuel percolation.

Healey also ripped out the stock exhaust system in favor of Bellanger custom headers and duals with resonators in place of mufflers. In addition to some 25 additional horsepower over stock, the T-Bird gained an authoritative rumble. Fired by a factory 427/425 transistorized ignition system with 35 degrees total advance, the engine bolted up to a beefed, high-rpm Cruise-O-Matic with a special pressure regulator as installed in A and B/SA 427/425 Galaxies.

"Under full-throttle acceleration, the transmission bang-shifts first-to-second at 5,400 rpm at 62 miles per hour and second-to-third at the same rpm at 97 miles per hour," said Tasca with a wall-to-wall grin. "It'll go to 60 miles per hour in six seconds, peg the speedo, and run in excess of 135 miles per hour. And I've done it!"

With much of the car's trim removed, the T-Bird looks longer than stock; it sits 3 inches lower as one coil was removed from each front spring and the rear leaf springs were de-arched. Stock hubcaps were retained.

The Alexander Brothers, best known for their flawless metal fabrication and show paint, customized the 427 Thunderbird. Front-end changes included a custom aluminum grille, a bumper handcrafted from Cadillac and Lincoln parts, and molded-in Cibie headlamps. All emblems were removed in favor of custom "Tasca 427" ID. A Ford Rotunda tach and a special electronic speedometer were added. For a finishing touch, more than twenty coats of Candy Apple Red lacquer were applied over Candy Gold.

After mechanical and custom upgrades, this unique Thunderbird actually weighed almost 160 pounds *less* than a stock 390 model. When I drove the car in 1964, I reported, "Engine idle was just a tick over 500 rpm and you could nail it at 110 miles per hour and get thrown back into the plush contoured bucket seat. It was agile, easy to drive, luxuriously appointed, and delivered musclecar performance."

FORD GT/101: PRELUDE TO LE MANS!

Lola-based GT prototype lays the groundwork for the GT40 and four consecutive Le Mans wins and four FIA International Championship titles.

Henry Ford II's aspirations for motorsports domination extended well beyond America's borders in 1963. Falcon and Mustang class wins at the Monte Carlo Rallye and Tour de France were certainly welcome. But what he really wanted was a Ford win in the most prestigious race on the International calendar—the 24 Hours of Le Mans. The race runs on the Circuit de la Sarthe and covers approximately 8.5 miles on closed public roads and a demanding racetrack.

On a scale of one to ten, Mr. Ford set his sights at eleven to bring the first-ever overall Grand Touring Prototype win to the United States. It was something never before accomplished by an American automobile manufacturer. To realize his most ambitious challenge yet, Ford would have to beat Ferrari, a marque that had dominated endurance racing with seven Le Mans wins between 1949 and 1963.

At the same time that Henry Ford II was planning to challenge the status quo at Le Mans, Ferrari founder and President Enzo Ferrari was interested in selling part or all of his company. Ferrari SpA was profitable, building cars in a modern

assembly plant and fielding a legendary racing team. He was looking for an infusion of cash and technology, as well as management support that could be used to grow the brand and expand racing activities.

In February 1963, Ferrari representatives distributed documents alluding to a possible sale of the company. They mailed letters outlining Mr. Ferrari's interests to Ford affiliates in Europe. Filmer "Phil" Paradise, president of Ford of Italy, received the letter and sent a copy with to Ford Motor Company president Arjay Miller, who passed it on to Henry Ford II. It included a handwritten note: "Recommended Ford of Italy acquire it [Ferrari] & announce acquisition. Send letters to dealers and have someone from your staff go with me to Ferrari."

Lee Iacocca, vice president of Ford Motor Company and general manager of Ford Division since 1960, and his assistant general manager and chief engineer Don Frey had been talking about acquiring a high-profile sports car brand. Iacocca recommended to Henry Ford II that Ford Division buy Ferrari. After discussions with Enzo Ferrari, his original $18 million asking price dropped to $10 million.

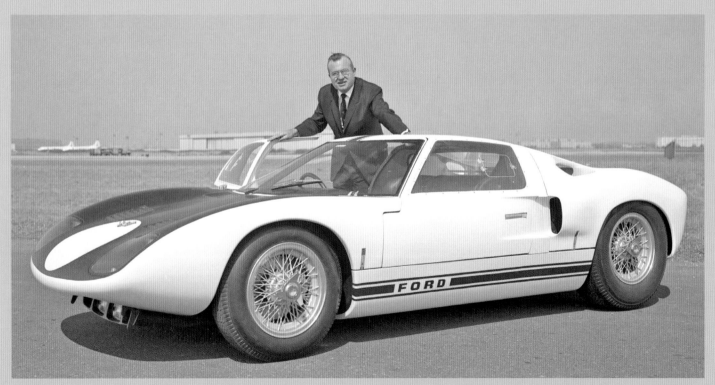

GT/101 prototype after being off-loaded at JFK Airport for press conferences on April 2, 1964. After an evening event at Essex House Hotel, it was shipped back to the United Kingdom for race-prepping and testing.

Ford's lead engineer on the GT40 Le Mans project was Roy Lunn, left, with John Wyer, general manager of the project and managing director of Ford's Ford Advanced Vehicles (FAV) in the United Kingdom. This photo was taken at the first press showing of the GT/101 in the United States.

Ford-Ferrari negotiations were fast-tracked in early spring 1963. On May 20, Ford Division News Bureau crafted the third and final "confidential" press release draft announcing the Ford-Ferrari purchase. I have copies of the Phil Paradise note and the three-page release with quotes from Messrs. Ferrari and Ford. Neither the release nor the Paradise note was released to the media.

One day later during final negotiations in Italy, Enzo Ferrari stood up and, with the help of his interpreter, delivered a bombshell. "My rights, my integrity, my very being as a manufacturer, as an entrepreneur, as the leader of the Ferrari Works, cannot work under the enormous machine, the suffocating bureaucracy of the Ford Motor Company." Mr. Ferrari was not happy with a clause in the purchase contract giving Ford some controls over racing decisions. That was it and Ford went home.

In July 1963, less than two months after negotiations had failed, Enzo Ferrari let Ford know that he was willing to revisit negotiations. Ford had started work on the GT project and was not interested. Thus began the legendary Ford versus Ferrari rivalry, one of the most famous in motorsports history.

One of the early Ford renderings of a Le Mans race car, based on Roy Lunn's Mustang I concept, finished in US racing colors. Note the left-hand drive, as used on Mustang I; all racing GT40s were right-hand drive. *Ford Motor Company*

Since Ford developed its lightweight aluminum small-block for Indy 500 racing in 1963, it was a natural for the GT40 project. Displacing 255.3 cubic inches, it was fitted with four Weber 48IDA carburetors and rated at 350 horsepower at 7,200 rpm and 294 pounds-feet of torque at 5,600 rpm.

Long before the Ferrari debacle, there was talk at Ford about conceptualizing a Le Mans race car. Roy Lunn and Len Bailey were responsible for engineering and developing the midengined 1962 Mustang I, an early concept for a potential racer. It was neither large nor powerful enough to be a Grand Touring Prototype, but its advanced chassis and suspension engineering and midengine placement helped facilitate building the prototype Le Mans racer.

Don Frey, working with Lunn and Ray Geddes, kicked off the Ford Le Mans race car project. Before coming to Ford in 1958, Lunn had worked as an engineer at Ford of Britain and as a lead chassis engineer for Aston Martin Lagonda. A contract was negotiated with Eric Broadley, owner of Lola Cars Ltd. in the UK, to develop a Ford version of the Mark 6 Lola GT. A new facility, Ford Advanced Vehicles Ltd. (FAV) in Slough, England, was chosen to handle construction of the new race car.

John Wyer, ex-manager of Aston Martin Racing, whose DBR1 had won Le Mans and the World Championship for Makes in 1959, was named GM of the GT40 program and managing director of FAV.

Ford's contract with Eric Broadley covered the sale of two Lola Mark 6 chassis built to Ford specs. Overseen by Harley Copp, the Broadley-Lunn-Wyer

team started work at Lola and then moved to the FAV facility. Master fabricator Phil Remington joined the team to build the first car. Ford supplied the money, computer-aided calculations, FAV facility, and, later, wind-tunnel testing for a full-size clay model. The approved clay model was shipped to Specialized Mouldings in the UK on October 23, 1963, for fiberglass body panels. Abby Panels of Coventry handled GT/101's semi-monocoque chassis construction. The prototype was completed on March 16, 1964.

Ford's GT/101, officially known as X40-101, was first shown to the press on April 1, 1964. It was then shipped overnight to JFK Airport in New York City for a press conference at the Essex House Hotel. It was then flown back to the United Kingdom for final race prepping.

Rarely written about in GT/101 media coverage, there was a private showing of the car by Roy Lunn and John Wyer for select automotive and business editors. Unlike the tony Essex House, the venue was Gotham Ford in Manhattan. It was held early on the day of the formal press conference. The purpose was to give "working media" an opportunity to talk with Lunn and Wyer about chassis, engine, and suspension details, and to sample the GT's semireclining driving position.

I was at the dealership when GT/101 arrived. Stunningly purposeful, GT/101 was developed and engineered by Ford and Lola Cars using the foundation of the Lola Mark 6/GT. Even though it hadn't been finished or sorted out, the midship-engined Lola coupe had been shown, for the first time, in January 1963 at the London Racing Show. Essential elements like the monocoque center section, broad sills that doubled as fuel tanks, and aerodynamic profile were carried over during the development of GT/101 and the subsequent GT40.

After talking with Lunn and Wyer, I had a better understanding about the relationship with Eric Broadley and Lola. Broadley came from the same school as Colin Chapman and, like Chapman, was committed to "adding lightness" for more performance. In the case of GT/101, this meant fabricating the chassis from lightweight materials. Lunn pushed for heavier steel construction so the GT platform could be adapted for a road car. Since Lunn controlled the purse strings, Broadley acquiesced. He sold two Lola Mark 6 chassis to Ford and signed a one-year consulting contract to collaborate on the GT40 prototype.

The main structure of the GT prototype was made of .024-inch steel and utilized the roof section as a stressed chassis member. Pontoon sections formed the sills that served as basic structural members through the car's midsection. Steel members extended fore and aft, providing mounting points for engine and suspension. The front-hinged doors incorporated roof sections and all body panels were of reinforced fiberglass construction. Inside were fixed semireclining bucket seats and a fully adjustable three-pedal assembly, as used on the Mustang I.

Ford's lightweight, aluminum Indy 500 small-block was the obvious choice for powering the prototype. Displacing 255.3 cubic inches and fitted with four Weber 48IDA carburetors and tuned headers, it was conservatively rated at 350 horsepower at 7,200 rpm and 294 pounds-feet of torque at 5,600 rpm. Backing up the Indy V-8 was a four-speed, non-synchro Coletti T37 limited-slip transaxle, fitted during R&D with 3.09 to 3.55:1 gearing.

An aerodynamic ducting system allowed air to be taken in at a high-pressure area under the nose and extracted from a low-pressure area on the hood. This system insured engine compartment and cockpit ventilation, even at normal road speeds. Lunn made more than a few references about the GT's feasibility as a road car. A road version GT40 and a Mark III variant would come a couple of years later. Sills on both sides of the GT housed 18.5-gallon neoprene fuel bladders. Each tank had its own large-diameter fuel filler and a pair of Bendix electric fuel pumps.

Working with proprietary computer programs, Ford engineers designed the GT's suspension to be tuned for specific road conditions and racetracks. GT/101 had fully adjustable, front coil-over-spring shocks working with tubular steel, double wishbone units. The rear suspension was also fully independent with two trailing links used with inverted lower A-arms, single strut upper arms, and adjustable coil-spring shocks.

Other GT/101 chassis details included hydraulically-dampened rack-and-pinion, 14:1 steering with an overall ratio of 2.8 turns lock to lock. Girling four-wheel disc brakes with 11.5-inch discs and dual master cylinders, allowing for tailoring of front/rear braking distribution, were installed on the prototype. Wheels were knock-off Borrani wires, 5.5-inch fronts and 7.25-inch rears.

Ford shipped GT/101 back to the UK after the April 2 press events and on April 8, 1964, testing began at the MIRA Lindley test track. The second car, GT/102, was completed on April 16 and both cars were tested at Silverstone before being shipped to France for the Le Mans Trials on April 18. On the eighth lap at the Trials, Jo Schlesser lost control of GT/101 and crashed. It was replaced by GT/103.

Ford entered three production Mark I GT40s at Le Mans on June 20, 1964. All three cars failed to finish. Three Ferraris—one 275P and two 330Ps—finished one-two-three. A Shelby Cobra Daytona Coupe, driven by Dan Gurney and Bob Bondurant, finished fourth. It would take two years before the GT40 matured and Ford ended Ferrari's domination of endurance racing.

Driven by Phill Hill and Bruce McLaren, the No. 10 GT40 dropped out after 192 laps at Le Mans in 1964. While GT40s set lap and speed records, not one of the three factory entries—GT/102, 103, and 104—finished.

Shelby Dragonsnake: A Cobra for the Quarter

Like his road-racing Cobras, Carroll Shelby's Dragonsnakes rewrote the record books . . . a quarter mile at a time.

Building drag racing Cobras was never part of Carroll Shelby's grand plan. You might say that the Dragonsnake was an "accidental" Cobra. It wasn't his idea. The Dragonsnake program originated in 1963 with three young employees—Jere Kirkpatrick, Randy Shaw, and Tony Stoer—and their boss, Leonard Parsons, Manager of Shelby's Production Department.

Kirkpatrick, Shaw, and Stoer wanted to build a drag racing car and pitched their boss on hot-rodding a 289 Fairlane from the company fleet. Parsons, an

experienced drag racer who had worked with legendary Shelby Cobra fabricator Phil Remington building Scarabs for Lance Reventlow, thought it would be a great morale-building exercise. He took their proposal to Carroll Shelby and he liked the concept but not their choice of car. He signed off on the project and donated a Cobra with the caveat that they had to work on the car at Shelby American on their own time.

Carroll Shelby donated a well-used, early worm-and-sector 260 Cobra, CSX2019, that had first been first used as a media test and marketing promotion car. It was then loaned to MGM for use in the movie *Viva Las Vegas*

The second Shelby American drag Cobra, CSX2357, now officially a Dragonsnake, set NHRA and AHRA National Records running in A/SP. It was powered with the first Stage II 289 with dual Carter AFB quads.

Mike Reimer, rear right with hand on helmet, and his crew at the NHRA Indy Nationals in September 1964 with his Stage III Dragonsnake. Shelby American built just one Stage III drag car, ordered by Mike's dad, John Reimer.

The rear fender graphics were applied when the Cobra was originally repainted yellow, later replicated by Steve Juliano. The chrome roll bar is visible through the convertible-top rear window. The original mufflered exhaust system was retained; capped collectors exit under the doors. *Steve Juliano*

CSX2472 was the final Dragonsnake customer car and the only one never drag raced. It was originally ordered as a Shelby Team car but was put in storage uncompleted. Later used to fill an order for a Stage II Dragonsnake, it was driven on the street and for autocross and hill climbs, winning more than 1,200 trophies. *Campbell Auto Restoration/Mark Schwartz*

starring Elvis Presley. Once back at Shelby American, it was repowered with a full-race 289 engine and painted blue metalflake with large, yellow "Cobra" lettering. They also added knock-off Halibrand mag wheels, 5.14:1 rear gears, a cowl-mounted Sun tach, and "Nassau" headers with outside pipes. The suspension was beefed with re-arched and lengthened front and rear leaf springs and Cure-Ride drag shocks.

The Cobra's first outing was in September 1963 at the NHRA Nationals in Indianapolis. Because it was such a high-profile event, they recruited Jim Wright, tech editor of *Motor Trend*, as the driver. Wright was doing well until he blew a half shaft while launching the Cobra at over 6,000 rpm!

Kirkpatrick, Shaw, and Stoer drove the car later. Still not officially a Dragonsnake, the Cobra set an AHRA A/SSP National Record—108.95 miles per hour in 12.81 seconds—in February 1964 at the Winter Nationals at Beeline Dragway in Scottsdale, Arizona. Stoer also drove it to class wins at Pomona and other NHRA tracks.

Before being retired in the Spring of 1964, the first Shelby Cobra drag car, competing in AA/SP, ran its best time ever, 119.20 miles per hour in 11.73 seconds. The next owner successfully raced it for a number of years. Restored to first-raced condition, it is now in Larry Miller's Total Performance Museum.

The first Dragonsnake's performance did not go unnoticed by Ford Motor Company or by Carroll Shelby. There was lots of media coverage and, suddenly, the Cobra was not *just* a sports car. Almost overnight, it unseated the Corvette's domination of Sports class drag racing and created a secondary market for Cobra performance equipment and accessories.

Instead of replacing CSX2019 with another used Cobra, Shelby offered Parson's group their choice of any Cobra in inventory. Stoer chose CSX2357, a

1964 Cobra with improved rack-and-pinion steering and a 289 engine. It was dubbed "Dragonsnake" by one of the team members.

At this point, Carroll Shelby became a believer and created a new line of Dragonsnake Cobras, engineered specifically for NHRA and AHRA competition. They were available with a choice of four 289-cubic-inch engines, rated at 271, 300, 325, and 380 horsepower. Listed under "Cobra Acceleration Package Options" was everything you could possibly need to win, from headers to drag slicks and complete Stage I, II, III, and IV engines. Only one Stage III Dragonsnake with a Weber-carbureted, 325-horsepower engine was built and records do not show any cars built with the Stage IV option that was specifically created for AHRA competition with a special #300R high-rev camshaft kit and machined heads.

Everything that Parson's team learned building and racing the first Cobra was applied to CSX2357. Since they wanted to run NHRA and AHRA meets, two engine combinations had to be developed. For legal NHRA A/SP, they were restricted to the Stage II 289 with dual Carter AFB four-barrels. Under more liberal AHRA class rules, they used the Stage IV package with special valvetrain and heads along with four Weber 48 IDA carburetors on a Shelby manifold.

Stoer was the primary builder of the second drag car and did much of the testing and evaluation before being drafted into the Army. Kirkpatrick then became the designated driver. At the Cobra's first outing on June 13, 1964, at the *Hot Rod* Magazine Championships at Riverside Raceway, he won class honors and set a new track record at 114.83 miles per hour in 12 seconds. After the race, Carroll Shelby received a congratulatory memo from Ford stating that they wanted the Dragonsnake to be entered in every major NHRA-AHRA meet with Jere Kirkpatrick as the driver. Shelby American was now, officially, in drag racing.

In mid-June, I flew to Los Angeles to meet with *CARS* West Coast editor Gordon Chittenden and visit Shelby American. I was then managing editor of the magazine and wanted to put the Dragonsnake on the cover. We met with Carroll Shelby and Don McCain. CSX2357, with unique Dragonsnake graphics on its rear fenders and a spare Stage II engine, was placed in front of the building for Gordon to shoot. The results appeared in a cover story in the October 1964 issue of *CARS* and became the year's best-selling issue!

On July 18, 1964, Kirkpatrick set the NHRA A/SP National Record at 116.27 miles per hour in 11.81 seconds at Freemont, California. With Kirkpatrick, McCain, and Ed Terry driving, CSX2357 went on to set records and win major events, including the 1965 AHRA Winter Nationals. The Dragonsnake continued its winning ways until summer 1965 when it was retired and sold.

The first Dragonsnake customer car was CSX2248, a Princess Blue, Stage II 1964 Cobra built for Hans Schmidt of Williamsville, New York, to run both A and B/Sports at AHRA events. Schmidt won the Daytona Beach Winter Nationals, West Coast Regional, and Big Go South in 1964. For the 1965 season, the Cobra was painted black with "El Cid" livery and took wins at the AHRA Winter Nationals and Arizona State Championships. Its best time was 124.36 miles

per hour in 10.86 seconds. It was restored by Mike McCluskey and resides today in Lynn Park's collection.

Shelby American built just one Stage III Dragonsnake, CSX2427, a Vineyard Green 1964 Cobra that was ordered by John J. Reimer of Gettysburg, Pennsylvania, for his son, Mike. The Weber-carbureted Cobra, shipped in August 1964, was repainted a special shade of yellow to match Reimer's Thunderbird tow car.

I first saw Reimer's Dragonsnake in the pits at the 1964 NHRA Nationals in September 1964 and didn't have a clue about its rarity. Even though I had spent time with the second factory drag car just a few months earlier, I was not aware that Reimer's car was a Dragonsnake. Back then, it was just another modified Cobra and, after chatting with the crew, I shot a photo and moved on. Until now I've had no reason to publish it.

After racing at the Indy Nationals, Mike and brother Don successfully raced at local tracks, including US 30 Drag-O-Way in York, Pennsylvania, until the summer of 1965. That's when Mike went back to school and the rare Dragonsnake was stored. John Reimer finally sold it in July 1966. In 2007, noted collector Steve Juliano purchased CSX2427 and restored it back to how

The Costilow and Larson drag Cobra CSX2093 started off as a road racer and later became one of the winningest Cobras in the country. Set up with single-four-barrel and Weber-carbureted engines, it won major events and set national records in A/SP and AA/SP with Larson driving.

Joel Rosen driving the MOTION *Dragginsnake* Cobra on August 22, 1965, at ATCO Dragway, New Jersey. He set the AA/SP class record at 118.42 miles per hour in 11.57 seconds running a Weber-carbureted 289.

NASCAR
National Record Holder

NASCAR Drag Race Division

proudly acknowledges

Motion Performance Inc.

as the

Official Record Holder

in the class A/SP
This record of 11.41 *ET* 120.80 *MPH*
was established at Atco Dragway
on September 18, 1966.

Edward Wetberger
NATIONAL CO-ORDINATOR

One of Rosen's many regional and national records set with his 289 Cobra. This one is for the NASCAR A/SP National Record set at 120.80 miles per hour in 11.41 seconds on September 18, 1966.

Two of the top Cobra drag racers from the 1960s with the author, left. Bruce Larson, center, and Joel Rosen dominated stock and modified Cobra drag racing on the East Coast.

it looked when Reimer raced at US 30. Even though it never won any major meets or set national records, it remains an incredibly important Cobra.

The final customer Dragonsnake, CSX2472, was ordered in June 1964 as a Shelby Racing Team car but was never completed. Finished in Bright Blue, it was put into storage until January 1965 when Shelby American received an order for a Stage II Dragonsnake from Cobra dealer, Ed Hugus of Continental Cars in Pittsburg, Pennsylvania. Hugus requested specific features not necessarily found on the drag racing model. In accordance with the order, CSX2472 was equipped with a 3.77 limited-slip rear, Koni adjustable shocks, roll bar, FIA Halibrand mags, fender flares, Belanger headers, and a hardtop. It was shipped to Hugus in August 1965 incorrectly fitted with a single four-barrel Stage I engine.

The Cobra was repainted British Racing Green and all "Shelby Cobra" and "Powered By Ford" emblems were removed before the first owner took delivery. It was used as a street car for almost two years before being sold to the second owner who actively campaigned it in autocross and hill climb competition. Before changing hands again, the green Dragonsnake had won over 1,200 trophies—not one on a drag strip!

Current owners Len and Linda Perham acquired the only Dragonsnake that was never drag raced in 2006. Perham had it restored to its first-owner condition. The Perhams have a number of Shelby cars in their collection, including the 427 Motion King Cobra.

In addition to the six Shelby American Dragonsnakes—five 289s and one 427—there were a number of *cloned* Dragonsnakes built and campaigned by record-setting drag racers. Some were as successful (if not more) than the two Shelby American team cars—CSX2019 and 2357—and the three customer Dragonsnakes—CSX2248, 2427, and 2472. The highest profile and national-record-holding privateer Cobra drag racers were Bruce Larson, Joel Rosen, and Gus Zuidema.

Campaigned by Bruce Larson for Jim Costilow of Ducannon, Pennsylvania, the Costilow and Larson Cobra, CSX2093, was sold to Costilow in 1964. It was first road raced and then entered in hill climbs before being converted to a Dragonsnake. Bruce Larson modified the Cobra and drove it in NHRA A/SP (with single four-barrel engine) and AA/SP (with Weber carburetors) competition on both coasts. Larson set NHRA National Records in both classes and took class wins at the 1965 Springnationals and Winternationals.

In 1966, Costilow sold the Cobra to Philadelphia's Ed Hedrick, who continued to campaign it in A, B, and C/Sports at NHRA Northeast Division 1 tracks. Hedrick set records, won Street Eliminator honors, was NHRA World's Point Champ, and set the C/SP record at 115 miles per hour in 11.51 seconds at the 1966 NHRA Nationals.

During 1965 and 1966, dyno-tuner and speed shop owner Joel Rosen of Motion Performance in Baldwin, New York, campaigned two national record-holding Cobras—the small-block Motion Cobra and Clem Hoppe's big-block *King Cobra*. While he did have help from Shelby American's Don McCain when converting his street 289 into *Dragginsnake*, Rosen prepared and drove the 427 Cobra without any outside support.

Not long after Rosen started racing his 289 Cobra, he and Motion Performance rocketed into the national drag racing spotlight. In one year's time, Rosen set ten East Coast track records, nailed the NASCAR B/MSP National Record, and won Street Eliminator honors at the 1965 Canadian Drag Nationals. On August 22, 1965, at ATCO Dragway, Rosen set both ends of the AA/SP class record at 118.42 miles per hour in 11.57 seconds.

"Without help from Shelby-American's Don McCain, I probably wouldn't have been able to set all those records," said Rosen. "He made it possible for me to replicate his 'factory' Stage II Dragonsnake."

Rosen started running Stock Sports classes with the 289/271 four-barrel engine, graduated to four Webers , then made the leap into the Modified ranks. He built a stroked, 340-inch small-block that could be fitted with either four Webers or Hilborn fuel injection, making the Cobra legal for AHRA, NHRA, and NASCAR Modified classes and ideal for match racing.

In addition to a Corvette four-speed with 2.54 First gear, Rosen's Motion Cobra was equipped with a Ford A/FX 427 SOHC Mustang rear end with a Detroit Locker, 5.67:1 gears, and thirty-one-spline axles. The fenders had to be flared to accommodate the big rear and 8-inch-wide Goodyears.

Rosen's gold metalflake Cobra was always a crowd-pleaser, especially when he ran match races against highly modified big-inch Chevys. His success at the track led to a relationship with Clem Hoppe, owner of 427 Cobra CSX3159. Shortly after turning his Cobra over to Motion Performance, Hoppe embellished its *King Cobra* graphics with Motion Cobra livery and started collecting 11-second time slips. Rosen's first run in the *King Cobra* was an 11.90 against an 11.40 NASCAR record. Later in the season, the *King Cobra* ran 10.30s and set a new NASCAR record at 131 miles per hour in 10.64 seconds.

Longtime friend Bill Kolb, a serious drag racer and high-performance sales manager at Larsen Ford in White Plains, New York, during the early to mid-1960s, remembers Hoppe. Kolb sold him CSX3159 on July 1, 1966: "I remember selling Hoppe a black Cobra that I had special ordered with optional rear fender flares like it was yesterday. He was the *only* guy who ever came into Larsen shopping for a Cobra to go drag racing."

At the 1967 NHRA Division 1 Record Meet at ATCO Dragway, Hoppe's *King*

Joel Rosen, left, with original owner Clem Hoppe and the King Cobra in 1966. The car was plated, driven on the street, and drag-raced on weekends. It was driven three hours to ATCO Dragway, New Jersey, for the Division 1 record meet, set AA/SP National Record at 10.67 seconds, and driven back to Motion Performance, Baldwin, NY.

Joel Rosen in 1966 with the Hilborn fuel injection that was used on the Cobra's Match race engine. Rosen ran stock and modified NHRA classes, and Hilborn injection was used on a 340-cubic-inch stroker motor used for match racing. The car was also fitted with Webers for NHRA-AHRA-NASCAR stock sports and modified classes.

Cobra annihilated the record. "My partner Jack Geiselmann and I drove the 427 Cobra, followed by a shop support car, for more than three hours to the track," Rosen recalls. "We changed plugs and tires and made a couple of passes. We set the AA/SP National Record at 10.67 seconds, then reinstalled the street plugs and tires and drove back to New York. Except for almost going deaf and my back taking a beating, it was a piece of cake."

In 1969, Hoppe retired from drag racing and stored *King Cobra* in a barn on his family's property. Hoppe's parents sold the Cobra in the 1970s and it was not until early 2004 that CSX3159 was back on the market. By that time, its drag racing livery as well as the 427 engine were long gone and it was being sold as a stock big-block Cobra. Shelby restoration specialist, Tony Conover, traced its history in the Shelby American Automobile Club's Cobra Registry and purchased it in 2004. He became the *King Cobra's* fourth owner.

After spending more than thirty years hiding in plain sight and masquerading as a stock 1966 Cobra, CSX3159, in full *King Cobra* livery and powered by a correct solid-lifter 427, was driven out of Conover Racing and Restoration. It looked and sounded like it did when raced in 1966–1967. Since 2005, *King Cobra* has resided in Len and Linda Perham's collection.

Gus Zuidema, Service Manager at Harr Ford in Worchester, Massachusetts, also raced two Cobras, CSX2109 and CSX3198. His first Cobra experience

came when Larry MacAlister, a Harr Ford customer, brought in his stock 289 Cobra, CSX2109, for service. He also inquired about upgrading it for drag racing. MacAlister had purchased his 1963 Cobra in early 1964 from its first owner, Bob Tasca. Other than a change from its original Princess Blue exterior to Candy Apple Red, CSX2109 was stock. Zuidema executed the conversion to Stage III Dragonsnake specs at Harr Ford.

Like the limited-production factory drag cars, MacAlister's Cobra was fitted with Koni adjustable shocks (90/10 front and 50/50 rear), NHRA-approved scattershield, competition clutch, 4.89:1 gears, rear-mounted batteries, and beefed springs. Zuidema also added an aluminum competition radiator, hood scoop, and fiberglass hardtop. Unlike most Cobras competing on the quarter-mile, CSX2109 retained its wire wheels.

During 1964, Zuidema racked up an impressive record of twenty straight wins plus track records in NHRA Division 1. His best times were in the 11.60s at trap speeds in the 120s and, after winning twenty races, he earned a spot at the 1964 NHRA Indy Nationals. After wading through a field of strong running cars, Zuidema lined up on the trophy run with the Shelby American Team Cobra driven by Ed Terry. Terry got the A/Sports class win. After the 1964 season, CSX2109 was converted into a road-racing car.

Officially, Shelby American did not build Dragonsnakes after the end of

289 Cobra production. They did, however, build CSX3198, a big-block 1966 Cobra ordered by Harr Ford for drag racing in late 1965. It was tagged as a Cobra Drag Unit and ordered with a gray primer exterior and black interior, and modified per instructions from Harr Ford's owner Gus Zuidema.

After it was received from AC Cars, Shelby American installed front and rear Koni adjustable shocks, roll bar, dual electric fuel pumps, road race exhaust system, rear mounted batteries, scooped hood, NHRA scattershield, 4.54:1 rear gears, and a cowl-mounted tach.

Zuidema campaigned the 427 Cobra in NHRA A/Sports and A/Modified Sports classes during 1966. Powered by a blueprinted and balanced

505-horsepower, 427 Side Oiler with 12.5:1 compression, the one-off 427 drag Cobra set both ends of the NHRA National A/Sports record at 127 miles per hour in 10.86 seconds and won both the NHRA Winternationals and Indy Nationals. Zuidema had an incredible NHRA Division 1 Street Eliminator win record during 1966. When he fitted the engine with Tunnel Port heads and induction, Zuidema was able to clock 138 miles per hour in 10.38 seconds in A/Modified Sports.

Rarely have so few done so much to enhance a brand's reputation and dominate a motorsports category. With just a handful of factory-built Dragonsnakes plus customer-converted drag racing Cobras, Shelby American and Ford "owned" the classes that were formerly the property of the Corvette.

Harr Ford ordered a 427 Dragonsnake from Shelby American in late 1965, after small-block Cobra and Dragonsnake production was over. Shelby built one 427 Cobra Drag Unit, sold to Harr in primer for Gus Zuidema to drive. In 1966, Zuidema set both ends of the NHRA A/SP record, 127 miles per hour in 10.86 seconds, and took class wins at the NHRA Winternationals and Indy Nationals. He also ran the big-block Cobra in A/MSP with 427 Tunnel Port engine, clocking 138 miles per hour in 10.38 seconds.

CHAPTER 6

1965

TOTAL PERFORMANCE: THE BEAT GOES ON!

Ford cars and engines prove to be unbeatable on the world's toughest proving grounds: Daytona, Indianapolis, Nürburgring, Pomona, Riverside, Sebring, Targa Florio.

1965 was a year of firsts and incredible accomplishments for Ford on racing circuits worldwide. No other American carmaker—and few European manufacturers—came close to Ford's seemingly unstoppable assault.

When Bob Bondurant crossed the finish line in a Cobra Daytona Coupe CSX2601 at the 12-hour race at Reims, France, he locked in the World Manufacturer's Championship, the first ever for an American carmaker. Jim Clark drove his Ford-powered Lotus into Victory Lane at the Indy 500, starting a revolution at the American classic. In NASCAR Grand National racing, Ford

Galaxies won forty-eight out of fifty-five races, including the Daytona 500. Ford driver Ned Jarrett was NASCAR Grand National Champion. Mustangs dominated SCCA C/Production racing in five of six divisions and a rally-prepped Mustang won the European Challenge Cup.

On the quarter-mile, A/FX 427 Mustangs won big in national events, helping Ford win NHRA's Manufacturers Award for the second year in a row. In AHRA's World Championship Series, Ford took seven of nine Eliminator brackets. Gas Ronda's 427 SOHC Mustang was Top Super/Stock Eliminator.

Henry Ford II was most impressed when Ford was presented with the 1965 Alec Ulmann Cup for the second year in a row. The silver bowl is presented annually to the American manufacturer whose engines earn the highest number

Tasca Ford was a mecca for high-performance Fords in the 1960s and in 1965, and Bob Tasca commissioned the build of the 505 Mustang to set his dealership apart from other Ford stores. It was powered by a 505-horsepower 289/271 small-block, stroked to 325 cubic inches and topped off with dual quads. Bob wasn't bashful about promoting it. *Tasca Family Archives*

Dick Brannan's red prototype was painted dark blue and later gold and white by the Alexander Brothers in Detroit. It carried Goldfinger livery and Brannan, captain of the Ford Drag Team, drove it to win the 1965 Super/Stock Nationals in York, Pennsylvania. *Dick Brannan Collection*

Specially prepared new Mustangs were very successful in European Touring Car races and rallies and won the European Challenge Cup. Here, Jack Brabham is pictured on his way to winning Gold Cup race at Oulton Park, England. *Ford Motor Company*

Prepared 289/271 Mustangs were quite successful in NHRA Stock competition, usually running in C/S. Sponsored by Grant Ford of Saint Petersburg, Florida, the *Flying Horse* was 1965 NHRA Southeastern Regional Champ. Photo shot at the 1965 NHRA Indy Nationals

of points in four of the world's toughest and longest road races—Le Mans, Nürburgring, Sebring, and Targa Florio.

Ford dealers had a lot to celebrate in 1965. The Mustang lineup grew to include a fastback coupe that was sexier and more appealing to enthusiasts than either the notchback coupe or convertible. While the engine lineup was carried over and the 289/271 was still the hottest option, new front disc brakes could be ordered for just $58. Mustang continued ownership of the pony-car market since it would be two more model years before Chevrolet would reveal its Camaro. In 1965, Ford dealers sold an incredible 559,451 Mustangs.

Dealers continued to push Total Performance and, in 1965, took an even more aggressive position marketing over-the-counter factory speed equipment and Shelby Cobra Kits to owners of Mustangs, Falcons, Fairlanes, and Comets. Kits included budget single four-barrel induction systems, cam kits, and the Weber carburetion packages that were used on championship Cobras.

Ford completely restyled and reengineered the full-size 1965 Galaxie with new sheet metal, chassis, and suspension updates. These could be ordered with 410-horsepower, single four-barrel and 425-horsepower, dual four-barrel 427 engines. Coil springs were used fore and aft for the first time, which improved ride quality.

Early production (up to January 1965) 427 Galaxies were powered with carryover big-block engines. The 1965½ production 427 Galaxie came with a new, side-oiler big-block fitted with a forged steel crank, high-rpm valvetrain with lightweight hollow-stem valves, and heads with machined combustion chambers. The same block was also used for the 427 SOHC race engine.

Even though the Galaxie was a big car with a 119-inch wheelbase, it offered surprisingly good performance on the street. Some of my old *CARS* magazine test notes show that a 427/425 Galaxie with four-speed and 3.50:1, Detroit Locker rear could sprint from 0 to 60 miles per hour in the low-5-second range.

On the drag strip, it was not unusual to run the quarter in the 15.0s at around 95 miles per hour. When equipped with headers, ignition tuning, and cheater slicks, a 427/425 Galaxie could clock high 14s.

In January 1965, I interviewed Jacque Passino for the May 1965 issue of *Rodder and Super/Stock*. He was then Ford Division competition manager working under Leo Beebe. Passino revealed drag racing initiatives for the year, primarily focused on participation at the NHRA Winternationals in February. "Ford will not be represented in Super/Stock competition in 1965 but will be well-represented in the stock classes, ranging from AA/S to J/S," Passino told me. "In Factory Experimental, we will have three hot machines—427 SOHC Mustang in A/FX, 427 Wedge Galaxie in B/FX, and a Weber-carbureted, 289 Cobra-powered Galaxie in C/FX. All these vehicles are being built strictly for drag racing and will not be streetable."

Dick Brannan was a key player in the development of the A/FX Mustang. He said, "We had Dearborn Steel Tubing build two prototype 427 SOHC Mustang fastbacks, one white and one red, in late 1964. In December, I shipped the red one, my car (VIN #5F09K380230) without any Ford racing livery, to California for testing. It was built and shipped with a single four-barrel, NASCAR-type cammer and I knew we would have to update with dual quads and get the car sorted out for the 1965 Winternationals at Pomona on February 5 through 7. I spent most of my track time working out suspension and chassis details with my boss, Charlie Gray, since high-speed handling left a lot to be desired. By the time it was track-ready, the color was changed to dark metallic blue. In midyear, color was changed again to gold with a Pearl White cove and it became known as the *Goldfinger* Mustang. I won the 1965 Super/Stock Nationals at York, Pennsylvania, in this car."

The ten production A/FX 427 Mustangs were built on 289/271 four-speed donor cars, shipped to Holman & Moody without doors, front fenders, bumpers, engines, windshields, radiators, rear seats, spare tires, jacks, and transmissions. Conversion from stock to A/FX race car cost approximately $11,000 per car; they were sold to Ford Drag Council members for $1.00 each.

In addition to Brannan's car, converted Mustangs were delivered to Ford's Bill Holbrook, Bill Lawton, Gas Ronda, Les Ritchey, Al Joniec, Clester Andrews, Len Richter, and Phil Bonner prior to the Winternationals. Holman & Moody retained one Mustang for driver Paul Norris. Ford's one-dollar drag-racing cars came without any warranty and with a disclaimer: "Not to be used as a passenger car on the street." Even though the A/FX Mustangs had legal VIN numbers, they were sold with special MSOs dated April 23, 1965, and could not be titled and registered for road use. After the ten AFX Mustang build at Holman & Moody was completed, they built some additional Wedge and SOHC Mustangs for dealers and private parties.

After its Winternationals debut, the 427 A/FX Mustang became *the* car to beat in stock-body vehicle competition. Bill Lawton, driving the Tasca Ford SOHC Mustang (VIN #5F09K380232), won the A/FX class and set the lowest elapsed time—10.88 seconds at 129.84 miles per hour—at the Winternationals. Lawton's Mustang was one of twelve built with 427 Wedge and SOHC engines, two at Dearborn Steel Tubing and ten at Holman & Moody. Len Richter set

the A/FX record at 10.91 seconds. Lawton later lowered the record to 10.63 seconds at over 131 miles per hour.

Ford dominated the tough Factory Experimental class at the Winternationals. Jerry Harvey captured the B/FX crown, running 119.68 miles per hour in 11.78 seconds in his one-of-one 427 SOHC Galaxie, *The Quiet One*. Bill Hoefer took the C/FX class win in his Weber-carbureted, 289 small-block Galaxie at 105 miles per hour in 13.58 seconds. In the showroom Stock classes, 1965 Galaxies won AA/S, AA/SA, and B/SA trophies!

Cars powered by Ford engines also excelled at the 1965 Winternationals. Bruce Larson won AA/SP with a 113-mile-per-hour, 12.09-second run in the Costilow & Larson 289 Cobra, and sixty-four-year-old Sam Perry drove his 427 Ford-powered Kurtis to victory in AA/Modified Sports.

Jacque Passino's drag racing plan for 1965 got off to an incredible start and gained even more momentum during the year. One week after the NHRA Winternationals, Fords and Ford-powered vehicles won twenty-eight classes at the AHRA Winter National Drag Races in Scottsdale, Arizona.

Ford Drag Council member Phil Bonner ran a 427 Falcon in 1964, one of two built by Dearborn Steel Tubing. There was also a third special 427 Falcon, built by Holman & Moody based on a 1965 model, for Bonner. It was Poppy

Gas Ronda was a Ford Drag Council member and received one of the original A/FX 427 SOHC Mustangs. At the AHRA World Finals, Ronda set the record at 134.73 miles per hour in 10.43 seconds. He crashed his original Mustang and Ford replaced it with this car, fitted with a drag chute.
Factory Lightweight Collection

After Tasca Ford moved on to an altered-wheelbase A/FX Mustang, the original one of ten built by Holman & Moody was sold to Bondy Long, right, with driver Carson Hyman. It was fitted with a 427 Wedge motor for Ultra/Stock-4 competition. In 1968, Bondy loaned the Mustang to Sam Auxier Jr., who drove it to beat Bill Jenkins and win the *CARS* Magazine Super/Stock meet at Cecil County Dragway, Maryland.

In mid-1965, Dick Brannan switched to an altered-wheelbase Mustang, still powered by a 427 cammer. This shot taken at the 1965 NHRA Indy Nationals shows Brannan on his way to beating "Dyno Don" Nicholson, who was driving one of a handful of altered-wheelbase cammer Comets built by Bill Stroppe. Brannan and Nicolson were factory racers and Brannan was an engineer at Ford. *Fran Hernandez Collection*

Red, powered by a 427 SOHC engine, and fitted with a small alloy Moon tank inset into the driver's side of the grille. At first, Bonner ran the car on race gas in Southern-style, match-race competition. He then added Hilborn fuel injection and filled the Moon tank with nitro. Sponsored by Frank Vega Ford, Bonner successfully campaigned his *Daddy Warbucks* Falcon from mid-1965 into the 1966 season.

Since Jacque Passino's 1965 drag racing program excluded Super/Stock cars, the Fairlane Thunderbolt program was not continued after the 1964 season. However, two special 1965 Fairlanes, one with a 427 and the other with a 289/271 engine, were built for Ford drag racers. Often referred to as "Thunderbolts," the B/Factory Experimental Fairlane was fitted with a 427 Wedge engine at the Ford X-Garage. Its sheetmetal work and shock tower modifications were farmed out to DST. It was later converted to 427 SOHC power. Campaigned by Darrel Droke of Downey, California, and sponsored by Doheny Ford, *The Wonder Colt* ran over 126 miles per hour in the quarter at Half Moon Bay during the Southwest US Divisional Championships. The biggest problem was rear end failures and, like many one-dollar Ford race cars, ended up in the crusher.

Ford built the second drag racing 1965 Fairlane, powered by a 289/271 small-block, specifically for NHRA Stock class racing. It was sold for $1.00 to Ford Drag Council member Les Ritchey, who prepped and tuned it at Performance Associates. It was driven by full-time police officer and part-time drag racer Ron Root.

In the world of stock car racing, 1965 could best be described as the "year of confrontation" with NASCAR's Bill France going head-to-head with Ford and Chrysler. It was all about engines and car size. Ford threatened to pull out if they couldn't run the SOHC 427 Galaxies against Plymouths and Dodges with 426 Hemis. Neither Hemis nor cammers were available in production models, so there was an issue of NASCAR legality to start with. Chrysler said if the Ford cammer was legal, they would be running dual overhead cams which, of course, they didn't have. Bill France had banned the 427 high-riser, which was primarily a drag-racing engine because it was not available in a production passenger car. There was also bickering about car size.

After the smoke had cleared, it was an all-new ballgame! NASCAR banned the Hemi, the cammer, and the Ford 427 high-riser and set up three classes for competition, starting with Class I for cars with a minimum 119-inch wheelbase and engines to 430 cubic inches. These cars were the only ones to be allowed on Super Speedways. Ford had the ideal car for this class—the 427 medium-riser Galaxie. Class II was for cars with 115- to 119-inch wheelbase and engines to 430 cubic inches. These cars could run anywhere except on Super Speedways. Class III was created for compact and sporty cars with less than 115-inch wheelbase and engines up to 335 cubic inches.

Ford dominated stock car racing in 1965 with teams run by Holman & Moody (Fred Lorenzen, Bobby Johns, Dick Hutcherson), Wood Brothers (Dan Gurney, Marvin Panch), Bondy Long (Ned Jarrett), independent Junior Johnson, and Bud Moore with Mercury (Darel Dieringer). Dan Gurney won the *Motor Trend* Riverside 500 for the third straight time. Ford debuted the new, NASCAR-legal 427 mid-riser engine at Riverside and the first eight place finishers were Fords and Mercurys. In 1965, Fords won forty-eight out of fifty-five NASCAR races, with Lorenzen winning the Daytona 500 and Dieringer coming in second in a Mercury. Ned Jarrett won thirteen races and was crowned NASCAR Grand National Champion.

The second '65 Fairlane drag car was built for Ford Drag Council member Les Ritchey, who also campaigned a 427 Mustang and prepped Gas Ronda's cars. This was built to run in NHRA D/Stock. Ron Root, a local police officer who had held records with Dodge Darts, drove it. Ron ran 14.4 second at over 91 miles per hour.

Fred Lorenzen won the Daytona 500 on February 14, 1965, in this first of three No. 28 Galaxies (C5HM-10047) built by Holman & Moody. He went on to also win the Martinsville, Virginia, NASCAR race three months later. Its owner, John Craft, who also drove it at Goodwood in 2004, restored it. It's since made two more appearances at Goodwood, driven by current owner Andrew Franzone. *John Craft Collection*

In 1965, Ford turned its GT racing program over to Shelby American. Ford committed to build fifty Ford GT40s with 385-horsepower, 289-cubic-inch small-blocks at Ford Advanced Vehicles in Slough, England, to be sold by Shelby American for $16,250 each. On February 28, 1965, with just a couple of months prep time, one of Shelby's GT40s, No. 73 with Ken Miles and Lloyd Ruby driving, won its first race, the Daytona 2,000 KM Continental. Bob Bondurant and Richie Ginther placed third in another GT40. The following month, a Shelby GT40 driven by Ken Miles and Bruce McLaren finished first in the Prototype class and second overall at the 12-Hour Sebring race. It was a great start for Shelby American and the Ford GT40.

Left: Ford gave control of its GT racing program to Shelby American and, with just two months' preparation, GT40 No. 73 driven by Ken Miles and Lloyd Ruby won the Daytona Continental. It was the first win for the GT40 and was followed a month later with a win by Miles and McLaren in a GT40 at the 12-hour Sebring. They finished first in the Prototype class and second overall. *Ford Motor Company*

Below: A flurry of activity at Shelby American's race car shop in 1965. In the foreground is a Cobra Daytona Coupe, then the No. 98 Competition 427 Cobra road-race car, Ford GT prototype, and, in the rear, '65 K-code Mustangs being converted into Shelby GT350s.

Ford's plans for challenging Ferrari at Le Mans centered on six GT40s, two entered by Shelby American and one each by Ford Advanced Vehicles and Ford of France. Additionally, George Filipenetti and Rob Walker each entered a GT40. The driver lineup included some of the world's finest endurance racers. Phil Hill/Richie Ginther and Ken Miles/Bruce McLaren drove the two Shelby American Mark II GT40s powered by big-block 427s. Bob Bondurant/Chris Amon and Innes Ireland/Herbert Mueller drove the privateer entries with stroked 325-cubic-inch small-blocks. Richard Attwood/Sir John Whitmore and Maurice Trintignant/Guy Lieger drove the 289-engined GT40s.

The two 427 Mark II GT40s were prototypes, GT/106 and GT/107, built at Kar Kraft under Roy Lunn's supervision and equipped with new Kar Kraft transaxles built around Ford four-speed transmissions. Prototype GT/106 was tested at over 210 miles per hour at Ford's Romeo test track and Riverside before going back to Kar Kraft for final race-prep. At Le Mans, Miles and McLaren set the fastest lap in the race at 212.51 miles per hour.

Unfortunately for Ford and Shelby American, Ferrari continued its winning ways at Le Mans, finishing one-two-three. Not one GT40 crossed the finish line on June 20, 1965, after all six were sidelined with mechanical issues. Henry Ford II would have to wait one more year before basking in the June sun and celebrating with his drivers.

Although its open-wheel racing program was still in its infancy in 1965, Ford rocked the Championship Car racing community at Indianapolis. "As far as the

Colin Chapman, Lotus Cars, and Ford started a revolution at the Indy 500 in 1965, with Jim Clark (No. 82) winning the Classic. Ford rear-engined cars finished one-two-three-four, and eight of the eleven finishing cars were Ford powered. It was the end of the front-engine-roadster dynasty. Colin Chapman is pictured at right, with Jim Clark in the pits. *Ford Motor Company*

One of Ford's secret weapons at the Indy 500 was the hiring of the Wood Brothers to run the pit operation. The legendary NASCAR team could refuel an Indy car in under 20 seconds. Nobody did it better! *Ford Motor Company*

car and the engine, they were both in order and ready for the win in 1965," said legendary Ford engine builder Mose Nowland. "The one thing Leo Beebe thought we could improve on was pit stop efficiency, so who is the best pit stop team of all? That would be the Wood Brothers. So that's who they went after and got."

With their well-rehearsed choreography and quick reflexes, the Wood Brothers had revolutionized modern-day pit-stop techniques on the NASCAR circuit. Brothers Glen, Leonard, Delano, and Ray Lee were the recognized leaders in their field and they made the transition from stock cars to open-wheel Indy car without missing a beat. They stunned competitors at the 1965 Indy 500 with under-20-second refueling stops. They were the best the Brickyard had ever seen.

Jim Clark led a Ford-engine assault at the Indy 500. Of the eleven cars that finished the 1965 Indy 500, including the first four finishers—Jim Clark, Parnelli Jones, Mario Andretti, and Al Miller—Ford engines powered eight. Clark led the race three times for a total of 190 laps and was the first non-American to win the 500-mile classic since 1916. Andretti came in third and also won the highly coveted Rookie of the Year honors.

While Mercury had minimal presence in NASCAR and USAC stock car competition in 1965, that was not the case in NHRA and AHRA drag racing. Lincoln-Mercury's Al Turner and Fran Hernandez mapped out a drag racing strategy for the Comet that would support dealers. Hernandez was the performance and evaluation coordinator and, in November 1965, became supervisor of the department.

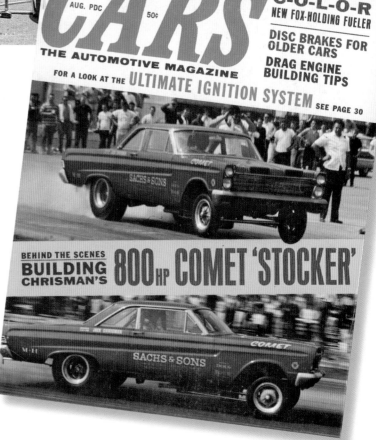

A small number of A/FX Comets were built by Stroppe for factory racers, not for sale to the public. After a season of running his Sachs & Sons Lincoln-Mercury Comet B/Fuel Dragster, Jack Chrisman built a '65 Comet lightweight that was even more a dragster. Powered by a supercharged and injected 427 cammer, Chrisman ran 160s in the mid-9s. Its construction was featured in a cover story in *CARS* in August 1965.

Turner and Hernandez contracted with Bill Stroppe Engineering to build fifteen Comet Lightweights similar to the 427 A/FX 1964 Comets, only with blueprinted 289/271 engines. Selected Lincoln-Mercury dealers were able to order full-blown drag racing Comets affordably priced at under $5,000!

Weighing approximately 2,600 pounds, these NHRA FX Comets came without radios, heaters, glove boxes, sound deadening, carpets, and back seats. Front fenders, bumpers, doors, hoods, deck lids, and panels covering the rear seat area were made of fiberglass. All Stroppe Comets had plexiglass side windows, lightweight bucket seats, and carryover 427 Comet traction bars.

Even though just fifteen Comet Lightweights were scheduled, purchasers could choose engine and performance options based on classes they wanted to compete in. The base Comet came with a single-four-barrel, solid-lifter 289 with Jardine headers rated at around 315 horsepower. Engine options included Shelby Cobra dual-quad intake for $250 and Shelby Cobra four 48IDA Weber carburetors on a special aluminum intake manifold for $600. A well-tuned, Weber-carbureted 289 was good for approximately 400 horsepower at 7,000 rpm.

Ford top loader four-speeds were standard, but FX Comet purchasers could opt for a 50-pound lighter Borg-Warner T-10 transmission. All Comets came with Ford 9-inch rears, thirty-one-spline axles, 5.67:11 gears, Detroit Lockers, and NHRA-approved scattershields. Depending on engine options, Stroppe's Comets could run 115 to 120 miles per hour in the mid-11s. Doug Nash, driving a factory B/FX Comet with Webers, set the NHRA record at 121.29 miles per hour, later setting low elapsed time of 11.54 seconds. By the end of the season, Nash was running 123 miles per hour in the 11.30s.

Stroppe also built approximately a half dozen A/FX Comet Lightweights powered by 427 Wedge and SOHC engines. Factory racer "Fast Eddie" Schartman received one of these cars and was running in the mid-10s before switching over to Nitro. The A/FX Comets were built specifically for high-profile racers like Arnie Beswick, George DeLorean, Don Nicholson, and Hayden Proffitt and could not be ordered from Lincoln-Mercury dealers.

Fresh from the previous year's Comet durability challenges and successes—100,000 miles at over 100 miles per hour at Daytona and dodging wild animals to finish the East Africa Safari Rally—Fran Hernandez planned a challenge for the newly styled 1965 Comet. The mission was to run three Comets for forty days and nights, on and off roads, from the bottom to the top of the world! Starting on September 12, 1964, the event ran from Ushuaia, the capital of Tierra del Fuego Province in Argentina, to Fairbanks, Alaska, covering 16,200 miles through fourteen countries under all possible extreme weather and road conditions. The route crossed the ice- and snow-covered Andes Mountains and traversed rain- and mud-soaked jungles. On October 22, all three Comets finished in Fairbanks, Alaska. The longest single leg, 2,049 miles, was Mexico City to Los Angeles. To many, the bragging rights earned through these durability events were much more relevant for increasing sales than those associated with racing.

After two successful speed and durability challenges in 1964—at Daytona and the East Africa Safari Rally—newly styled '65 Mercury Comets ran for forty days and nights from the tip of South America (Cape Horn) to Fairbanks, Alaska. They covered 16,200 miles through fourteen countries and the most extreme weather and road conditions imaginable. *Ford Motor Company*

1965 Shelby GT350: Mustang with Cobra Bite!

Converting a Mustang into a GT350 may not have been rocket science, but the results were unmatched sound and fury—*and* the SCCA B/Production National Championship.

In 1964, Mustang created its own sporty-car market segment. Ford further enhanced its image in 1965 with a slick fastback coupe and available front disc brakes. But it was still a sporty car, not a *sports car*. The two-place Corvette was "America's Sports Car" and, in 1965, Chevrolet confirmed its title by offering an optional 396 big-block engine and standard four-wheel disc brakes.

Ford market surveys revealed that a sizeable percentage of young Mustang shoppers who didn't buy Mustangs *did* buy Corvettes and imported sports cars. Marketing manager Bob Johnson shared the details with Ray Geddes at Ford Special Vehicles. At the time, there was a small, low-profile group at Ford trying to get SCCA approval for a modified 289/271 Mustang notchback. But they weren't getting anywhere.

Ray Geddes went to Jacque Passino, who felt that participating in SCCA road racing was the key to creating an upscale sports car image for the Mustang. "If you want to get a Mustang homologated for Production class racing, it should be built by Carroll Shelby," said Passino. He had worked with Shelby during the early days of Ford's involvement in the Cobra program and knew that he had the resources to make it happen. Lee Iacocca agreed.

"I was called into Lee Iacocca's office and he asked me what we had to do to road race the Mustang, said Carroll Shelby in an interview with Joe Oldham for 'Striped Lightning, The Shelby Mustang' in *Automobile Quarterly*, Volume 16, Number 3, 1978. 'Build a hundred of 'em,' I told him. That's how the GT350 happened," Shelby would actually deliver *far* more than Iacocca

The hand-built first or prototype GT350, #5S003, has been restored and is owned by Mark Hovander. Note the front fender decal used only on a couple of early cars. Wheels are stock steel originals and the only option (dealer or purchaser installed) is the Le Mans stripe package. *Mark Hovander*

Above: Gus Zuidema, who drove the record-setting Harr Ford Cobras, also handled the reins of the dealership's '65 Shelby GT350 Mustang. Prepared at Harr Ford, the GT350 was very successful in NHRA Division 1 B/SP competition. This photo was shot at the 1965 NHRA Indy Nationals.

The Shelby GT350 Mustang display in the Ford Pavilion at the 1964–1965 New York World's Fair. The production GT350 is believed to be #5S065 with optional alloy wheels designed by Peter Brock. *Ford Motor Company*

Peter Brock, designer of the World Championship Cobra Daytona coupe, is responsible for the GT350's graphics, emblems, interior treatments, and optional wheels. He also wrote the copy and produced the first GT350 advertisement that featured Mark Hovander's first-built GT350. Brock drove #5S003 for the advertising shoot. *Gary Jean*

ever anticipated. Shelby American won the B/Production Championship in five of the SCCA's six regional divisions. Jerry Titus drove #5R001 to win the 1965 American Road Race of Champions and SCCA National Championship.

In order to homologate a car for SCCA racing, there had to be a minimum of one hundred produced that followed modifications and safety equipment guidelines. Shelby was a little ahead of the curve since Cobra racer Ken Miles had been experimenting with a couple of modified Mustang notchbacks. He was brought in along with ex-GM engineer Chuck Cantwell, an active SCCA racer, to head up the "Cobra Mustang Project." In the Fall of 1964, Cantwell was named Project Manager and worked with Ray Geddes, Sam Smith, and Klaus Arning at Ford in Dearborn. It was Arning who plotted the GT350's final suspension geometry settings on a computer after testing a "mule." Interestingly, he also designed a fully independent rear with disc brakes for the GT350.

Unlike anything else available, regardless of brand, Shelby's GT350 Mustang was a pure driver's car. It was hairy, loud (engine, exhaust, and Detroit Locker),

and a handful at low speeds. Brakes and steering were manual and driving a GT350 required full, undivided attention at all times.

In January 1965, Cobra, GT350, and race car production moved to a new facility at the Los Anges International Airport. Mustangs for GT350 conversions—all Wimbledon White, K-code fastbacks with 289/271 engines and Shelby-spec changes, were ordered on DSOs and built at Ford's San Jose assembly plant. The total production of 1965 Shelby GT350 Mustangs was 562—522 "S" street models, four earmarked for drag racing, and 36 "R" race cars.

GT350 Mustangs started life as stripped, or KD (knock-down), donor cars. They arrived at Shelby American without wheel covers, seat belts, grille trim, rear seats, side trim, and hoods. Each car had six-cylinder model fenders without emblems. The stock stamped cowl-to-shock-tower braces were replaced with a single forged steel brace as used on export models. Before leaving San Jose, donor Mustangs were fitted with narrowed Galaxie nine-inch rears with big

The engine compartment of #5R535, with an aftermarket air cleaner that was installed when it was street driven. Note the one-piece cowl brace, Monte Carlo bar, original Competition "tin" valve covers with tall breather tubes, and oil cooler mounted off to the side of the radiator.
Miller Motorsports Park/Jeremy Henrie

police/taxi drum brakes. They also substituted lighter, alloy-case, Borg-Warner T-10 four-speed transmissions (2.36 first gear) in place of the Ford units.

Structural rigidity was increased by the addition of an underhood, fender-to-fender, tubular steel Monte Carlo bar. Holman & Moody first used Monte Carlo bars in 1963 and 1964 on the winning Monte Carlo Rally Falcons and in 1964 on the Holman & Moody/Alan Mann Racing Mustang that won the Tour de France.

Peter Brock, designer of the Cobra Daytona Coupe, was responsible for making the GT350 look unique and stand out in a sea of Mustangs. He penned the exterior graphics, racing stripes, hood scoop, wheels, exterior, interior badges, and instrument cluster.

The GT350 (#5S003) featured in the first advertisement and driven by Brock in Benedict Canyon, near Venice, California, was the first GT Mustang hand-built at Shelby American. Its T-10 four-speed, Galaxie rear, and other special components were installed at Shelby American, not at the San Jose plant. Today, Mark Hovander owns #5S003 that has been restored it to original condition.

What immediately grabbed your attention as you looked at a GT350 was the scooped fiberglass hood with NASCAR-style locking pins, side-exit exhausts, two-seat interior with Ray Brown competition belts, wood-rim Cobra steering wheel, and a large tach and oil pressure gauge mounted in the center of the dash. A fiberglass panel and spare tire mount replaced the Mustang's rear seat. Berry Plasti-Glass was a fiberglass supplier to Shelby-Ford programs. The GT350 rode on speed-rated Goodyear 7.75 x 15-inch Blue Dot tires. If you looked closely at an alloy-wheeled GT350, you would notice the 11.3-inch Kelsey-Hayes front disc brakes with semimetallic pads. At the rear, the 10.5-inch rear drums had metallic linings. When cold, a GT350 was a bear to stop!

You had to drive a GT350 to understand just how special it was. A stock 289/271 Mustang with HP suspension and disc brakes was a very decent handling road car. The GT350 was an outstanding sports car with ride control, handling, and braking capabilities achieved only from extensive suspension and chassis tuning.

The GT350's chassis and suspension preparation was what turned the pony car into a sports racing car. The relocation of the 1-inch lower upper control arms improved front-end geometry and increased front roll center height. This small change decreased front wheel "lean," caused by body roll, by 30 percent, resulting in more traction and usable power under hard cornering. Increasing the roll center height reduced body roll by 8 percent. Two degrees of positive caster helped increase directional stability.

Shelby American engineers favored keeping the stock Mustang spring rates and adjusting the GT350's Koni shocks for increased control. Custom idler/Pitman arms reduced the steering ratio from 21:1 to 19:1 and reduction of 3.75 to 3.5 turns lock to lock. A 1-inch-diameter antisway bar replaced the stock component. To combat rear spring windup and wheel hop, Traction Master supplied traction bars that ran forward from brackets welded atop the axles to floor-pan-mounted brackets, in line with the front pivot point of the rear springs. Aircraft cable loops limited rear axle movement. Each GT350 was fitted with a driveshaft safety loop, like those on drag cars. While a Galaxie rear was down for installation of traction bar mounting brackets, a Detroit No-Spin (Detroit Locker) differential was installed. The most popular final drive ratios were 3.89 and 4.11, but 3.70 and 4.33 gears could be ordered.

All GT350 street Mustangs were Wimbledon White with Guardsman Blue rocker panel stripes, GT350 identification, and 15x5.5-inch steel wheels. Full bumper-to-bumper racing stripes were available for dealer or purchaser installation, and a handful of GT350s left Shelby's facility with stripes already in place. The only Shelby-installed option was unique 6-inch-wide alloy wheels designed by Peter Brock and manufactured by Cragar.

Engines were modified at Shelby American and covered by the vehicle's factory warranty. The stock, solid-lifter 289/271 engine retained all internal components and was bolstered by intake, exhaust, and lubrication upgrades. Shelby junked the stock intake manifold and Ford carburetor in favor of a high-rise manifold with a 715 cfm, center-pivot-float Holley four-barrel. Often referred to as a Le Mans Holley, it was used in road racing cars to insure fuel delivery during hard cornering. The GT350 engine was rated at 306 horsepower at 4,200 rpm or 1.06 horsepower per cubic inch!

The changeover to a larger, baffled Cobra aluminum oil pan improved oil cooling and prevented oil from sloshing away from the pickup under high G-loads. Made by Buddy Bar Casting, the finned oil pan increased capacity from 5 to 6.5 quarts. Cyclone and Belanger supplied tubular steel headers and glass-pack mufflers for the GT350's side-exit dual exhausts. A large capacity radiator aided cooling.

Both street (S) and competition (R) model GT350s were originally programmed to receive trunk-mount batteries that took weight off the front and relocated it over the right rear wheel for improved traction. Since the trunk was not totally isolated, there were many complaints from owners about odors from battery fumes. According to Mark Hovander, "They tried to control fume leakage by installing Cobra battery caps, but that really didn't work."

All GT350s selected for racing were built with trunk-mount batteries. Competition models also had shorter-than-stock plexiglass backlights that were open at the top for extracting interior pressure and battery fumes. R-model donor Mustangs left the plant without insulation, weather stripping, sound deadening materials, interior trim, glove box door, front and rear bumpers, front lower valence panels, glass side windows and backlight, and side window channels and hardware.

Race car conversion included installation of an engine oil cooler, ducts for front and rear brake cooling, metallic brake pads, 34-gallon fuel tank, fiberglass front valance, roll bar, shoulder harness and belts, fire extinguisher, flame-resistant interior materials, fender flares, and a unique instrument panel. Race engines were built to order; a typical blueprinted and balanced 289 with machined, ported, and polished heads; flycut 11.5:1 forged pistons; and headers produced 330 to 350-plus horsepower at 6,500 rpm.

Ready-to-race R models weighed approximately 2,500 to 2,600 pounds and were as quick and fast as they sounded. The debut of Shelby's GT350R was at an SCCA event at Green Valley Raceway in North Richland Hills, Texas, with Ken Miles driving. He took the D/P class win, beating Corvette Sting Rays and E-Type Jags. During the year, R models driven by Jerry Titus, Bob Johnson, Mark Donahue, and Chuck Cantwell dominated SCCA B/P competition.

GT350 Mustangs were priced at $4,547, approximately $1,000 more than a well-equipped 289/271 fastback. Track-ready Rs retailed for $5,950. Drag racing models were priced at $5,441. Shelby American turned a production Mustang into viable choice for Corvette-shopping enthusiasts. And that's exactly what Lee Iacocca wanted!

SHELBY COBRA DAYTONA COUPE:
WORLD CHAMPION

Because Cobra roadsters were not suitable for long, high-speed circuits in Europe, Shelby's solution was a streamlined coupe. Born out of necessity, the Daytona Cobra trounced Ferrari to win the 1965 World Championship.

November 11, 1965, was one of Carroll Shelby's happiest days. He received a cable from G. William Fleming, executive director, Automobile Competition Committee for the United States (ACCUS), Fédération Internationale de l'Automobile (FIA): "Confirm Shelby American won Group 3 World Manufacturers Championship. Our deepest congratulations and best wishes for a 1966 repeat of this signal honor."

In his quest for the GT World Championship in 1964, Carroll Shelby was handicapped by the Cobra's top-speed limitations. Cobras hit an aerodynamic "brick wall" at 140 to 150 miles per hour and were not competitive with archrival Ferrari's 250 GTO. Increasing horsepower was not the answer. The problem was the roadster's less-than-aerodynamic styling.

Stylist Peter Brock, a graduate of the Art Center College of Design in Pasadena, California, had designed the stunning Corvette Sting Ray racer for William Mitchell while working at GM Design. He was Carroll Shelby's

first employee and had become a major creative force at Shelby American. In late 1963, he explained to Carroll that the cheapest "free" horsepower had nothing to do with engine modifications. It was all about superior aerodynamics, something sorely missing in the Cobra roadster. He convinced Shelby that a streamlined coupe body could increase a Cobra's top speed and make it competitive with the world's fastest and most successful GT, the Ferrari 250 GTO.

Brock sketched a coupe body proposal for Shelby and, with his knowledge of aerodynamics and racing, projected that it could increase a Cobra's top speed by at least 20 miles per hour. There was also a good chance that fuel consumption would drop based on the body's wind-cheating attributes. Shelby gave it a green light and Brock, working with chief engineer and master fabricator Phil Remington and racing director Ken Miles, created the first of what would be six Cobra coupes.

The prototype coupe was CSX2287 (the actual second chassis) with an aluminum body crafted by California Metal Shaping in Los Angeles. It was the first built, first raced, and the only coupe bodied in the United States.

Jo Schlesser and Harold Keck drove CSX2299 at the 1965 Daytona Continental, shown here on its way to taking first in class, second overall.

CSX2287, the first Daytona Coupe built (though actually the second chassis), in the No. 10 livery used at Sebring. Though sidelined due to complications from a pit fire at its first race, it won its second race at the Daytona 12-Hour on March 21, 1964. *Ford Motor Company*

Here's CSX2287 at Shelby American in Venice, California, being primered after its rear vents have been filled in, which proved to not be a good idea according to Daytona designer Pete Brock.

Carroll Shelby accomplished what no other racing team owner had ever done before or has done since: he brought the FIA GT World Championship to the United States in 1965.

For its first race at Daytona, CSX2287 carried No. 14. While it did not finish, it did earn the pole position, leading the winning Ferraris by a big margin for the majority of the race. *Ford Motor Company*

Five other Cobra chassis earmarked for coupe production were shipped to Carrozzeria Grand Sport in Modena, Italy.

The first track tests were held at Riverside Raceway. The prototype was run with a "tired" test engine, 3.54 rear, and without windows. It top-ended at 175 miles per hour and the Weber-carbureted 289 engine pulled 6,000 rpm in fourth gear. A well-tuned, sorted-out coupe would have 200-mile-per-hour potential—exactly what Shelby was looking for.

Brock, Miles, and Remington scrambled to get the coupe ready for its first public outing on February 14, 1964, at the Daytona Continental. Driven by Dave MacDonald and Al Holbert, the Viking Blue No. 14 Cobra, now known as the Daytona Cobra Coupe because of its debut at Daytona, almost stole the Ferrari GTO's thunder. Holbert qualified the coupe at 106.93 miles per hour to win the pole. The new, barely tested Cobra led for nearly 200 of the 330 laps but had to drop out on the 204th lap because of complications after a fire when Holbert came into the pits for fuel. Three Cobra roadsters finished fourth, seventh, and tenth. Ferrari finished one-two-three.

Wearing No. 10 livery, CSX2287 was back on the track approximately one month later at the Sebring 12-Hour race. Piloted again by Holbert and MacDonald, the first-built Daytona Cobra finished first in the GT Class and fourth Overall, losing to the latest Ferrari prototypes.

In addition to being road raced by Shelby American in 1964 and 1965, CSX2287 set twenty-three National and International speed records at the Bonneville Salt Flats in November 1965. Land speed racers Craig Breedlove and Bobby Tatroe broke records that had been in the USAC book for approximately

three decades. Breedlove and Tatroe logged more than 1,931 miles and averaged 150 miles per hour, breaking an existing speed/durability record set by a Bugatti in the 1930s. Interestingly, the Bugatti and CSX2287 are both on display at the Simeone Foundation Museum in Philadelphia.

Between 1966 and 1971, CSX2287 was used (and abused) as a street driver by producer/songwriter Phil Spector. It was then passed on to his bodyguard, who didn't treat it any better. The neglected Daytona was stored for a number of years by Spector's sister before she committed suicide. In 2009, Spector was convicted of murdering actress Lana Clarkson and began serving a nineteen-year prison sentence. After being purchased by Fred Simeone, CSX2287 was the subject of a detailed preservation/restoration by Bob Ash.

Daytona Cobra CSX2299 was the second built and the one credited with the best racing record, leading the charge to winning the World Championship for Shelby American in 1965. In addition to first in GT Class at Le Mans and Goodwood Tourist Trophy races in 1964, it won the GT Class at the Daytona Continental, Sebring 12-Hour, and Oulton Park, and took a second at Le Mans, Reims, and the Coppa de Enna races in 1965. It is owned the Miller Total Performance Museum at Miller Motorsport Park in Tooele, Utah.

Between February and September 1965, Shelby American Cobras, competing in the FIA GT category, won six road races and a hill climb: Daytona; Sebring; Monza, Italy; Oulton Park, England; Nürburgring, Germany; Rossfeld, Germany; Reims, France; Enna, Italy; and Bridgehampton, New York.

Shelby celebrated the GT World Championship win with a cross-country, twenty-six-state road trip. The Cobra Caravan road show featured a Cobra Daytona Coupe, a 427 Competition Cobra, a Ford GT40, and a new Shelby GT350R road-racing Mustang.

Using a Best Seven Event matrix (six road races and one hill climb), the FIA awarded Ferrari 71.3 points. They awarded Cobra 90.3 points and the championship. Some of the drivers responsible for winning the championship include Bob Bondurant, Allen Grant, Dan Gurney, Phil Hill, Bob Johnson, Jo Schlesser, Jack Sears, Lew Spencer, Dr. Dick Thompson, and Sir John Whitmore.

On January 22, 2014, the Historic Vehicle Association (HVA) announced that 1964 Shelby Cobra Daytona Coupe CSX2287 would be the first automobile to be recorded under the Secretary of the Interior's Standards for Heritage Documentation. The documentation will be part of the HVA's National Historic Vehicle Register and Historic American Engineering Record (HAER) that is permanently archived in the Library of Congress

At the announcement, Peter Brock, of Brock Racing Enterprises and the designer of the car, said: "Having my Shelby Cobra Daytona Coupe design recognized as the very first car to be included in the permanent archives of the Library of Congress is a great honor and the thrill of a lifetime. I'm very proud that the Shelby Cobra Daytona Coupe helped lead the way to American's first win in the FIA International Manufacturer's GT Championship in 1965. The Coupe's revolutionary design contributed to new standards for automotive aerodynamic efficiency."

Decades later, the Ford-powered Shelby Cobra Daytona Coupe remains the only US-built car to win the coveted FIA Grand Touring World Championship. All six coupes are accounted for, some in collections and museums, some still being raced.

The engine in CSX2299 is typical of the 289 Ford small-blocks installed in Daytona Coupes for GT Class competition. Induction is by Weber: four 48IDA two-barrel carburetors mounted on a Shelby aluminum intake manifold.
Miller Motorsports Park/Jeremy Henrie

1965 USRRC:
Cobra-Powered Lola T70 Spyder

AC/DC rocker Brian Johnson's T70 Spyder, which has been powered by Ford since it was new, is considerably faster than when first raced in California a half-century ago.

In 1962, John Bishop, then executive director of the Sports Car Club of America (SCCA), helped create the United States Road Racing Championship (USRRC), SCCA's first racing series for professional drivers. The goal was to recover the races that rival United States Auto Club (USAC) had taken for its Road Racing Championship Series. Shortly after, the USAC series folded.

The USRRC races ran from 1963 to 1968, when it was dropped in favor of the hugely successful Can-Am Series, also run by SCCA. During its first three seasons, the USRRC showcased open sports cars as well as serious, high-powered GT cars. Shelby American vehicles dominated the Over-Two-Liter class, while Porsche took home the Under-Two-Liter gold. In 1963, Bob Holbert drove a Shelby Cobra to win the championship, followed by Jim Hall in 1964 and George Follmer the following year in Shelby American entries.

Lola was the premier race car constructor in the UK and, under Eric Broadley's management and working with Ford's Roy Lunn, was responsible for creating the Ford GT prototype in 1963–1964. That prototype would become the ultrasuccessful Le Mans winning GT40. They also built incredibly advanced Chevrolet and Ford small-block-powered T70 coupes and open cars specifically for USRRC. While at first glance they looked like Can-Am cars, they were actually one step down from the big-block racers of *Thunder Road* fame. Almost a half-century later, many are competing in historic racing events both here and abroad. One that looks like it was just delivered by Lola in 1965 is the blue and white T70 Spyder owned and campaigned by rock band AC/DC frontman Brian Johnson.

Brian Johnson is as passionate about race cars and racing as he is about music. His current love, a real 1965 Lola T70 Spyder (SL 70/15), is a seriously fast machine that first competed in the heyday of both Can-Am and USRRC competition. Unlike many Lolas that had left Slough, UK, with 289 Ford power and years later converted to Chevrolet, Brian's Lola is still Ford-powered. It's currently seeing service on tracks from coast to coast, powered by a 598-horsepower, 347-cubic-inch small-block. His stunning Lola tips the scales at under 2,000 pounds!

The rocker's Lola is finished in its original blue with white stripes and No. 12 livery, as it was driven by Ronnie Bucknum and Dave Jordan. Bucknum was a

Brian Johnson on the corkscrew at Laguna Seca during the Monterey Historics. Lola has the same livery as when it raced in 1965–1966. *Michael Alan Ross*

popular USRRC, Formula One, and Can-Am pilot who also raced a GT40 at Le Mans. He drove Lola No. SL 70/15 for Haskell Wexler who campaigned it when new for owner Jim Russell, President of Russkit models. Russell was a pioneer of slot racing cars, the first to offer models with dual engines and four-wheel drive. Brian Johnson's Lola was the first of a new series of $^1/_{24}$-scale models that launched Russkit's enormously popular *Black Widow* line.

"When Eric Broadley first introduced his Lola Mark VI GT coupe in 1964, he started a revolution in sports car racing that swiftly led to the T70, said Lola expert, author, and racer John Starkey in his book *Lola: The Sports-Prototype and Can-Am Cars*, the acknowledged bible of "everything Lola," including the history of SL 70/15. "It developed into a Can-Am open version and a World Championship coupe version."

Over the years, SL 70/15 was painted blue and white with power by both Chevrolet and Ford engines. At one time, it actually ran without a body when then-owner Bob Bondurant converted it into a drivable chassis configured as a movie camera car. According to original owner Haskell Wexler in Starkey's book, it was used as a camera car for the Paul Newman movie, *Winning*. "Newman

may have actually driven it at some point," said Starkey. "This is when he was starting to get hooked on racing."

Lola T70s were used as camera cars for racing films. A T70 Spyder, identical to Brian Johnson's and powered by Ford, was used in the making of the UK film *Day of the Champion*.

It was Starkey who found SL 70/15 for Brian Johnson. Its previous owner, Skip Shattuck, had dismantled the Lola and was going to restore it. It never happened. It just sat in pieces until Starkey located it.

Predator Performance in Largo, Florida, a company that competition preps and restores vintage race cars, executed the restoration and initial race-prep of Brian Johnson's Lola T70 Spyder. They installed a new Mark I body on the mostly steel original Mark I tub. Except for an aluminum scoop attached to the roll bar to channel fresh air to the Webers, the Lola looks exactly as it did in 1965–1966, right down to its white-trimmed, blue No. 12 livery.

While originally powered by a 289-cubic-inch Ford small-block, the latest powerplant is larger, considerably stronger, and much more powerful. Ted Wenz at Savannah Race Engineering in Georgia built the Lola's 347-cubic-inch "289." It pumps out 598 horsepower at 6,500 rpm and 514 pounds-feet of torque at 5,500 rpm. Topped with four Weber 48 IDA two-barrel carburetors and ported and polished aluminum heads, the blueprinted small-block is fitted with Crower steel crank and rods along with 13:1 forged aluminum pistons. The 3.25-inch stroke, 3.40-inch bore engine bolts up to a Predator-installed Hewland D6500 transaxle.

Johnson's first time out in No. 12 was at the 2011 Monterey Motorsports Reunion at Laguna Seca. In a field of forty-six 1960 to 1968 USRRC Sports Racing cars, he finished eighth. Not too shabby for its first outing. Brian's Lola is maintained by David Hinton's Heritage Motorsports in Clearwater, Florida. Hinton had been a partner at Predator Performance and is also President of Historic Sportscar Racing (HSR). Steeped in history and supported with pages of racing provenance, Johnson feels his Lola is not only scary fast, but beautiful enough to park in his den!

Above: This stunning, envelope-bodied T70 Spyder has all the makings of a wonderful road car, yet it is a purpose-built race car from the foremost constructor of the time. *Michael Alan Ross*

Right: The big-inch, small-block Ford is fitted with big-valve aluminum heads, photographed here after the powertrain was installed in the platform. The transaxle is a Hewland D6500.

Brian Johnson with Stuart Schorr, vice president of communications, Jaguar Land Rover at the Quail. Brian has a Range Rover and has driven a C-Type Jaguar at the Millie Miglia and other Jaguar Heritage Trust vehicles at Goodwood and other venues.

1965 De Tomaso Sport 5000: Sole Survivor!

Alejandro de Tomaso brought Carroll Shelby and Peter Brock in to help create a racer that Shelby could race in Can-Am and de Tomaso could run in FIA competition. The results: a stunning sports racer with a convoluted heritage.

In 1959, Alejandro de Tomaso and his wife, Isabelle Haskell, formed De Tomaso Automobili SpA in Modena, located close to Ferrari. Haskell, like de Tomaso, came from a privileged background and raced sports cars. De Tomaso grew up in a prominent political family in Buenos Aires and, after being linked in 1955 to an assassination attempt on President Juan Peron, fled to Italy. Haskell was an heir to the Rowan Industries of Red Bank, New Jersey, fortune.

In 1964, de Tomaso approached Carroll Shelby and Peter Brock for powertrain and design assistance on a new sports racer. Shelby viewed the project as a potential source for a replacement for his Cooper-based King Cobra. Shelby was concerned about Chevy-powered cars dominating competition and Ford's lack of support for his King Cobras. De Tomaso offered Shelby a large displacement variant of the 289 Ford which would give him a leg up racing against Chevy-engined cars, especially in the upcoming Can-Am series. Shelby was in and he took Brock along with him.

The story of this project is somewhat fuzzy because Alejandro de Tomaso continually spent much of his time wheeling, dealing, and trolling for investors

The De Tomaso Sport 5000, with Fantuzzi body styled after Peter Brock's design for a 7-liter Can-Am racer, did not meet FIA specifications. The original P70 design did not have doors or an accepted windscreen. *Bill Noon/Symbolic Motor Car Co.*

for his next project. After looking at Brock's early renderings, Shelby felt that a relationship with de Tomaso represented a win-win situation. For his and Brock's help, Shelby American would receive a potent race car with a powerful 7-liter engine. It would replace the Cooper-based King Cobra. De Tomaso Automobili would end up with a Brock-designed sports racer powered by a Weber-carbureted 289 Cobra engine.

In January 1965, De Tomaso revealed the Ghia–de Tomaso Sport 5000 mock-up chassis with a poorly interpreted, Brock-designed body. It was later dubbed the P70. Neither Shelby nor Brock was happy, so Brock went to Italy to supervise styling revisions at Carrozzeria Fantuzzi in Modena. This was the first sign of confusion—Ghia badges on a car designed and built by Fantuzzi. Shelby withdrew support of the project based on de Tomaso's failure to come up with the promised 7-liter engine.

The heart of the P70/Sport 5000 race car was de Tomaso's rigid steel backbone chassis with fully independent suspension and a 575-horsepower, 289 Cobra engine that served as a stressed member of the chassis. The engine was bolted to a five-speed Coletti transaxle similar to the one used on early GT40s. Fantuzzi built the car but never got credit. It appeared on the cover of the March 1966 *Road & Track* as the Ghia–De Tomaso Sport 5000.

"I actually didn't design the Sport 5000," said Peter Brock. "Back when it was the Ghia–De Tomaso Sport 5-Liter, later called the P70, I did do the design. There was to be a Ford-powered Can-Am racer to be built by De Tomaso for Carroll. He promised us a 7-liter version of the 289 and never delivered. Shelby never paid him. So the Shelby–De Tomaso deal was done."

After de Tomaso took the Ghia-badged car to the 1965 Turin Motor Show, it made the cover of *Road & Track*. Shelby was obviously no longer involved and there was only one car, the P70 with the small-block Cobra engine originally designed for future Can-Am and FIA Group 7 competition.

Brock added, "Since the car didn't comply with FIA Sports Car rules, de Tomaso took the body off and had Fantuzzi build a similar body with FIA-

approved doors and legal height windscreen. It officially became the De Tomaso Sport 5000. My original design was renamed P70, Prototipo 7 Liter."

Brock feels that the De Tomaso Sport 5000 was definitely influenced by his P70 design. Since the P70 would not be legal under FIA rules, de Tomaso promoted the Sport 5000, but not Fantuzzi. The sports racer was entered and ran one time at Mugello. It was doing well until sidelined with electrical problems. He entered it for races at Nürburgring and Sebring, but never showed.

The De Tomaso Sport 5000 was stored in 1967 and did not surface until 2004. Even with its convoluted heritage, the car remains a stunning, powerful, and valuable machine.

The first and only race the Sport 5000 competed in was at Mugello in Italy. It initially blew off Ferraris before being plagued by electrical problems, causing a DNF.

COMPETITION PROVEN:
HOLMAN & MOODY

The rise, fall, and rise of John Holman and Ralph Moody's NASCAR-centric temple of testosterone.

Often, the most successful partnerships are those where the partners bring unique and complementary talents to the relationship. They don't have to share similar political or social views, or even like each other, to build a successful business. John Holman and Ralph Moody, two very different people who did not get along and often fought, shared a common goal—winning! They built many of the most winning and iconic Ford race cars on the planet.

Holman & Moody represented a potent partnership of two driven men of opposite persona—race car driver and technical wizard Ralph Moody and the tireless hustler and promoter John Holman. Together, they grew a tiny rented garage into a multimillion-dollar center for Ford racing. At its peak in the mid-to-late 1960s, Holman & Moody's "Competition Proven" logo was on the fenders of more winning Ford stock cars than any other shops involved in NASCAR competition.

Ironically, Holman & Moody's race shop grew out of the 1957 Automobile Manufacturer's Association racing ban. John Holman and Ralph Moody's unlikely partnership began shortly after the AMA banned factory participation in racing. At the time, Holman was manager of Pete DePaolo's Ford factory stock car racing team in Charlotte. Moody was a top-ranked Ford driver and mechanic. The racing ban essentially left both men unemployed.

With Ford shutting off the financial pipeline, DePaolo wanted out. Ford-sponsored racers on both coasts were given race cars, transporters, and spare part, then cut loose. Fortunately, there was one person who came up with a solution for circumventing the AMA ban and to keep Ford racing—Jacque Passino, a recent engineering-marketing hire assigned to racing activities at Ford. His solution was to get Holman and Moody to buy DePaolo's inventory at fire-sale prices and create a new home for Ford stock car racing. In order to raise funds for the buyout and open a shop, Moody took out a $12,000 loan on his airplane.

John Holman was a character—a wheeler-dealer, a ferocious competitor, and a pioneering spirit. When he was fifteen, his father died and family finances forced him to work while struggling to get enough credits to graduate high school.

Working in shipyards during World War II, Holman began a new career as a tool and die maker. After the war, he went back to trucking. His reputation as a tireless over-the-road trucker is what got him into racing. In 1952, he went to work for Bill Stroppe and Clay Smith, who had convinced Ford Motor Company that a Lincoln could win the Mexican Road Race. They needed a part-timer who could drive their support truck over each leg of the race on the night before and stay ahead of the racers. Holman was their man and the Smith-Stroppe Lincolns won the race in 1952, 1953, and 1954.

Following the 1952 race victory, Holman became a parts man and mechanic for Smith and Stroppe at their shop in Long Beach, California. Stroppe took over the business when Clay Smith was killed in a freak racing accident in 1954. Holman continued in Stroppe's employ until 1956, when he started work at Pete DePaolo Racing. Essentially, he was hired by Ford to run DePaolo's shop. This move set in motion the chain of events that would lead to the creation of Holman & Moody. Less than ten years later, Holman & Moody would buy out Bill Stroppe. The California facility would become Holman-Moody-Stroppe, the west coast branch of the H&M empire that included a Marine Division in Long Beach and Miami.

John Holman with a '65 Ford Medium-Riser 427 engine on the dyno at Holman & Moody. It was homologated for NASCAR and used first in Dan Gurney's Galaxie that won the Riverside 500. It also powered Fred Lorenzen's Daytona 500–winning Galaxie. *Holman Collection*

Ralph Moody, far left, often worked in the pits at races. That's Fred Lorenzen in one of his early 1962 No. 28 Fords, powered by a 406-cubic-inch, 385-horsepower big-block. *Fran Hernandez Collection*

Dan Gurney with his Holman & Moody fastback '63½ 427 Galaxie during testing at Daytona. Gurney would go on to win the Motor Trend 500 at Riverside Raceway in 1963, 1964, 1965, 1966, and 1968 in 427 Fords. *Ford Motor Company*

Benson Ford in the specially prepared '64½ Holman & Moody Mustang built to pace the 1964 Indy 500. The blueprinted 289 engine with special cam and valvetrain pumped out 450 horsepower, and the one-off convertible had a top speed of 140 miles per hour. *Ford Motor Company*

The John Holman–Ralph Moody partnership was a study in contrasts. Whereas Holman was larger than life and in your face, Moody was taciturn beyond belief. Born and raised in Massachusetts, Moody was a typical New Englander and a man of few words. Yet together, the two men made a significant historical impact in the world of motorsports.

Often reluctant to talk about it, Ralph Moody was a successful racer. He started racing midgets and sprint cars shortly after graduation from high school in the 1930s. He operated two speed shops in New England before moving to Florida after World War II where he opened a race car shop in Fort Lauderdale. One of the early stars of NASCAR, Moody had five Grand National wins prior to joining forces with Holman.

One of Moody's chief responsibilities was finding and coaching drivers. His most famous discovery was "Fearless" Fred Lorenzen, one of NASCAR's all-time greats who retired in 1967 after more than six years driving Holman & Moody Fords. One of Moody's most famous coaching tactics, especially with drivers who weren't getting it, was to hop in their race car to demonstrate. Legendary racer Dan Gurney came under Moody's wing in 1963, the first year he drove an H&M Ford at Riverside. Gurney had difficulty adjusting his sports car and open-wheel driving techniques to the big 427 Galaxie. When he complained, Moody jumped in his car and ran a couple of laps some six seconds faster than Gurney. On race day, Gurney blew off everyone and won. He followed up by winning the Riverside *Motor Trend* 500 in Fords in 1964, 1965, 1966, and 1968!

At the beginning of each season, Moody would determine the powertrain and chassis packaging for new model Fords. During races he could always be found in the pits, formulating strategy and, often, jumping in as a member of the crew. He would also counsel other teams running H&M-equipped Fords. After an illustrious career, Ralph Moody passed away in June 2004 at age 85.

Personalities aside, John Holman and Ralph Moody shared the power of a singular vision—an unparalleled dedication to winning. Shortly after joining forces in 1957, Holman & Moody Fords won their first two races. They entered two cars, driven by Curtis Turner and Joe Weatherly, in the final two races on the Daytona Beach course in 1958. The Fords finished first and third in one race, followed by second and fourth finishes in the second race.

Next, H&M changed direction from a racing team to a racing factory. As Ford increased financial support, they started building race cars for other teams at their Charlotte airport facility.

At the first Daytona 500 on February 22, 1959, Johnny Beauchamp's Holman & Moody T-Bird crossed the finish line fender-to-fender with Lee Petty's Oldsmobile. It was a dead heat, a photo finish. A couple of days later, Petty was declared the winner. The two cars averaged 135.521 miles per hour, which made the Daytona 500 the fastest stock car race in history up to that time.

Holman & Moody continued to grow their Ford race car business and in 1961 started building engines for the Wood Brothers No. 21 Galaxie. That year, they also introduced the first NASCAR three-piece sway bar and Fred Lorenzen drove H&M Fords to wins at Martinsville, Darlington, and Atlanta. In 1962,

H&M built tube-framed "long nose" Mustangs with setback 427 SOHC cammer engines primarily for match racing and in some fuel classes in NHRA in 1965–1966. Here is Tasca's Bill Lawton running against Phil "Daddy Warbucks" Bonner in the H&M 427 SOHC Falcon at Cecil County Dragoway. Both cars ran Hilborn fuel injection. *Tasca Family Archives*

Holman & Moody star driver Fred Lorenzen won at Atlanta, Bristol, Charlotte, Darlington, Martinsville, and North Wilkesboro in '64 Galaxies. *Ford Motor Company*

the dynamic duo branched out into sports car racing with their Falcon Challenger, dubbed "The World's Fastest Falcon," and driven at the 12 Hours of Sebring by Marvin Panch and Jocko Maggiacomo. H&M also prepared an early Cobra, driven by Augie Pabst, for Nassau Speed Week. Nelson Stacy won in a Holman & Moody Galaxie at Darlington, Charlotte, and Martinsville. The company continued to build engines, grind cams, and supply parts for other Ford teams, services that lasted into the 1990s.

While Holman & Moody started by building and racing stock cars, by 1963 its reputation had spread to the UK and Europe. Their 1963 Monte Carlo Rallye Falcons made history, taking a class win and laying the groundwork for a win the following year. Alan Mann Racing in the UK took notice and started a relationship with H&M that resulted in years of collaboration for road-racing Falcons, Galaxies, and Mustangs.

According to author and NASCAR historian John Craft, "H&M's racing factory had an everything-built-in-house approach to motorsports in a day when many NASCAR stock cars were still being built in small garages. It was a window on the future of what the sport was to become. Legions of mechanics, chassis men, engine builders, and fabricators honed their racing skills 'at the airport' and then went on to guide many great teams to victories in the years after their work for Holman & Moody."

H&M built thirty-two Omega sports cars in 1966 and 1967, twenty-five with K-code 289/271 engines. Designed by Bob Cumberford and produced in Italy by Frank Reisner's Automobili Intermeccanica, "rollers" were shipped to Charlotte for powertrains and completion. Originally the Griffith GT, it was renamed Omega when ownership went to Steve Wilder, an editor at *Car and Driver*. *Holman Collection*

In 1964, racers in the UK and Europe were having great success in Touring Car racing with Holman & Moody powertrains and modified cars. UK racers Rob Beck and Geoff Richardson came up with the concept of putting a Holman & Moody 427 Galaxie big-block in Beck's 1962 Jaguar E-Type. They ordered a race-ready, single four-barrel, 470-horsepower 427 side-oiler, dyno tested at 500 pounds-feet of torque. It was the birth of the Jaguar E-Gal.

With Rob Beck driving, the EGAL won two firsts—in the Sports Car and Libra classes—the first time out at the Nottingham Sports Car Club race at Silverstone. Second time out, Beck trounced Ferrari GTOs and won at Castle Combe. He followed that up with a win at Oulton Park. The 427 E-Gal was a successful club racer for a many years. It's been restored by Vantage Motors in Stamford, Connecticut, and is owned Charles and Wendy Fuchs.

For the 1965 NASCAR season, Holman & Moody fielded Ford's A-Team: A. J. Foyt, Dick Hutcherson, Ned Jarrett, Junior Johnson, Fred Lorenzen, Curtis Turner, and Cale Yarborough. Lorenzen won three major races, including the Daytona 500, while Hutcherson won nine events. Ned Jarrett had thirteen wins out of fifty-four starts and was named 1965 NASCAR Grand National Champion. The newly homologated 427 medium-riser debuted in Dan Gurney's winning Galaxie on January 17, 1965, at the *Motor Trend* 500 at Riverside Raceway. Holman & Moody Fords won forty-eight of fifty-five NASCAR Grand National races in 1965.

Ford's big news in 1966 was winning Le Mans in a one-two-three sweep with Shelby and Holman & Moody GT40 Mark IIs. Mark IIs also took a one-two-three win at the Daytona 24-Hour and the first two slots at the 12 Hours of Sebring that year. During 1966, Holman & Moody Mark II driven by Walt Hansgen and Mark Donahue finished third at Daytona, and Walt Hansgen and Mark

Donahue's Mark II finished second at Sebring. Over the following years, dozens of GT40s would be race-prepped, rebuilt, and restored at Holman & Moody.

NASCAR superstars Fred Lorenzen and Dick Hutcherson continued winning for Holman & Moody. New for 1966 was the conversion of midsize unibody Fairlanes and Comets using 1965 Galaxie front clips, or snouts, forward of the firewall with tubular steel members running inside the rockers, tied into roll cages and the pressed steel platforms. Holman & Moody installed Galaxie snouts on Bud Moore's second and third of three 1966 Mercury Comets driven by Darel Dieringer.

Mario Andretti and Fred Lorenzen, driving Holman & Moody 427 Fords, owned Daytona in 1967. Lorenzen won the Daytona 500 Qualifier and Andretti took the win at the 500. It was an all-Ford, all–Holman & Moody show! During midseason, David Pearson, the 1966 NASCAR Grand National Champion, joined Holman & Moody.

Lorenzen was the star of the H&M team for six and a half years before retiring in 1967. In 1963, he had made the most money of all drivers in a single season—$113,570. He drove his legendary No. 28 Ford to an unparalleled place in NASCAR record books, holding the record for the most career victories, twenty-one, in 250-mile or longer events. "Fearless Fred" was the only driver in history to have won a major race on each of the five NASCAR super-speedways—Atlanta, Charlotte, Darlington, Daytona, and Rockingham.

David Pearson's move from Cotton Owens' Dodge team to Holman & Moody would pay off in 1968. In spite of finishing fifth at the Daytona 500, he managed to win sixteen NASCAR races and was named Grand National Champion for the second time. His winning streak continued into 1969, when

Holman & Moody also offered specialty car services to individuals, creating one-off super-high-performance cars such as this sinister-looking '66 Ford Fairlane powered by a 427 SOHC cammer. Documented by Lee Holman and Howard Dehart, it was fitted with NASCAR steering, hubs, spindles, full-floating rear, oil cooler, and beefed Toploader four-speed. *Charlie Lillard*

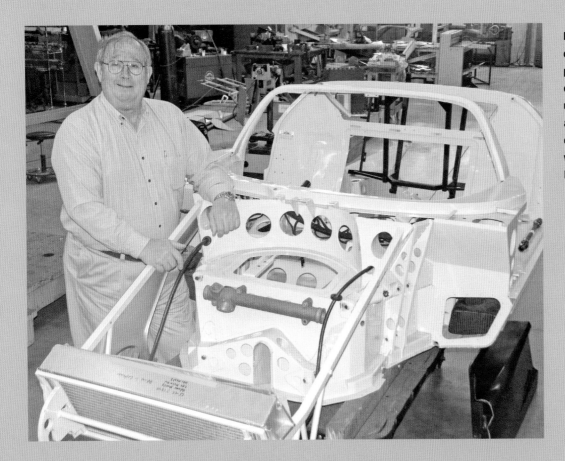

he took eleven firsts in his Torino Talladega. He won the Daytona 500 Qualifier and finished sixth at the 500. For the third time, David Pearson was crowned NASCAR Grand National Champion.

Ford made a big splash on March 30, 1969, at the Atlanta 500 by introducing the Boss 429 engine with big-valve aluminum heads with crescent-shaped combustion chambers. Standard equipment in the Boss 429 Mustang, it replaced the 427 that had been the mainstay of Ford's racing programs since 1963. Cale Yarborough won the 500 driving a Junior Johnson Mercury Cyclone and David Pearson took a second in the H&M Torino Talladega. Pearson would go on to win the Richmond 250, Northern 300, Volunteer 500, and the Yankee 600.

Purolator Corporation, manufacturer of oil and air filters and a race car sponsor, approached John Holman in 1969 regarding a buyout. Purolator wanted to own the Holman & Moody brand and its racing operation. There was a substantial offer on the table. Holman called Henry Ford II to get his opinion. According to Holman's son, Lee, "Henry told Dad, 'Don't do it. You're our guy and we're going to be racing for years.'"

John Holman turned Purolator down, a decision he would soon regret. Even though Ford was winning on a regular basis, its financial commitment to racing was coming under scrutiny in 1970, internally and in Washington at Congressional hearings on auto safety. Henry Ford II, with input from Ford Division head Lee Iacocca and Comptroller Harold "Red" Polling, decided it was time to pull the plug on racing. By the time John Holman got the message, it was too late. Purolator had made other plans.

Holman received two extremely impersonal letters from Ford's Product Development Group, dated December 16 and December 22, 1970. The first was from department head Harold C. MacDonald, essentially telling Holman, "Your services are no longer necessary and we will be auditing your records." The second was from engineer John H. Cowley, letting him know, "It's over." This situation prompted Ralph Moody to sell his stock back to the company. He stayed with Holman & Moody as an employee until the fall of 1971. After leaving, he set up a small shop and prepared a 1969 Mercury Cyclone for Bobby Allison that won eleven NASCAR races.

Although Moody left, the company name remained the same. Holman & Moody held its first auction of old race cars and engines to raise capital and make room for future projects. After John Holman passed away in 1975, a local bank administered control of H&M. By 1978, Holman's son, Lee, had sold his boat business and took over as president of Holman & Moody, injecting new life into the struggling business.

In 1982, Lee Holman opened a new 75,000-square-foot Holman & Moody and Holman Automotive facility. In addition to performance services, Lee started handcrafting continuation 427-powered GT40 Mark IIs in the early 1990s, built using original tooling, components, and GT40 suppliers. Today, H&M also builds new Tour de France tribute Mustangs.

"Holman & Moody changed the entire face of NASCAR racing on a number of levels," said John Craft, who has restored a number of vintage H&M race cars. "Its refinements and innovations resulted in durable, high-quality race car components that became the standard of the industry. In some cases, those components continued to be used until the late 1980s. It is hard to imagine the NASCAR series becoming what it is today without the influence of John Holman and Ralph Moody."

CHAPTER 7

1966

Christmas Comes Early to Dearborn!

By June 1966, victories at the Indy 500, Daytona, Le Mans, and Sebring had already confirmed Ford as a dominating force in International motorsports.

In 1966, Ford dealers looking for the ultimate in "Sunday wins" to help generate "Monday sales" celebrated once-in-a-lifetime opportunities. GT40s not only won big at Daytona and Sebring but also ended Ferrari's rule at Le Mans with a one-two-three finish.

At the Indy 500, Ford engines powered the first four cars and, of the seven cars running at the finish, five were Ford-powered. On drag strips from coast to coast, Mustangs continued their winning ways. And, even with

Henry Ford II's part-year boycott of NASCAR, Fords and Mercurys won twelve races. Total Performance was alive and well at Ford Motor Company and in dealer showrooms.

For 1966, the ultrasuccessful Mustang, with 289 engines up to 271 horsepower, was basically carried over with minor trim changes. Ford concentrated its efforts on the mid-and full-size models, the Fairlane and the Galaxie, with the newly styled unibody Fairlane getting the most attention. The Galaxie was face-lifted and still available with 427 engine and four-speed options. However, the big-car line was expanded to include a 7-liter

Dick Brannan, Ford Special Vehicles Activity's resident drag racer, with the first altered-wheelbase (standard) '66 Mustang powered by a Hilborn-injected 427 SOHC engine. Photo taken during testing at the Dearborn Proving Ground.
Ford Motor Company

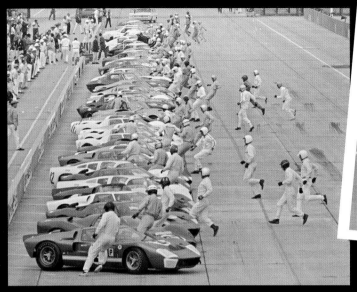

Six weeks after finishing one-two-three at the Daytona 24-Hour race on February 5–6, 1966, GT40s ran the Sebring 12-Hour endure and racked up first, second, and twelfth slots with the X1 roadster and two Mark IIs powered by 289 and 427 engines. Here's the Le Mans start of the Sebring race, GT40s in front. Next came Le Mans, where Mark IIs finished one-two three. *Ford Motor Company*

Dick Hutcherson competed in NASCAR in 1966 with this much-altered Holman & Moody '66 Galaxie. Not as radical as Junior Johnson's legendary "Banana" Galaxie, this cheater car had a dropped front end with headlights obviously below the bumper, raked windshield and backlight and mildly chopped top. *Ford Motor Company*

Scott Davies has been racing one of the fifty-seven R-code 427 Fairlanes built in 1966 since purchasing it as a roller with 1,100 miles on it in 1974. It has never been titled or driven on the street. Davies runs 10.3s with a dual-quad 427 Low-Riser in Nostalgia Super/Stock competition. *Scott Davies*

Ford DOHC-engined cars finished one-two-three-four at the fiftieth anniversary of the Indy 500. Graham Hill in the No. 24 Lola-Ford won the race. At the end of the race, there were just seven cars running, five of them powered by Ford engines. *Ford Motor Company*

model with a new 428 big-block, beautiful bucket-seat interior, and unique trim. Rated at 345 horsepower at 4,800 rpm, the 428 had a 406-inch bore (4.13-inch) and 410-inch Mercury stroke (3.98-inch). There was also a special Police Interceptor version, with an aluminum four-barrel manifold, rated at 360 horsepower at 5,400 rpm. Both 428s were available only with an upgraded C6 automatic.

In the highly competitive midsize field, Ford and Lincoln-Mercury had been busy playing catch-up to GM's enormously popular and more powerful GTO and Chevelle. For 1966, new 390 Fairlane GT/GTA and Comet Cyclone GT models were Ford's entries in the youth-driven supercar market. Ford nailed it midyear with a street-legal 427 Fairlane powered by the R-code, medium-riser side oiler. Dick Brannan worked on the 427 Fairlane's development and Vern Tinsler was involved in making it production ready as an LPO (Limited Production Option) vehicle. There were two 427 Fairlane development cars built for the program at the X-Garage. Not a true lightweight, the 427 Fairlane had a Plaza Fiberglass lift-off hood with a functional scoop and ram-air induction. Ford built fifty-seven Wimbledon White 427 Fairlanes with four-speeds and 9-inch rears at the Atlanta plant, thus meeting NHRA's fifty-vehicle minimum to be legal in Stock classes.

Bill Stroppe and Holman & Moody built a number of race-prepped 1966–1967 Super/Stock 427 Fairlanes, including Hubert Platt's SS/C record-holder and Dave Lyall's Fastbacks Club SS/CA entry.

In 1966, a 427/425 Fairlane, campaigned by John Downing from Downing and Ryan Engineering in Rutherford, New Jersey, set the NHRA B/Stock National Record at 11.42 seconds. Ford 427 Fairlanes also won A/Stock at the NHRA Springnationals and the Super/Stock Nationals.

New Jersey drag racer Scott Davies has been running a real R-code 1966 Fairlane, VIN 6A43R249133, since 1974. He purchased it in 1974 as a roller with 1,100 miles from Downing and Ryan. It has never been titled or driven on the street. Over the years, he has raced his rare Fairlane in a variety of NHRA Stock classes with 390 and 427 low- and medium-riser engines. "I find the low-riser 427 to be the most reliable and consistent engine of the two 427s," Davies said. "Running in Nostalgia Super/Stock, my best time this year has been a 10.31 ET."

After January 1966, a 335-horsepower version of the Fairlane and Comet with Holley four-barrel carburetor and low-restriction dual exhausts was

announced. Even with 335 horsepower, they were short on power compared with the tri-power GTO, Olds 442, and big-block Chevelle.

In late 1965, I spent a week with a one-off 1966 Fairlane 390 GTA that had come from Holman & Moody. In its glove box was a two-page letter from H&M Project Engineer John Wanderer to Ford PR dated November 2, 1965. The letter listed more than thirty parts, with part numbers, used to modify this Fairlane.

Ford Public Relations originally ordered a 335-horspower Fairlane for a *Car & Driver* magazine supercar comparison test. When they couldn't get the latest high-performance Fairlane, they settled for a 315-horsepower model that was sent to Holman & Moody for prepping. The comparison test venue was the Bridgehampton Race Circuit in New York. Unfortunately, the Springtime Yellow Fairlane was not prepped for road racing and did not do well against a Royal Pontiac GTO, Bud Moore Comet, and factory-prepared Chevelle SS396, Olds 442, and Buick Skylark GS. Except for the Fairlane, they were all "cheater" cars set up to run on a road course. The Fairlane was modified primarily for street and drag use.

I had a great time with the H&M Fairlane. I *guesstimate* that Wanderer's massaged engine produced 350-plus horsepower. Modifications ranged from stock 335-horsepower parts to front sway bar, shocks, front coil springs, and 9-inch rear fitted with 3.70 gears and a locker. The Fairlane was lowered about 1.5 inches and the engine had a deep sump oil pan that showed the scars of daily driving. The 390's heads were blueprinted and fitted with new valves and valvetrain from a 427 engine. Its distributor had full centrifugal advance, dual points, and special spark plug wires. At Holman & Moody, the Fairlane received 14x6-inch Mag Star I wheels, a console-mounted Sun tach, and a North Carolina Manufacturer license plate.

SCCA sanctioned the first Trans-Am race series in 1966, and Ford won the Championship for cars powered by over-2-liter engines. While two-seat Shelby GT350 Mustangs competed in B/Production, Shelby and others built notchback, four-seat, 289 Mustangs for "sedan racing" in the Trans-Am. Jerry Titus won the seventh and final race of the season on September 7 at Riverside International Raceway and locked in the Championship for Ford. *Ford Motor Company*

We had a lot of fun with the Fairlane and especially loved the super-quick-shifting modified C-6 Sportshift transmission and throaty exhaust note. We took it to the track and ran consistent 99 miles per hour in the mid 14s with street tires and closed exhausts. Our best elapsed time was 14.50 seconds. Masten Gregory ran the same miles per hour as I did, only a quicker 14.26-second ET. The Bud Moore prepared Comet was much more of a cheater car than any of the others. *Car & Driver* clocked it at 103.8 miles per hour in 13.98 seconds!

Thanks to the efforts of Special Vehicles Activity's Leo Beebe and Jacque Passino, supported by Holman & Moody, Kar Kraft, and Shelby American, Henry Ford II's quest for motorsports domination became reality in 1966. An American carmaker won the prestigious 24 Hours of Le Mans for the first time. Ford

One of two 427 SOHC '66 Galaxies, built for evaluation. This Wimbledon White Galaxie was assigned to SVA head Jacque Passino when I photographed it in 1966 at the Dearborn Proving Ground. There was also an Emberglo Galaxie that was used for a limited time by astronaut Gordon Cooper.

The engine compartment of this 427 SOHC Galaxie almost looks production. If Ford could have seen the way to offering the 427 as an optional engine in the Galaxie line, Bill France would have approved it for NASCAR in 1966 (without a weight penalty). Dual carbs are smaller than those used on race engines, more tractable on the street.

also won the 1966 International Manufacturers Championship; International Championship For Sports Cars, Division II; and the SCCA Trans-Am Championship. Ford teams entered twenty GT40s in races in the United States and Europe, finishing in eleven and winning the most significant endurance events.

The rumor mill was working overtime in 1966, churning out misinformation about Ford building 427 SOHC Galaxies with four-speeds and 9-inch rears with Detroit Lockers. Since Ford was having difficulty getting the engine into NASCAR, they were searching for ways to make it optional in production cars. Hoping to sway Bill France, they also made SOHC engines available to the public, initially priced at $2,000 to $2,400

Officially, there was no street 427 SOHC Galaxie. Unofficially, there were at least two built by the X-Garage—a Wimbledon White evaluation car, often signed out to Jack Passino, and an Emberglo variant that was loaned to astronaut Gordon Cooper for promotional purposes.

In July 1966, I managed to get some seat time in the Wimbledon White Galaxie cammer on the Dearborn Proving Ground road course. I held the story, waiting for production confirmation that never came. I finally wrote about it in the June 1967 issue of *Super/Stock & FX*. I found the car a little clumsy on the tight road course, but the engine felt like it had an unlimited redline—it just revved and revved and made power.

Factory racers Mike Schmidt and Ed Terry received special Galaxies that were race-prepped for NHRA FX classes. Terry's Galaxie had a fiberglass hood covering a blueprinted 289 with four Weber 48IDA carbs on a Cobra manifold. He shifted the small-block at almost 8,000 rpm and set the C/FX record at 12.90. Later in the year, he got into the 11s. Schmidt's 3,400-pound, 427 SOHC Galaxie ran low 11s in B/FX. It was also set up to run in AHRA B/Modified Production.

In order to stay competitive with Dodge and Plymouth in 1966, Ford's drag racing group knew they would have to start building altered wheelbase, tube-framed Mustangs and at times switch from gas to nitro. The first of those programs was the altered-wheelbase, 427 SOHC Mustang with fiberglass hood, fenders, doors, and deck lid. It also had a full roll cage, onboard fire suppression, and a 9-inch rear with Detroit Locker and 4.88 gears.

Photo of ready-to-race NASCAR 427 cammer was taken at the Holman & Moody garage in early-December 1965 at Daytona International Speedway during tests at Daytona. An SOHC engine was used in Fred Lorenzen's '65 H&M Galaxie, updated with '66 body parts, to evaluate performance. The 626-horsepower cammer powered the Galaxie to a fastest lap average of 177.51 miles per hour and top speed of 180 miles per hour on the straightaway.

SVA's Charlie Gray shipped some 1966 Mustang fastbacks to Howard DeHart at Holman & Moody for conversion into altered stock and stretched wheelbase race cars. They were tagged for Dick Brannan, Bill Lawton, and others for racing and promotional uses. The Mustangs received carbureted and Hilborn-injected SOHC engines.

Brannan and Lawton took their Mustangs to Irwindale, California, for the AHRA Winternationals and, together with Les Ritchey, turned it into a Ford show. Ritchey won Super/Stock Eliminator in his 427 SOHC, stock-wheelbase Mustang while Brannan won Unlimited Fuel Stock and Lawton took Unlimited Gas Stock honors in their new stretched Mustangs.

Holman & Moody also built extended-chassis, long-nose 427 SOHC Mustangs for Dick Brannan, Gas Ronda, Phil Bonner, and others. These were tube-frame Mustangs with fiberglass bodies. One of Brannan's 118-inch-wheelbase, long-nose Mustangs was the last of that short series.

Thanks to Bill France's rule changes, along with Chrysler and Ford threatening pullouts over rules affecting car size/weight and engines, NASCAR fans and drivers suffered. The previous year, it was Chrysler that took its "toys" and went home after the Hemi engine was banned. In 1966, it was Ford's turn after France allowed the Hemi based on production Dodges and Plymouths being built with optional 426 Street Hemis. Since the Ford SOHC cammer was not available in any production cars, France allowed the engine providing it would be installed in a car with an approximate 450-pound-plus handicap. It would have to run in a big Galaxie, not the new, midsize Fairlane. France sweetened the pot by permitting Ford to equip the Wedge engine with a second four-barrel carb. Ford was still not happy.

After tests conducted by Holman & Moody at Daytona in early December 1965, Ford knew what the SOHC Hemi could deliver in NASCAR competition. In an intracompany letter to Special Vehicles Activity's John Cowley, Leo Beebe, and Jacque Passino dated December 13, 1965, SVA Special Events Manager

Don D. A. Wahrman outlined the results of the Daytona tests. They ran three Holman & Moody cars with the single four-barrel, 427 Wedge and dual four-barrel, SOHC engines. The 626-horsepower SOHC engine was in Fred Lorenzen's No. 28 1965 Galaxie (C5HM-10047) updated with 1966 sheet metal. Its fastest lap average was 177.51 miles per hour and it hit 180.00 miles per hour on the straightaway. The 1966 Galaxie with a 530-horsepower 427 Wedge had a fastest lap average of 170.78 miles per hour, clocking 172.41 miles per hour on the straightaway. The 1966 Fairlane with full chassis mods and a 510-horsepower 427 Wedge averaged 168.85 miles per hour and 170.77 on the straightaway.

Bud Moore, right, pitched in with the pit crew on Darel Dieringer's Mercury Comet. Either the second or third of three Comets campaigned by Moore, it had a destroked 427 and a Holman & Moody modified chassis with narrowed Galaxie snout from the firewall forward. The first Comet ran with a dual-scoop Cyclone GT hood.

In 1966, Lincoln-Mercury's Fran Hernandez and Al Turner contracted for four replica Comet-bodied flip-top race cars, forerunners of the fuel Funny Cars. For exhibition and match racing, the Comets were campaigned by Jack Chrisman, Kenz & Leslie, "Dyno Don" Nicholson and "Fast Eddie" Shartman. With a full fuel-dragster chassis and 1,000-horsepower SOHC 427 running 80 percent nitro, these 1,700-pound exhibitionists shook the ground. Here's Shartman checking his new ride out.
Fran Hernandez Collection

"Dyno Don" Nicholson, one of Lincoln-Mercury's most successful drag racers, with his *Eliminator 1* Comet powered by a fuel-burning 427 SOHC cammer. *Fran Hernandez Collection*

Ford's Indy 500 juggernaut continued in 1966 at the fiftieth anniversary of the American Classic. With Mario Andretti on the pole in the Dean Van Lines Hawk-Ford, there was a first lap crash that eliminated eleven cars from the field. By the time Graham Hill crossed the finish line first in the Mecom/American Red Ball Lola-Ford, there were only seven cars running. Of the seven finishers, Ford DOHC Indy engines powered five.

Graham Hill won the race, averaging 144.31 miles per hour for 500 miles. Jim Clark in the STP/Team Lotus-Ford, Jim McElrath in a Brabham-Ford, and Gordon Johncock in a Gerhardt-Ford followed him. Jackie Stewart finished sixth in a Mecom Lola T90-Ford. In spite of not finishing the race, Stewart was named USAC Rookie of the Year.

While Ford was having Holman & Moody build tube-framed long-nose 427 SOHC Mustangs for match racing, Hernandez and Turner went one step beyond. They managed the build of four 427 SOHC exhibition Comets, forerunners of flip-top Funny Cars. Powered by blown and injected 427 cammers that generated over 1,000 horsepower at 8,000 rpm on an 80 percent nitro mix, the four cars were given to professional racers Jack Chrisman, Kenz & Leslie, Don Nicholson, and Eddie Schartman. They were strategically placed to cover top marketing areas across the country. Fitted with one-piece, fiberglass Comet replica bodies, the heart of these cars was a fuel dragster chassis. Chrisman's Comet was the only roadster built, with the chassis designed and built by Ron and Gene Logghe at Logghe Stamping in Fraser, Michigan. These tire-smoking exhibitionists weighed approximately 1,700 pounds and delivered ground-shaking performance.

For the 1966 model year, Ford outsold Chevrolet for the first time in five years. Together with Mercury, they sold in excess of 2.5 million vehicles. It was a great year for racing and car sales.

On April 15, 1966, at the North Wilkesboro, North Carolina, racetrack, Henry Ford II announced that Ford was boycotting NASCAR and warned its contract drivers that if they attempted to run as independents or drive other make cars, they would be terminated. He told the *Detroit News*, "We're out of stock car racing. We don't like Mr. France's new rules—we think the rules are unfair to us, so we're out for the year."

After the 1967 NASCAR rules were announced in August 1966, Ford contract teams returned to stock car racing. They ran a variety of engines displacing 396 to 427 cubic inches. Fords won ten races and Mercury won two races. Dan Gurney won at Riverside again, and Dick Hutcherson, Fred Lorenzen, Elmo Langley, and Tiny Lund put Fords in winners' circles. Bill France was happy, Henry Ford II was happy, and, most importantly, drivers and fans were happy.

Darel Dieringer, driving Mercurys for Bud Moore, won two races, including the Southern 500 at Darlington. Whereas Holman & Moody was still being funded by Ford, Bud Moore Engineering only received minor support from Lincoln-Mercury. Fortunately, Moore had a great relationship with Lincoln-Mercury's Fran Hernandez.

Hernandez worked a deal to get Moore three new, unibody Comet Cyclones with 390 big-blocks. Moore and Dieringer ran the first one with minimal changes, later using destroked 427s displacing 403 cubic inches. The second and third Comets were sent to Holman & Moody where they received narrowed 1965 Galaxie "snouts" forward of the firewall and tubular steel rails tied into the Comet's roll cages and pressed steel floor pans.

Bud Moore sold the No. 16 Comet that had won the Southern 500 to successful NASCAR team owner and racer Hoss Ellington, who later crashed it.

Ford's Dick Brannan, center, after winning the 1966 NASCAR Grand Finale. The Mustang cammer is an altered-wheelbase, extended chassis with a Hilborn injected 427 cammer. It's one of a handful built by Holman & Moody for Ford Special Vehicles Activity. *Dick Brannan Collection*

1966 SHELBY GT350:
LESS SHELBY, MORE SALES!

A decontented Mustang offered shoppers more options and sales quadrupled. It was a win-win situation for Shelby American, Ford, and Hertz Rent-A-Car.

Sometimes, less is actually more. The original Shelby GT350 Mustang was a serious driver's car, a two-seat sports car that was more racer than daily driver. While it had maximum appeal and obvious Cobra heritage, sales were lackluster. Just 562 were sold, including R-Model race cars. They were way too expensive to build and way too hairy for the average enthusiast. Almost from the start of 1965 production, Ford bean counters tried to save money by shifting some GT350 conversion work from Shelby American to the assembly plant.

For 1966, the Shelby GT350 delivered Carroll Shelby and Cobra cred without the high production costs and racer-oriented content of the original. Its option list was expanded, from alloy wheels and do-it-yourself racing stripes to choices of four-speed stick or three-speed automatic, folding rear seat, alloy wheels, five colors, and supercharger, plus dealer-installed Detroit Locker and Le Mans racing stripes. The optional $50 folding rear seat was installed on just about all GT350s, making the 1966 GT350 much more user-friendly.

Because there were a lot of unsold 1965 GT350 Mustangs at Shelby American, the first 252 1966 Shelby GT350s were actually Wimbledon White carryovers, called "carryover" or "changeover" or "1965½" models, depending on who you ask, with Shelby 1966 VIN plates mounted atop the factory-stamped 1965 VIN numbers. They received key 1966 updates—plexiglass side quarter windows, folding rear seats and undercar exhausts—in all but 78 cars. Most of the carryover "1965/1966" GT350s kept their 9-inch rears with Detroit Lockers, adjustable Koni shocks, lowered A-frame pivot points, driveshaft safety

New for 1966 were colors other than Wimbledon White, functional rear brake cooling scoops, and a supercharger option. One of approximately a dozen built, this ultra-rare Candy Apple Red GT350 was built with the Shelby-Paxton supercharger option that added $700 to its cost and is in the Kevin Suydam Collection.

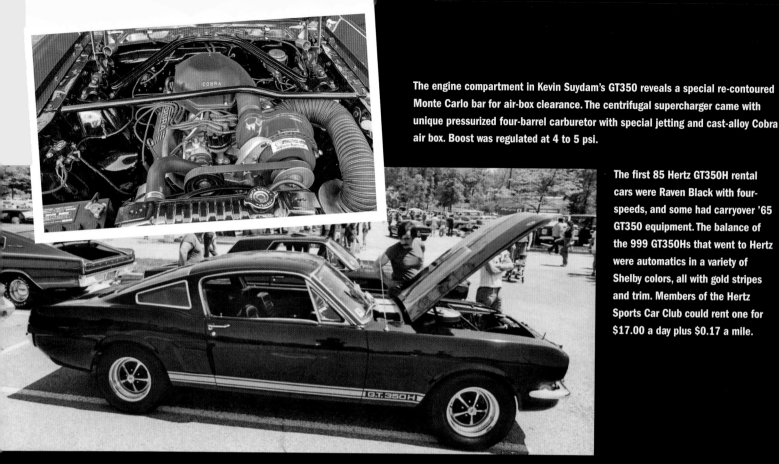

The engine compartment in Kevin Suydam's GT350 reveals a special re-contoured Monte Carlo bar for air-box clearance. The centrifugal supercharger came with unique pressurized four-barrel carburetor with special jetting and cast-alloy Cobra air box. Boost was regulated at 4 to 5 psi.

The first 85 Hertz GT350H rental cars were Raven Black with four-speeds, and some had carryover '65 GT350 equipment. The balance of the 999 GT350Hs that went to Hertz were automatics in a variety of Shelby colors, all with gold stripes and trim. Members of the Hertz Sports Car Club could rent one for $17.00 a day plus $0.17 a mile.

loops, over-axle traction bars, and axle-limiting aircraft safety wires. Those cars came with 15-inch wheels with Goodyear Blue Dots. That stuff was gone for 1966 production.

For those who thought there was life after Wimbledon White, color choices were available in 1966: Candy Apple Red, Sapphire Blue, Ivy Green, Raven Black, and, of course, Wimbledon White. The interior was simpler, utilizing a Mustang GT dash and simulated wood steering wheel, and the spare tire was returned to its stock trunk-mounted location. The original fiberglass hood was replaced with a steel unit and new functional rear brake cooling scoops were added.

Gone were the loud, side-exit exhausts. They were replaced by stock K-code Mustang undercar duals connected to Shelby headers. But the 306-horsepower 289 engine with big center-pivot-float Holley four-barrel on a Cobra manifold was carried over in four-speed cars. GT350s with upgraded three-speed C-4 automatics received smaller 460-cfm Autolite/Ford four-barrel carburetors. Since narrowed 9-inch rears with thirty-one-spline axles and Detroit Lockers were expensive and noisy, they were replaced with smaller rears with twenty-eight-spline axles and Ford Traction-Lok or Equa-Lok limited-slip differentials. Shocks were still adjustable, but they weren't Konis.

During midyear production, you could order a GT350 with a $700 optional Paxton centrifugal supercharger with a pressurized, custom-jetted 460cfm Ford/Autolite four-barrel, cast aluminum air pressure box, HD fuel pump, and fuel and blower pressure gauges mounted on a small panel below the dash. With 4 to 5 psi boost, Shelby claimed a highly optimistic 46 percent power boost. It is estimated that twelve supercharged GT350s, including one prototype, were built. Shelby American also marketed supercharger kits to dealers and individuals for GT350 and Mustang installations.

Hertz Rent-A-Car contributed to the success of the 1966 Shelby program by ordering 1,000 GT350H Mustangs for its Hertz Sports Car Club. Hertz already had a deal with Chevrolet for Corvettes. Carroll Shelby and Shelby American General Manager Peyton Cramer sold the program that turned out to be lucrative for Ford and Shelby. Club members could rent a GT350H for $17 a day and 17 cents a mile.

The first eighty-five GT350H Rent-A-Racers were black, four-speed Shelby GT350s with gold trim. Some of the earliest Hertz cars had carryover 1965 GT350 performance features. In addition to Raven Black, GT350Hs were produced in a variety of Shelby GT350 colors, all with gold stripes and trim. After the initial run of four-speed cars, all were equipped with C-4 automatic transmissions and Ford/Autolite 460-cfm four-barrel carburetors.

Carroll Shelby loved open cars, yet there were only four GT350 convertibles built for the 1966 model year. Some records show a total of six Shelby VINs reserved for convertibles, but only four convertibles were built—6S2375, 6S2376, 6S2377, and 6S2378. Each was a different color: Sapphire Blue, Springtime Yellow, Candy Apple Red, and Ivy Green. The four-speed, air-conditioned red convertible, 6S2377, was sold new to the popular Kingston Trio's Bob Shane and is now in Len and Linda Perham's outstanding collection.

While Shelby American did not produce specific 1966 GT350Rs, they did build notchback Mustangs for the new SCCA Trans-American Sedan Championship Series (Trans-Am) and FIA Appendix J Groups 1 and 2 for racing and rally competition. Shelby race-prepped approximately fifteen road-racing Mustangs with 289 engines, steel hoods, and seating for four. These cars contributed to Ford winning the first Trans-Am Championship for Over-Two-Liter cars.

Ford GT40: The Taking of Le Mans One-Two-Three!

Variants of Roy Lunn's 1964 prototype Ford GT changed the landscape of International endurance car racing and won the ultimate prizes: Le Mans victories in 1966, 1967, 1968, and 1969.

In the spring of 1966, Henry Ford II received a personal letter from a friend of Enzo Ferrari. "Mr. Ferrari assured me he is ready at any time to reconsider and close the deal with you at conditions already discussed." It was the second such letter he had received after the Ford-Ferrari negotiations had fallen apart in 1963. Once again, Ford was not interested. At that point there was little reason for Henry Ford II to buy Ferrari. Ford had already developed the GT40 and, in just a couple of months, GT40s would finish one-two-three at the 24 Hours of Le Mans on the Circuit de la Sarthe, the world's most important sports car endurance race. Henry Ford II would be celebrating with his drivers on the podium while Enzo Ferrari was on his way home in defeat for the first time in many years. It was something that Mr. Ferrari would have to get used to!

On Sunday, June 19, 1966, there was a light rain falling and gray clouds hung low over the rolling countryside southeast of Paris as three Ford GT40 Mark II-A Sports/Prototypes crossed the finish line at 4:00 p.m. In the thirty-four-year history of the world premier endurance race, it was the first time an American car had won. Three Ford GT40s finished one-two-three and terminated Ferrari's ownership of endurance racing.

Ford's smooth and aggressively dynamic GT40 Mark IIs, powered by 427 engines, ended Ferrari's multiyear domination of Le Mans and international endurance racing. In 1967, 1968, and 1969, GT40 variants with small- and big-block engines would continue winning at Le Mans, thus confirming that Ford's GT40 was not a one-trick pony. The timeline of events leading to Ford's first of four consecutive wins at Le Man, started in June 1962. That is when Henry Ford II announced the company's withdrawal from the AMA antiracing agreement.

Prior to the 1966 Le Mans race, GT40s had not proven to be successful endurance racers. They usually qualified well and even set lap records, but finishing was not their strong suit.

For the 1965 season, Ford contracted with Shelby American to update the GT40s and manage the team. During the winter of 1964, GT40s received more than twenty modifications, including the addition of Dana transaxle couplings, 289-cubic-inch Cobra wet-sump engines, and wider alloy wheels.

Ken Miles and Lloyd Ruby won the 1965 Daytona Continental endurance race in GT/103, prepared by Shelby. It was the first Ford GT or GT40 to win a race. A Weber-carbureted 256-cubic-inch Ford Indy engine with a Colotti T37 four-speed transaxle powered it. *Ford Motor Company*

Shelby's upgraded GT40s debuted at the 1965 Daytona Continental. Ken Miles and Lloyd Ruby won the race driving a GT40 to a new event record with a 99.9-mile-per-hour average for 12 hours. Another GT40 took third place. Shelby entered two GT40s at the 12 Hours of Sebring and one, driven by Ken Miles and Bruce McLaren, won first in class and second overall. Unfortunately, finishing at Le Mans proved to be an elusive dream once again.

Based on wins at Daytona and Sebring, Ford decided to manufacture fifty GT40s for FIA homologation. There was little doubt that the GT40 was more than just competitive as far as performance was concerned. But reliability was still an issue. All fifty were completed with the Shelby upgrades and new ZF five speed transaxles replacing unreliable Colotti units. GT40s were produced at Ford Advanced Vehicles in Slough, England, and sold to privateer racers and teams.

In the fall of 1964, Leo Beebe took charge of Ford Special Vehicles Activity, including the GT racing program, and moved FAV operations to Dearborn.

A very happy Henry Ford II at Le Mans after the unprecedented one-two-three victory for an American carmaker. He was also celebrating his decision not to buy Ferrari and produce a Ford-badged endurance racer. Enzo Ferrari was not happy as this event ended Ferrari's domination of endurance racing. *Ford Motor Company*

This classic photo of three GT40s crossing the line in the rain was taken at Le Mans in 1966. The first two were Shelby prepared; the third-place car was a Holman & Moody entry. *Ford Motor Company*

Ken Miles and Denny Hulme would have taken first at Le Mans in 1966 in No. 1 Mark II P/1015 had it not been a staged finish. Miles backed off the throttle, allowing the McLaren/Amon entry to win. Shown here in "Mercury" livery. *Miller Motorsports Park / Jeremy Henrie*

Dan Gurney driving the Gurney-Grant GT40 P/1031 at 1966 Sebring 12 Hours. He almost won the race but was disqualified after pushing the car when it broke down. Originally prepared by Shelby, it went to Holman & Moody to be prepped for Le Mans. *Ford Motor Company*

The second of the four production Mark IVs built, driven only once in a race—to win Le Mans. Shelby prepared J-6 set a new record in 1967, 3,215.5 miles with an average speed of 135.48 miles per hour over 24 hours. Owned by the Henry Ford Museum, it has not been restored, just given preservation upgrades under Dan Gurney's supervision. *Ford Motor Company*

Jacque Passino was appointed head all Ford racing. Roy Lunn, Ford's advanced concepts manager who set up the FAV operation in Slough, relocated the GT40 team to Michigan. Development of the GT40 would continue at Kar Kraft, maintained by Ford Division as an off-site skunk works. Once at Kar Kraft, Lunn and his team concentrated on improving the GT40's reliability and performance.

When interviewed, Lunn said: "Although work was progressing on correcting durability problems, it was obvious that the GT40's performance in this fast-moving racing field would soon be outmoded. Therefore the problem was how to get an improved power-to-weight factor and, at the same time, achieve a high durability level."

Lunn's group at Kar Kraft evaluated two concepts—increasing the 289's output and swapping to a 427 big-block. Once the 427 was given the nod, a beefier transaxle and driveline had to be engineered, and potential handling and braking issues had to be addressed. Estimates were that a heavier-duty transaxle and 427 engine would add approximately 250 pounds. This was the birth of the Mark II GT40.

Initiated in the winter of 1964, the Mark II project started as a test bed to generate information for a future model. At the time, there was no intention of racing the new car. The production-ready Mark II was scheduled for completion during the summer of 1965 after the Le Mans race in June. However, Leo Beebe was eager to show Ferrari just how serious Ford was.

The Mark II's lead designer, Ed Hull, came up with a solution to the GT40 drivetrain's weak link—the transaxle. Working at Kar Kraft, Hull came up with a drive unit incorporating a bulletproof Ford top loader four-speed, already proven in stock car and drag racing. While heavier and somewhat less efficient than a direct transfer unit, it had the advantage of using already developed components. The housing was cast of magnesium and a pair of quick-change gears transmitted the power to the pinion shaft. Between the new driveline and larger 427 engine, the Mark II required new front and rear structures and body shell. It was slightly bigger, heavier, and considerably more powerful.

The ready-to-race, 485-horsepower 427 Mark II, less fuel and driver, weighed 2,400 pounds with a horsepower-to-pound ratio of .202. The advantage was obvious as the production GT40 weighed 2,150 pounds (with a 289/385 engine), delivering .179 horsepower-per-pound.

Little more than a month before Le Mans, a prototype was tested at Ford's Dearborn Proving Ground, then run on the banked 5-mile oval at the Romeo test facility. With Ken Miles at the wheel, the Mark II's first high-speed runs showed great promise. Miles ran 201.5 miles per hour average laps and clocked 210-plus miles per hour on the straightaway. They calculated that the 427 GT40 Mark II could run 3:30 laps at Le Mans while observing a maximum engine redline of 6,200 rpm. The Mark II had the potential to win at Le Mans.

Based on these results and brief tests at Riverside Raceway, Beebe made the decision to ship the prototype and a hurriedly constructed second Mark II to France for the big race. On the second evening of prerace practice, Phil Hill, in the second car, set an all-time lap record of 3:33 at an average speed of 141 miles per hour!

One of the cars qualified in first place for the 24-hour race and both drivers led the pack without having to rev the big-blocks over 6,000 rpm. Unfortunately, on race day, both cars, driven by Ken Miles/Bruce McLaren and Phil Hill/Chris Amon, dropped out by the 7-hour mark with mechanical issues. Four other GT40s with small-block engines did not finish.

The Ford pits prior to the start of the 1967 24 Hours of Le Mans. Dan Gurney and A. J. Foyt drove the Mark IV J-6 in the foreground to the win. It was the first time an all-American car had won at Le Mans. *Ford Motor Company*

Ford's second year at Le Mans proved to be no better than its first. Sunday evening, just 4 hours after the 1965 race had ended, Beebe called a meeting for all those involved with the GT40 racing program. He opened that meeting saying, "I want you to know that this is a victory celebration. We're celebrating our victory in the 1966 race!"

In preparation for the 1966 racing season, specifically endurance racing at Daytona, Le Mans, and Sebring, Roy Lunn laid out plans for racetrack testing plus participation in a proprietary engine dynamometer test cycle developed by Ford. There was also some new engine, ignition, electrical, transaxle, and brake component updates that were covered in a number of SAE papers.

Ford engineers developed a unique dynamometer testing program that could run the engine and driveline units under simulated road conditions that were prerecorded on tape in an instrumented test vehicle. This allowed component testing to proceed independently of vehicle availability and specific climate conditions for a total of 48 hours. The tape represented a map of the 8.3-mile Le Mans circuit, plotting exact shift, accelerating, decelerating, and braking locations for the drivers and team managers. At the time, this kind of racing strategy was "rocket science."

On-track testing by Shelby American and Holman & Moody, along with data collected from the dynamometer program, resulted in a number of mechanical and design upgrades that converted the original Mark II into a 1966 Mark II-A. On the design side, the nose was shortened to reduce weight and improve aerodynamics, and brake cooling scoops and ducts to radiator, carburetor, and brakes were added. To improve efficiency, performance, and reliability, the Mark II-A received new radiators, live rear hubs, a crossover fuel system with a single filler, an internal oil scavenger pump, and quick-change, ventilated brake discs for quicker pits stops.

During the development of the Mark II-A, Lunn's group worked with Corporate Styling Studios on a parallel GT40 project dubbed "J-Car." The name came from

revised FIA Appendix J competition rules. Lighter than the Mark II-A, the J-Car was designed around an adhesive-bonded, honeycomb-aluminum chassis concept developed originally by the Brunswick Corporation for the aircraft industry. Chuck Mountain, a Ford engineer working with Lunn at Kar Kraft, proposed that it be used for what would become a totally American GT40. While the GT40 Mark II and its engine and component parts were developed in the United States, the body structure was modified from the original GT40 design and still produced in England. Equipped with a 427 engine and automatic transmission, the J-Car was tested at the Le Mans trials in April 1966. Although it posted the fastest times, subsequent tests indicated that it was not ready for prime time and it was pulled from the lineup. It would become the mule for the 1967 Mark IV.

The first upgraded GT40 Mark II-As debuted on February 5 and 6, 1966, at the Daytona 24-hour Continental, America's premier sports car endurance race. Three GT40s virtually led the race from the start, finishing one-two-three for their first victory.

Prior to shipping GT40 Mark II-As to Europe for the 1,000-kilometer race at Circuit de Spa-Francorchamps in Belgium and the 24 Hours of Le Mans, testing continued at one more racetrack. One month later at the 12-hour race at Sebring, two GT40s powered by small-block 289s with Weber carburetors took first and second and set new distance and lap records. Miles and Ruby won in the Shelby American-prepared GT40 X-1 roadster with an aluminum underbody. Donahue and Hansgen drove the Holman & Moody Mark II to second place. A big-block Mark II-A, also entered by H&M and driven by Ronnie Bucknum and A. J. Foyt, came in twelfth.

A total of eight Mark II GT40s were entered at Le Mans, three by Shelby American, three by Holman & Moody, and two by Alan Mann Racing. The teams were managed by the best in the business, and cars qualified in the first four places and set a lap record of 3:31 (142 miles per hour). The fastest Ferrari time was 3:33. At the end of 24 hours, Ford GT40 Mark II-As finished an unprecedented one-two-three. The first two cars were Shelby American entries driven by Bruce McLaren/Chris Amon and Ken Miles/Denny Hulme. Ronnie Bucknum and Dick Hutcherson, in a Holman & Moody car finished third. An American carmaker had won Le Mans for the first time, but it was not without theatrics and political intrigue among Ford, the first and second place drivers, and track officials.

A decision was made by Ford to stage a photo finish and have the three GT40s finish side by side in a dead heat, a first in Le Mans history. Negotiations with track officials revealed the rule that, in case of a tie, the car that had started farther back on the grid had traveled the farther distance and, therefore, would be the winner. It was determined that the McLaren/Amon No. 2 car had started 60 feet behind Miles and Hume in No. 1, so it was declared the winner. Not a good plan.

At the end of the race, Miles was ahead of McLaren and had the opportunity, not only to win Le Mans but also win the Triple Crown of endurance racing—Daytona, Sebring, and Le Mans. He was asked to slow down and let the No. 2

car get ahead. As a Ford team driver, he played the game. As the three GT40s neared the finish line, Miles allowed McLaren to pull ahead by about a car's length, giving him the win.

The win demonstrated that production engines could compete with pure racing powerplants and that an American-built car could beat Europe's best.

Ford had done what no other American carmaker had ever done—and it was the greatest Ford victory in the company's history. After the win at Le Mans, the August 1966 issue of *Sports Car Graphic* featured a split cover with Roy Lunn and a GT40 on one side and Zora Duntov with a Corvette on the other. The title of the issue's cover story: "The Men From Advanced Vehicle Concepts."

The Mark IV, no longer referenced as a "GT40," was developed at the same time as the Mark II-A. Employing unitized construction, the Mark IV chassis was made entirely of an expanded aluminum honeycomb, sandwiched between .016-inch aluminum sheets. The sheets were bonded together with epoxy resin and riveted at the highest stress points. Front and rear body sections and doors were reinforced fiberglass construction. For 1967, the aluminum head, 10.75:1 compression 427 engine, with dry deck, lightweight cast-iron block with O-ring

One of the rarest, most important GT40 racecars GT40 P/1075 in Gulf livery. This was originally Mirage M.10003 and converted back into a GT40 Lightweight by John Wyer, JWA Racing. It is the only car to have ever won the 24 Hours of Le Mans twice—1968 and 1969. Shown here on way to winning in 1969. It's currently vintage-raced by Rob Walton. *Ford Motor Company*

sealing, received new heads and intake manifold with two Holley 652-cfm four-barrel carburetors. The 560-pound 427 generated 500 horsepower at 6,400 rpm and 470 pounds-feet of torque at 5,000 rpm. Designed and built by Lunn's team at Kar Kraft, the Mark IV was produced in accordance to FIA Group Six, Appendix J regulations.

For 1967, all factory efforts were dedicated to campaigning the Mark IV. However, at the 12 Hours of Sebring, GT40s finished first and second, one a Mark IV and the other a carryover Mark II-A. Mario Andretti and Bruce McLaren drove the Shelby American Mark IV to the win, followed by A. J. Foyt and Lloyd Ruby in the Holman & Moody Mark II-A. Following Sebring, the Mark II-A was updated to Mark II-B status and fitted with the Mark IV 500-horsepower 427 engine. The lighter Mark II-B featured new nose and tail sections without the previous model air induction snorkels.

The ultimate test for the Mark IV came in June 1967 at Le Mans. Dan Gurney and A. J. Foyt, in the Shelby American Mark IV, won the race and a second Shelby American Mark IV, driven by Mark Donahue and Bruce McLaren, finished fourth. While not as dramatic as the one-two-three finish the year before, it was the first win at Le Mans for an American carmaker with an American designed and built race car powered by an American engine. Ford also won the coveted Index of Thermal Efficiency award for the 427 engine in the winning Mark IV. This award was given to the engine that delivered the most performance on the least amount of fuel.

Unlike the Anglo-American GT40s, the Mark IV was made entirely in Michigan. Lunn summed it up best after the win: "To have an all-American winning car in 1967, having started from a clean sheet of paper in 1963, was a thrilling culmination to the program."

After winning Le Mans in 1966 and 1967, Henry Ford II had accomplished his original goal and, in 1968, withdrew from endurance racing. Ford left GT40 racing up to privateer teams and individuals. The FIA changed the rules in 1968, limiting Prototype Group 6 cars to 3-liter engines and Group 4 to 5-liter engines. Grady Davis' Gulf Oil Team, managed by John Wyer, was the most successful GT40 privateer operation. Wyer partnered with Ford UK megadealer John Willment to form JWA Racing. For the 1968 season, JWA converted three of its GT40-based, Len Bailey-designed 1967 Mirages into lightweight GT40s. The most significant, the Mirage M-10002, became GT40 P/1074 and the Mirage M-10003 became GT40 P/1075.

In 1968, JWA GT40s won six of the season's seven races: Brands Hatch, Le Mans, Monza, Spa, Watkins Glen, and Kyalami in South Africa. Pedro Rodriguez and Lucian Bianchi won at Le Mans in P/1075, powered by a Gurney-Weslake 289, by five laps. The same car also won at Brands Hatch, Spa, and Watkins Glen.

Past its prime as an endurance racer, the GT40 went out in a blaze of glory in 1969, winning Le Mans in the closest legitimate finish in history. Jackie Ickx, racing with Jackie Oliver in JWA's old P/1075 that had won Le Mans the previous year, crossed the finish line approximately 300 feet in front of Porsche racing legend Hans Hermann in a 908. It was the first time the *same* car had won twice at Le Mans.

Ford's original GT40 and Mark II and Mark IV variants changed the face of international endurance road racing in the 1960s. Henry Ford II's "dream that became reality" generated some of the most beautiful, iconic cars in the history of sports car racing. Thanks to Ford, the building of 2005-2006 GTs meant that enthusiasts could enjoy driving modern-day GT40s on the road.

GT40 and Mark IV: Last of the Legends!

Two iconic GTs—including the only one to have ever raced at Bonneville—signaled the end of Ford's endurance racing programs.

Ford's GT40, P/1083, was the last of forty-eight original Mark I race cars constructed in the period and the only new GT40 advertised by the factory for sale to the public. Finished in Carnival Red, John Wyer's JWA-built P/1083 was constructed in 1969 to P/1075 "lightweight" specs. Gurney-Weslake 289s with Webers powered both GT40s.

When the Mark IV replaced the GT40 Mark II, a total of twelve all-American Mark IVs were planned. Only ten were completed at Kar Kraft, and the final two spare tubs, chassis numbers J-11 and J-12, were never finished in period. They were sold in the 1970s and J-11 was completed in 1986, almost two decades after Mark IV J6 won Le Mans. The Mark IVs with honeycomb-aluminum chassis from Brunswick Corporation were powered by 427s with dual four-barrel carbs mated to Ford/Kar Kraft T-44 four-speed transaxles.

It's safe to say that only a miniscule number of enthusiasts have ever experienced seat time. Even fewer have driven a real GT40 or Mark IV. Archie Urciuoli is one of the fortunate few who has not only owned and raced both, but they were GT40 P/1083 and Mark IV J-11. A road racer since the 1950s, he competed in British sports cars, including a Jaguar XK-140 MC and E-Types, in SCCA's New England Region. He raced before, during, and after his thirty-five-year career on Wall Street.

In the late 1980s, Urciuoli started racing in vintage/historic events and, between 1990 and 1996, successfully raced a Jaguar D-Type, Formula Two Ralt, and Mark IV J-11. In addition to a number of podium finishes over the years, Urciuoli won the Skip Barber Racing Cup in 1994. Between 1999 and 2011, when he retired from racing, Archie drove a variety of serious race cars—Chevron B-36, Porsche 956 GTP, GT40, and a Lola T70 Spyder in SVRA and HSR events. He also codrove in three Daytona 24-hour races.

After purchasing Mark IV J-11 in 1993, Urciuoli raced it for four seasons before selling it. Powered by its original 427 engine, blueprinted in 1989 by Holman & Moody, it saw some success on the historic racing circuit. At the Merrill Lynch/Brian Redman International Challenge at Road America in 1997, Urciuoli clocked 198 miles per hour and set a new track record. His Mark IV won the Monterey Historic Award for Post-War Cars at Laguna Seca that year. It was also featured on a GT40 poster and calendar, and on the cover of *Vintage Motorsport*, Volume 4, Number 3.

However, one of Urciuoli's most exciting driving experiences was not on a road course. "I had always wanted to drive at the Bonneville Salt Flats but I spent my entire racing career on sports car tracks," he said. "In 1996, I realized that my Mark IV would go past Wendover, Utah, on its way home from Laguna Seca. I decided to have the necessary chute installed and register for Speed Week. My first run was 175 miles per hour on the short course, faster than

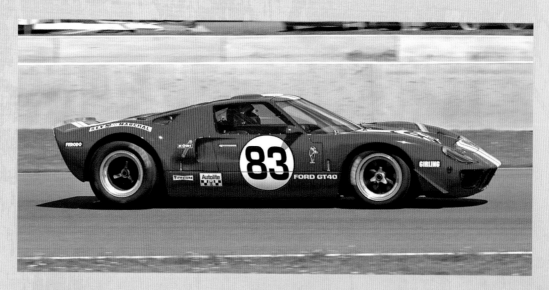

GT40 P/1083 at speed at Mont Tremblant Circuit, Quebec, Canada, at historic racing event. It was the last GT40 Mark I built in period and the only one ever advertised for sale to the public. Its second owner was Formula One great, Emerson Fitttipaldi's Fittipaldi Racing in Brazil. *Archie Urciuoli Collection*

In order to run at Speed Week at Bonneville, you need a competition license issued by the Southern California Timing Association (SCTA) for each class. Licenses cover Categories B, C, and E. It was the first and only time a GT40-series car has raced on the Salt Flats.

Archie Urciuoli, right, with codriver Dale Lang and wife Joan (Lang) and GT40 P/1083, smiling in the pits at Le Mans, after finishing (nineteenth overall) the 24-hour Le Mans Classic in 2004. They were able to run 200 miles per hour on the Mulsanne Straight. *Archie Urciuoli Collection*

Archie Urciuoli, left, with his crew at the Bonneville Salt Flats in 1996 after running over 200 miles per hour on the "long" course, going through the traps at over 180 miles per hour backwards. Known as *The Big Red One*, the GT40 Mark IV he drove is in the Bonneville books with a 1-mile average speed of 187 miles per hour. *Archie Urciuoli Collection*

I was supposed to go. But nothing ever quite equaled spinning across the damp, 7-mile long course on too-wide road-racing slicks at over 200 miles per hour in eerie silence. Then going through the traps at over 180 miles per hour backwards with, thankfully, no harm done. It brought to mind a Winston Churchill quote while serving in the military in 1898: 'Nothing in life is so exhilarating as to be shot at without result.' That's exactly how I felt."

Urciuoli's Mark IV was the only Ford GT series car ever run on the Salt Flats and is listed in the official Bonneville book as *The Big Red One* with an average speed of 187 miles per hour.

P/1083, the last GT40 constructed, was tested by David Hobbs at Thruxton, the UK's fastest race circuit, prior to its sale in 1969 to Sidney Cardoso's CAI Racing Team in Rio de Janeiro. In 1971, P/1083 was sold to Fittipaldi Racing and driven by Wilson Fittipaldi and Carlos Pace for approximately ten years. Team principal and Formula One great, Emerson Fittipaldi, sold it to George Stauffer in the United States in 1982. It was raced for a couple of decades, re-powered with a modified dry-sump engine, and acquired in 2002 by Archie.

After taking delivery, P/1083 was restored to original specs by Bob Ash at FAV Company and Jeff Sime at Jeff*Works. The GT40's original wet-sump 289 with Gurney-Weslake heads and Weber carburetors was located and blueprinted. Dynoed at 450 horsepower, it bolts up its original five-speed NR 1009 ZF transaxle. Urciuoli applied for and received FIA HTP papers #USA-5097.

"During my 'real' racing days, I'd never raced at Le Mans and the advent of the 24-hour Le Mans Classic presented a chance to go back in time," said Urciuoli. "Most of the 8.5-mile Circuit de la Sarthe is run flat-out on narrow public roads and is a truly awesome experience. Although I had driven faster in my Porsche 956 GTP car at Daytona, racing my GT40 at 200 miles per hour on the Mulsanne Straight in 2004 was a near religious moment."

Between 2003 and 2011, Urciuoli successfully raced P/1083 at major historic events from coast to coast. It won the Monterey Historics Award in 2004. Additional honors include the Best Race Car Award at the 2005 Greenwich Concours, Amelia Award in 2006 at the Amelia Island Concours, and the *Road & Track* Award at the 2007 Lime Rock Concours. He continues to serve as a member of the Governing Council of the International Racing Research Center at Watkins Glen and is on the board of the Road Racing Drivers Club (RRDC). Both GT40 P/1083 and Mark IV J-11 continue to do what they were originally constructed for—win races.

BILL KOLB JR.: MR. MONDAY!

As long as Shelby American was winning on Sunday, Bill Kolb was selling Cobras, Shelby Mustangs, and GT40s on Monday—more than anyone else in the country.

Bill Kolb is truly the poster boy for Ford's Total Performance and Win on Sunday, Sell on Monday marketing concepts. Since 1961 when he came out of the service, he has spent his entire adult life involved in the automotive retail business and building, racing, and selling specialty cars. His sales records of Shelby Cobras and Mustang GTs from 1965 to 1970 are legendary. What's even more impressive is that he turned both Larsen Ford—a small mom-and-pop dealership in suburban White Plains, New York—and Gotham Ford—a factory store located in New York City, one of the least car-friendly cities in the United States—into the country's two top-selling Shelby dealers.

When Shelby Cobra and Mustang GT sales numbers were tallied after the 1970 model year, Kolb's unique Shelby dealership-within-a-dealership at Gotham Ford ranked number one of sixty-four Shelby dealers. Between 1966

and 1970, Gotham sold 479 Shelby-branded cars. The Number Two spot went to Larsen Ford with 319 cars. Kolb is also credited with selling the most big-block Cobras, 18, including CSX3140, the first 427 Cobra shipped to Ford's New York District.

Like so many successful racers, car builders, and marketers of performance cars in the 1960s and 1970s, Kolb was a hot rodder first. His romance with high-performance Fords dates back to his days at White Plains High School when he street-raced a 1932 Ford with a modified flathead. By the time he graduated in 1959, the flathead gave way to a 312-inch Y-block with a home-brewed induction system consisting of dual four-barrel carbs and a pair of McCulloch-Paxton superchargers.

Kolb's next project was stuffing a bored-out 390 Ford tri-power engine, displacing close to 406 cubic inches, into a 1959 Corvette. Built in his parent's garage, Kolb successfully drag raced it at Dover Drag Strip in Wingdale, New York, winning Middle Eliminator on a regular basis.

Bill Kolb with his '06 Ford Tungsten Grey and Heritage GTs. Both GT models were released in 2006 to commemorate Ford GT40 wins at Le Mans: the Tungsten Grey for the fortieth anniversary of Ford's one-two-three win at Le Mans in 1966 and the Heritage for its wins in 1968 and 1969.

In 1961, Kolb purchased one of the first 375-horsepower, big-block Ford Starliner coupes sold in Ford's New York District. He later installed a factory tri-power package and upgraded the 390 to 401 horsepower.

"Since I was spending so much time and money at Larsen Ford buying high-performance parts, I thought it might be more fun and profitable to be on the other side of the counter," said Kolb. Later in the year, Carl Larsen hired Kolb as a salesman and high-performance director at Larsen Ford.

By the time Kolb adjusted to being called "the Kid" by the other salesmen, who were closer in age to Bill's father, he was outselling them all. In his second month on the job, he sold more than forty cars! His secret was customer service. "I would go into the dealership at seven in the morning when people were dropping their cars off for service, offer to drive them home, then give them my business card," he said. "Next, I divided the city of White Plains into quarters. I took one quarter at a time and gave out my card at all the businesses."

Starting in 1963 when Bill Kolb was racing a factory 1963½ 427/425 Lightweight Galaxie for Larsen Ford and I was editing automotive magazines, he became my go-to guy for Ford racing and high-performance parts information. The following year, Kolb received one of the early automatic-equipped 427 Thunderbolt Super/Stocks. He campaigned it primarily on the East Coast, where it could generate sales at Larsen Ford, traveling to the Midwest only for major meets.

As our relationship grew stronger, Kolb became an invaluable asset when I started editing CARS magazine in 1964. Whenever I needed special cars for photography or a story that Ford couldn't supply, he always came through. Our friendship continues to this day.

Tasca Ford sold 17 Cobras and GT350 Mustangs in 1965 and was the country's top-ranked Shelby dealer. Larsen Ford sold nine Shelbys and landed in fifteenth place. Kolb started slow but by the end of the 1966 model year, he had moved 160 Shelbys out the door and put Larsen Ford in the Number One spot.

Committed to "winning on Sunday and selling on Monday," Kolb's next drag racing venture was more entertainment than eliminator. Enter the *Little Yellow Wagon*, a raucous 427-powered "billboard" capable of running the quarter mile on its rear wheels. It actually proved to be more effective as a sales tool than previous Super/Stock race cars.

Kolb and his 1965 Ford Econoline pickup joined the ranks of wheel-standing exhibitionists, headed by Bill "Maverick" Golden, who, driving his Dodge *Little Red Wagon*, pioneered the genre. The *Little Yellow Wagon* was built by Armand "Monty" Gatti, a friend and brilliant fabricator, and was powered by a Hilborn-injected 427 side oiler built by Tasca Ford's John Healey. The engine was mounted on a subframe behind the cab. Kolb worked with Larsen Ford mechanic and friend, John Sachs, and Monty Gatti to tune and race-prep the truck. Kolb did all the driving and experienced the first of a number of crashes at a small track in Vermont.

There's little doubt that the car that saved the Shelby GT350 Mustang program from going south at the end of 1965 was the 1966 GT350H Hertz *Rent-A-Racer*. If Hertz hadn't ordered a thousand for its Sports Car Club, there might not have ever been a 1967 model. That order came close to not happening had it not been for a chance meeting between Kolb and a Hertz executive who had been road testing a prototype GT350H. The executive

Bill Kolb presents the Super/Stock class trophy to Carl Laren, Larsen Ford owner and sponsor of Bill's '63½ 427/425 Lightweight Galaxie. Photo taken in 1963 at Larsen Ford, White Plains, New York.

Kolb's wheel-standing 427 Econoline pickup proved to be more effective than race cars in attracting customers. The truck was powered by a pro-built, Hilborn-injected 427 side oiler. It was the subject of the cover story for the December 1965 issue of *Super/Stockers in Action* magazine.

mistakenly dropped the car off at Larsen Ford at 80 Westchester Avenue instead of Ford's New York District Office at 250 Westchester Avenue in White Plains.

Kolb recalls, "I was walking through the Service Department when this guy comes in, drops off a modified Mustang, gives me the keys, and says, 'I want to drop off this hunk of junk. I can't take the loud noises and clunks every time I go over a bump. I'm testing it before we sign off on buying a thousand and there's no way I would ever buy this car.' I knew exactly what the problem was and asked if he would give us an hour or so to check it out.

"The problem was that the bolts used for mounting the Traction Masters were too long, essentially causing a bottoming-out problem over dips and bumps in the road. I had written to Shelby about this problem on 1966 GT350s and never heard back. My head-tech, John Sachs, and I had come up with a solution. While the guy from Hertz was out, we shortened the bolts, reinstalled them, and took the Mustang out for a test ride. It was perfect. Then we let him drive it and he loved the car. He went on his way, dropped the car off at the Ford Office, and went back to work. Not long after, Hertz signed off on the GT350H.

"I believe if he hadn't dropped the car off with us instead of returning it to Ford, more than likely the order would have been seriously delayed or not

happened at all. Our reward was an increased allotment of Shelby Mustangs."

Carroll Shelby was keenly aware that while his Cobras and Mustangs were selling like proverbial hotcakes at Larsen Ford, sales at the high-profile factory store on Manhattan's posh east side, located at Sixty-First Street and First Avenue, were embarrassing. Gotham Ford had sold one Shelby and was in last place nationally.

"In 1966 I was approached by Lee Iacocca, then vice president of Ford's Car and Truck Group," says Kolb. "Familiar with the transformation of sleepy Larsen Ford into the Number One Shelby store in the country, he offered me an opportunity that I couldn't refuse—running my own exclusive Shelby sales and service operation inside Gotham Ford. Essentially, Iacocca created the first dealership-within-a-dealership, selling and servicing only Shelby automobiles.

After making the transition from suburbia to Manhattan, Kolb sold thirty-six Shelbys in five months, moving Gotham from the bottom rung of 1965 Shelby sales to eleventh place in 1966. He laid the groundwork for creating a model metro-area Shelby dealership. One of his rewards was an invitation to join Ford's Dealer Council for Performance Cars, the only salesman to be part of this group.

Kolb often drove for Ford-product road tests in *Hi-Performance CARS* magazine. Here he is behind the wheel of CSX3140, the first 427 Cobra shipped by Shelby to the New York area.

By 1967, the Shelby outlet at Gotham Ford had become the country's epicenter for Cobra and GT350/GT500 Mustangs. One-third of all the Shelbys sold on the east coast came from Gotham. In 1967, Kolb sold 108 Shelby-badged vehicles and that year, and again in 1968, Kolb won every Shelby sales contest. Monthly sales reached as high as sixty units.

Based on his success at managing the Shelby/Gotham Ford operation, in March 1968 Kolb was invited to participate in a special Shelby marketing forum for Ford executives in Dearborn. In a letter dated May 28, 1968, from Ray Geddes, manager of Shelby Automotive marketing, Kolb was thanked for a recent presentation he made to the group: "Many of the recommendations you made at the March 19, 1968, meeting have been passed on to senior management, including continuing the Shelby GT350-500 series for at least the 1969 and 1970 model years. In accordance with your collective recommendations, we have designated the 428 Cobra Jet Shelby GT as the GT500KR—*King Of The Road.*"

Kolb became a key player in Ford's Shelby marketing programs. Ford hired him to be the national spokesperson for the Shelby dealer network and he consulted on the scripting and production of sales training films. Between 1968 and 1969, Kolb also sold more Ford GT40 road cars and Mark III models than anyone else in the country.

"I was asked to sell off a handful of GT40s that had been used as demos, executive cars, and for auto shows," Kolb recalls. "They were stored in a Ford warehouse in Secaucus, New Jersey, and one was actually left outside on an open trailer at the Ford Parts Depot. Cars had flat tires, bent Borranis, dents, and scratches. The one left outside and unprotected had to have its fuel bladders flushed before it could be driven. All the cars had to be refurbished. Included in the fleet was the prototype Mark III, GT40 M3/1101, which had been shown for the first time at the 1967 New York International Auto Show. It's

also the GT40 that Marty Schorr and I road tested for the July 1967 issue of *Hi-Performance CARS* magazine. Our cost on the cars was a little over $5,000 each. Before selling them all, I drove one from New York City to visit Bob Tasca at his dealership in Rhode Island. I couldn't believe what it felt and sounded like cruising at 150 miles per hour."

By late 1969, Ford decided to shut down its Gotham Manhattan location and Kolb moved on. He found an opportunity at Hory Chevrolet, a dealership in Larchmont, New York, that had been losing money for eleven straight years. Focusing on building and marketing specialty Corvettes and customized vans, he turned Hory into a profitable store.

Kolb returned to his Ford roots in 1975 when Ross Roberts, head of sales at Ford Division, offered him a sweetheart deal to take over the old Larsen store for very little cash down. He accepted and partnered with his old pal, John Sachs. That was thirteen years after Kolb was hired at Larsen as a salesman. They renamed the dealership White Plains Ford and, between 1975 and 1981, built it into one of the top dealerships in the New York District.

Before opening Bill Kolb Jr. Ford in 1984, Kolb enhanced his relationship with Ford as a manufacturer by creating Spoilers-Plus, a company that produced aerodynamic styling and ground-effects kits for slow-selling vehicles like the Ford EXP. The line was expanded to include bolt-on RFP (Flexible Resin Process) and urethane restyling components for Mustangs and Thunderbirds. Spoilers-Plus became the first aftermarket company to sell aero-enhancing body kits to Ford. In 1982 when Ford discontinued the front air dam on the GT Mustang, Kolb sold more than 5,000 precolored, bolt-on air dams to Ford dealers.

In the October 30, 1983, edition of the *New York Times*, Rich Taylor wrote, "Ford Motor Company copied Kolb's customized 1979 Mustang Indy Pace Car replica when it came out with the 1982 Mustang GT. This year's EXP Turbo is a virtual replica of the Spoilers-Plus model."

When Kolb opened Bill Kolb Jr. Ford, he moved the Spoilers-Plus operation into the dealership. Over the next couple of years, the company shipped more than 4,000 aero kits with custom grilles, air dams, side-skirt panels, and rear spoilers for Thunderbird Turbo Coupes to Ford dealers.

For three years, Atlanta Motor Speedway contracted with Spoilers-Plus to build aero-model Thunderbird official pace cars for NASCAR events. Approximately two years later, Masco Corporation, an automotive industry supplier, approached Kolb to purchase Spoilers-Plus. The deal was closed in 1986.

One of Kolb's most rewarding projects was building an air dam for Bill Elliott's 1987 Daytona 500 winning Thunderbird. "Ford had tested Elliott's NASCAR Thunderbird in the wind tunnel and was able to get an 11.2-mile-per-hour increase with their prototype air dam design," said Kolb. "The problem was that Ford needed 60 days to create a race-worthy air dam and get NASCAR

approval. Ford tested Elliott's racecar with my Spoilers-Plus air dam and recorded a 9.8-mile-per-hour gain over stock. I was able to ship Elliott our air dam within a week and they got it approved. He qualified at Daytona, got the pole, and won the 500 averaging over 176 miles per hour to set a record. After the race he sent me a note: 'Thanks for the air dam, it has the record.'"

Since 1998, Kolb and his wife, Maryann, a former Ford marketing executive, own Bill Kolb Jr. Subaru in Orangeburg, New York, just down the road from his last Ford dealership. It's one of the brand's top sales leaders on the East Coast.

Total Performance is still a way of life for Kolb, who parlayed a passion for racing and high-performance cars into a legendary career. A master at building and marketing specialty vehicles, he keeps his decades-old Ford connection alive with a pair of 2006 Ford GTs, Tungsten Grey and Heritage Blue.

In early 1963, Bill Kolb took delivery the first factory 427/425 fastback Galaxie lightweight in the New York District. Set up for Super/Stock racing, Bill was the driver and worked with Larsen's top tech, John Sachs, to prep and tune it for the track.

AC 289:
COBRAS FROM ACROSS THE POND

Old Shel' never touched COB/COX ACs, but they are authentic Cobras.

Carroll Shelby's Cobras started life as AC Ace roadsters shipped from AC Cars, Ltd. Thames Ditton, Surrey, England, to Shelby American in Southern California. Once in Shelby's hands, they received Ford small- and big-block engines and were finished to Shelby Cobra specs. In 1965, a new, improved coil-spring chassis designed with help from Ford, more aggressive styling, and 427- or 428-inch Ford engines changed the look and performance of the Cobra. AC shipped rolling wide-body chassis to Shelby until the end of 1966.

Not long after Shelby Cobra production started, AC Cars started building AC Cobras, with 289 engines and four-speeds supplied by Shelby, for distribution in the UK and Europe. AC Cobras were constructed in two versions: COB (CObra Britain) as a right-hand-drive domestic model and COX (CObra eXport) as a left-hand-drive export model.

The AC Cobra did not have "Powered By Ford" badging, but it had a Cobra emblem on its nose and an AC emblem on the deck. Total production was sixty-two cars—forty-five COB and seventeen COX models. Chassis numbers started at COX6001 that was built in October 1963. The last leaf-spring AC Cobra, COX6062, was completed in May 1965. After the end of leaf-spring Cobra

production, there remained an extensive inventory of leftover parts. They were used to assemble some cars after all AC and Shelby Cobra production ended.

In 1966, AC Cars continued in the Cobra business to produce domestic and export AC 289 Sports in COB and COX trim. Unlike Shelby's Cobras, the latest coil-spring chassis AC Sports did not come with big-block engines, or with Cobra emblems or "Powered By Ford" badges. AC had little use for big-block engines because of high fuel costs, taxes, and fees related to engine displacement in the UK and Europe. The combination of a high-revving small-block and much-improved chassis and suspension produced one of the most roadworthy, best driving Cobras. Out of a total of twenty-five AC 289 Sports built between 1966 and 1969, eighteen were right-hand-drive while just seven were left-hand-drive.

The "wild cards" were two unfinished leaf-spring chassis or, possibly, two reserved early chassis number plates. Chassis numbers COX2610 and COX2620 appear to be sequenced with the end of leaf-spring Cobra production. The last small-block Cobra chassis produced for Shelby American was CSX2602, the last of six Cobra Daytona Coupes and invoiced on August 31, 1964. The twenty-five COB/COX coil-spring cars continued the

Owned by Ned Scudder, this is AC 289 Sports chassis number COX6111. It is the second of seven LHD models, built on the improved coil-spring Cobra chassis with "narrow-hip" body, and was the first to leave AC on October 15, 1966. Scudder has owned it since 2005 and participated in the inaugural Cobras in the Mountains Tour in 2006 and the Moonshine Tour in 2007.

All five original FIA roadsters built for the Shelby American Team were painted Viking Blue; three had unique colors of fender-nose stripe, and two had white. Note the standard hood scoop, flared fenders, and KO pin-drive Halibrands.

6000-series chassis numbering, starting with COB6101. AC Cars produced two custom cars for John Willment Racing built on leaf-spring chassis. The Willment Coupe was actually CSX2131 and the roadster CS2131.

The next-to-last AC 289 was COX6126, a left-hand-drive car exported to the United States without an engine in January 1969. It ended up at Holman & Moody, where it received a 427. The last car, COB6127, left the factory unfinished in 1968 and, in the late 1980s, was repowered with a Holman & Moody 427. It was converted to left-hand-drive. Confusing? Wait, there's more.

Those two never-completed chassis numbers—CSX2610 and CSX2620—appear to have remained unfinished long after the last AC 289 left the factory on July 15, 1968. However, in 2002–2003 they appeared as complete and obviously finished as continuation or remanufactured cars.

In 1968, Don Zucker visited AC Cars in England to check out an AC 428, the Frua-bodied GT coupe. At AC, he discovered a leftover 289 Sports that had been "deposited" and never picked up. He made an offer, bought the car, and had it put on a Pan Am flight to JFK in New York. That car was COB6123, but instead of having right-hand-drive, it had been built to COX left-hand-drive specs. They never changed the chassis tag!

Today, Archie Urciuoli owns COX2610, a striking, Viking Blue, FIA-bodied 1965 AC Cobra that captures the spirit of Shelby's five Viking Blue 289 FIA Cobra competition cars. It's a dead-ringer for a Shelby team car because it has the same aluminum body and was produced at AC Cars using original tooling and buck.

Like Shelby's race cars, Urciuoli's roadster, purchased in 2005, has a high-compression 289 with four Weber 48 IDA carburetors on a Cobra manifold; headers leading to outside exhausts; knock-off, pin-drive Halibrands;

Raydyot mirrors; FIA dash layout; hood scoop; and flared fenders. The trunk accommodates an FIA-legal "suitcase." Unlike the five FIA team race cars, Urciuoli's roadster was built on a standard chassis and is driven on the street.

Jim Price, owner of AC Cars in 2006, researched COX2610. In a letter to Urciuoli dated June 12, 2006, he stated, "With reference to your AC FIA 289, chassis number 2610, I can confirm that it was, according to my knowledge, the last car assembled and shipped from the AC Firmley Plant. It was built using original tooling and from the original drawings and specifications."

COX2610 was not built at the time AC Cars was producing leaf-spring Cobras and, even though it has an authentic FIA aluminum body and early chassis, it's classified as an AC Cars "factory continuation car." It was bodied or rebodied as an FIA model and purchased by its previous owner in 2003. It came with a Certificate of Newness on AC letterhead dated February 2003 and signed by John Owen, Chief Engineer, AC Cars.

Like the mythical Phoenix, AC Cars—in one iteration or another—keeps rising from the ashes. The brand was based in the UK and Malta, and has experienced a number of owners, partnerships, joint ventures, and bankruptcies. Steve Gray continues to build AC 289 and 427 "Cobra" variants at AC Heritage Ltd., Brooklands Motor Company, Weybridge, United Kingdom. AC Cars celebrated its centennial in 2001 and will probably be around to celebrate its bicentennial.

Don Zucker purchased COB6123 at the AC factory as a leftover model. When Carroll Shelby used the new body style, he did not allow AC to call it a Cobra or use any Cobra badging. Powered by a 289 K-code motor with a single four-barrel carb, it is essentially the same engine used by Shelby in its small-block cars. When new, it was dyno-tuned and modified by Motion Performance and was featured in the August 1969 issue of *Hi-Performance CARS*.

SUNBEAM TIGER: A COBRA FOR THE REST OF US!

The usual suspects at Shelby American helped turn a mild-mannered Sunbeam Alpine into a Cobra-fanged cat.

Almost four decades before Shelby American prototyped a V-8-powered Sunbeam Alpine, Sunbeam already had serious racing cred. In 1920, Sunbeam merged with French carmaker Darracq. They produced the first Sunbeam Tiger, a race car powered by a 4-liter V-12 engine. The one-off 1926 Sunbeam Tiger was the first car to exceed 150 miles per hour and held the record for the smallest displacement engine to set the land speed record.

The 1964 *through* 1967 Sunbeam Tiger was a low-volume series production car powered by a Ford small-block V-8 and capable, in 289, trim of hitting an estimated 128 miles per hour. The 1926 Tiger was a pure, raucous race car constructed for Major Henry Seagrave to contest Malcolm Campbell's 150.76-mile-per-hour land speed record, set in the legendary Bluebird. On March 16, 1926, Seagrave set the new land speed record at 152.33 miles per hour on the Southport sands course. Unlike most land speed record cars, the Tiger was the last known, true dual-purpose racer, built for circuit racing as well as land speed record attempts.

In the 1960s, only racing historians and land speed record aficionados knew of the original Tiger's achievements. However, the V-8-powered Tiger, built off the instantly recognized Alpine, became a small part of 1960s American culture. Don Adams' character, Maxwell Smart, drove a 1965 Sunbeam Tiger to "Control Headquarters" at the start of every television episode of the hit comedy series *Get Smart*.

In 1953, the first Sunbeam-Talbot Alpine was introduced as a GT-type touring convertible and, in 1959, the totally new two-place Alpine sports roadster was added to the line. Sunbeam and Talbot had been taken over by the British Rootes Group in 1935. At that point, the sporty but anemic Sunbeam Alpine was an attractive, two-place sports roadster and the only brand in the Rootes stable that appealed to sports car enthusiasts in the United States, a primary market for British exports.

There was little interest in American V-8-engined sports cars at the Rootes Group in the UK. But they were aware that, in order to stay competitive in the United States, the Alpine needed a shot of adrenalin. The man running Rootes West Coast, the US sales and distribution center in Los Angeles, was John Panks. He and Sales Manager, Ian Garrad, knew that the Alpine needed an American V-8 engine. Garrad approached Carroll Shelby and race-car builder Ken Miles in the spring of 1963 to construct a pair of V-8 Alpines.

Miles did a quickie conversion with a 260 V-8 and an automatic transmission for under $1,000, while Shelby produced a close-to-production-ready, four-speed prototype for $10,000. Shelby's prototype had a set-back engine for close to 50/50 weight distribution, Borg-Warner T-10 four-speed, and Dana 44 rear. MG rack-and-pinion steering was also added.

After testing, Panks and Garrad shipped the Shelby prototype across the pond for evaluation by Rootes Group engineers and Lord Rootes of Ramsbury himself. Shelby's V-8 Alpine was a big hit and management contracted with Jensen Motors, Ltd. in West Bromwich, England, for conversions of Alpines to Tigers. There were some small changes from prototype to production, including the substitution of Ford's four-speed in place of the smoother-shifting but pricier T-10.

The production Sunbeam Alpine had 82-horsepower single carburetor and 93-horsepower dual carburetor four-cylinder engines. Ford's 260 hydraulic-lifter, two-barrel engines rated at 164 horsepower were used in 1964–1966 Tigers, while 1967 Mark II Tigers received 289 versions rated at 200 horsepower. Because the Ford engine was so easily modified using Ford and Shelby speed equipment, Tigers became potent road cars and track racers.

The first Sunbeam Tiger was a raucous race car with a V-12 engine that, in 1926, was the first car to exceed 150 miles per hour. It set the land speed record at 152.33 miles per hour and eclipsed the 150.76-mile-per-hour record set by Malcolm Campbell in the legendary Bluebird.

One of two Lister-bodied Tiger coupes during practice at Le Mans prior to the 1964 24-hour race. It ran consistent 150-mile-per-hour speeds and was clocked at 160 on the Mulsanne straight. There were three Prototype Class Tigers in the 1966 race, competing against Ferraris and Cobra-Lolas. Unfortunately, none finished.

Max Pahmeier owns this 1964½ Sunbeam Tiger, a "transition" car with squared-off doors and hood. The trunk is rounded and the body seams unfilled, an economy move by Chrysler. *Max Pahmeier*

Tigers were raced in Europe as well as road and drag raced in the United States. Two modified Tiger coupes, bodied by Lister, ran in the 1964 24 Hours of Le Mans. One was timed at over 160 miles per hour, but neither car finished. However, Tigers finished one-two-three in the Geneva Rally and finished fourth and eleventh overall in the 1965 Monte Carlo Rally. Hollywood Sports Cars' road-racing Tiger, built by hot rodder Doane Spencer and driven by Jim Adams, was incredibly successful in B/P competition in the SCCA Pacific Coast Region.

Gordon Chittenden, West Coast editor at *Hi-Performance CARS,* set the AHRA National Record at 108 miles per hour in 12.95 seconds driving the Larry Reed Sports Cars' 245-horsepower Tiger. Gordon was also the 1965 AHRA Class World Champion and held the record until 1967. The Tiger was powered by a 260/245 four-barrel engine built by Les Ritchey's Performance Associates.

At the time, the Rootes Group's Sunbeam Tiger Division in Los Angeles approved the LAT (Los Angeles Tiger) option 194- and 245-horsepower engine modifications. Sunbeam dealers offered a full complement of COBRA/LAT performance options, including traction bars, four-barrel Edelbrock/Holley induction, headers, and mag wheels. We covered the building of Gordon's record-setting Tiger in the February 1967 issue of *Speed and Supercar.*

Jensen Motors converted 7,003, 7,005, or 7,067 Alpines into Tigers between 1964 and 1967 or 1964 and 1968, depending on research sources. After this project started, Chrysler Corporation became a majority stakeholder in Rootes. Going with 7,005 Tigers and an end date of 1967, there were 3,763 Mark I 260 Tigers with doors with rounded corners, metal convertible boot, and leaded body seams. Additionally, there were 2,706 Mark I-A 260 Tigers with doors with squared-off corners, vinyl boots, and unfilled body seams. The final run of Mark II Tigers with 289/200 Ford engines and unique egg-crate grilles were produced after Chrysler acquired 100 percent of Rootes. Some records show Tiger production into 1968, but most likely they were leftover 1967s. Approximately 70 percent of Tigers were exported to the United States.

The Tiger offered enthusiasts a fast, attractive sports car with Cobra roots for $3,500—approximately half the price of a Cobra. Chrysler didn't want to continue marketing a Ford-engined car and didn't have a suitable engine for the Tiger. It just faded away after the last Mark II was built.

Steve Sorenson's Tiger has been a race car since it was new, converted by Lew Spenser and later sold to Art Firmes. The heavily modified Tiger has been maintained and race-prepped over the years by Corvette racing legend Dick Guldstrand at Guldstrand Engineering. *M. M. "Mike" Matune Jr.*

Lotus-Cortina: The Mouse That Roared

Ford of Britain and Colin Chapman created a twin-cam "giant killer" that wreaked havoc in Touring Car competition.

Not long after its introduction in 1963, the Lotus-Cortina, powered by a DOHC, 1.5-liter four-cylinder with dual Weber carburetors, started winning races and striking fear in the hearts of Jaguar racers and sports car owners. Ford's Consul Cortina Lotus, best know as the Lotus-Cortina, was built on a rather uninspiring two-door econo-sedan platform. The relationship with Lotus' Colin Chapman accelerated the Cortina from a sedate sedan into a screamer. In addition to a twin-cam engine, the Lotus-Cortina received Chapman's suspension upgrades and signature "lightness" in the form of aluminum body panels.

Cortinas with Lotus bragging rights were built from 1963 to 1966 in Mark I trim and from 1966 to 1970 as the less angular, facelifted Mark II. Ford started exporting Lotus-Cortinas to the United States. in 1966. Chapman started developing Ford's 1.5-liter Kent engine in 1961. By the time it was ready for the Lotus-Cortina, it had received a slight overbore and displacement increased to approximately 1.6 liters. At first, the 1.6-liter engine, rated at 105 horsepower, was offered as a special option and then it was phased in as standard equipment. When the Mark II model was introduced in 1966, the 1.6-liter engine, now rated at 109 horsepower, was standard. Primarily a right-hand-drive car, the Lotus-Cortina was available with left-hand-drive toward the end of 1966 model year production.

Initially, the Lotus twin-overhead-cam conversion of Ford's engine was part of Colin Chapman's 1961–1962 strategy to develop a powerful, less expensive powerplant than the Coventry Climax he was using in the Lotus 23 race car and Elan road car. Chapman contracted with Harry Mundy to design the DOHC head

Developed by Lotus' Colin Chapman, the DOHC 1.5-liter engine in the Mark I Lotus-Cortina looks like it belongs in a race car. The Mark II engine came with a huge silencer that looked like a muffler, filtering air for the side-draft Webers. *Ford Motor Company*

A rare Alan Mann Racing '68 Twin-Cam Escort, the car that replaced the Lotus-Cortina as Ford's road-racing and rally competition car. It was driven by Henry Mann and Jackie Oliver. Photographed here in the pits at Goodwood, this race car has the 1.6-liter Cosworth FVA Twin-Cam engine with fuel injection, rated at 215 horsepower, set up for FIA Group 5 Saloon competition. *Stuart Schorr*

conversion and with Keith Duckworth at Cosworth Engines for tuning specs. The donor engine was the tried-and-true Ford 116E four displacing 1.5 liters. By the time the conversion was completed, components were used in the 1.6-liter engine.

The key player in the creation of the Lotus-Cortina was Walter Hayes, then head of public relations at Ford of Britain. A confidant of Henry Ford II, he shared Ford's passion for racing and the Total Performance marketing concept. Hayes entered into a relationship with Colin Chapman, not unlike the one Ford had with Carroll Shelby. Chapman agreed to build one thousand Lotus-engined Cortinas so that the nameplate could be homologated for FIA Group 2 Saloon Racing and the British Touring Car Championship Series.

Unlike so many cars available new with larger high-performance engines, suspension tweaks, and status emblems, the Lotus-Cortina was a serious, well-balanced machine. Generating 105 horsepower with a Lotus DOHC alloy head and twin side-draft Webers, it looked like no other Ford engine. Its four-speed

transmission was used in the Lotus Elan and, along with the differential, cased in aluminum.

In true Colin Chapman style, lightness was added via aluminum door skins, hood, and deck lid. Suspension upgrades included shorter-than-stock front struts, forged control arms, and 9.5-inch Girling disc brakes. At the rear, leaf springs were replaced with coils and a pair of trailing arms located the rear axle. For improved balance and traction, the battery was moved to the trunk over the right wheel. Except for some red cars for Alan Mann Racing, all Lotus-Cortinas were white with a green stripe. One was custom finished with a blue stripe.

Other unique Lotus-Cortina features included split front bumpers, Lotus badging, and an interior with center console, fully instrumented dash, special bucket seats, and wood-rimmed steering wheel. Until 1966, subcontractors built Lotus-Cortina engines, then production moved in-house at Lotus' Hethel, Norwich facility. From late 1964 to early 1965, models were slightly facelifted and alloy body panels became an extra-cost option. Restyled 1966 to 1970

Mark II Lotus-Cortinas with 109-horsepower DOHC engines were produced at the Dagenham plant without support from Lotus. There were small transmission and final drive ratio changes, and the Webers breathed through a top-mounted fixture that looked more like a muffler than an air cleaner. Lotus badges gave way to "Twin Cam" emblems.

After the Lotus-Cortina was introduced, Ford sponsored two Lotus-Cortina racing teams for competition in the United Kingdom and Europe—Team Lotus and Alan Mann Racing. In the first outing at the 1963 Oulton Park Gold Cup races, Lotus-Cortinas finished third and fourth overall behind Ford Galaxies. They beat Jaguar 3.8 sedans, at the time the dominant force in Saloon racing in the United Kingdom.

By 1964, Lotus-Cortinas had won the Swedish Ice Championship, the Wills Six-Hour in New Zealand, the South African National Saloon Championship, and the Austrian Saloon Car Championship. Red and gold Alan Mann cars finished one-two at the *Motor* Six-Hours International Touring car race at Brands Hatch. In the United States, Jackie Stewart and Mike Beck won the 12-Hour at Marlboro Motor Raceway. Jim Clark drove a Lotus-Cortina to win the 1964 British Saloon Championship, and an Alan Mann Lotus-Cortina, driven by Sir John Whitmore, took the 1965 European Touring Car Championship. He won his class in every race entered! In the inaugural Trans-Am Series in 1966, Allan Moffat won the Under-Two-Liter Class in the third round race at Bryar Motorsports Park in Loudon, New Hampshire.

In 1968, Ford of Britain introduced the Escort, the car that would eventually replace the Cortina. The Twin-Cam Escort was a brand-new, modern car homologated for FIA Group 2 racing. A new Twin-Cam Escort won the 1968 British Saloon Car Championship as Escorts became virtually unbeatable in professional rally competition. The first twenty-five Twin-Cam Escorts were "Works" competition cars, with five supplied to Alan Mann for the British and European Touring Car Championship series. Twin-Cam Escorts were equipped with 1.6-liter DOHC engines rated at 109 horsepower at 6,600 rpm and 107 pounds-feet of torque at 4,700 rpm.

Later, there were some Alan Mann Twin-Cam Escorts built to FIA Group 5 Saloon racing specs with Cosworth 1.6-liter FVA Formula Two engines. The red and gold Twin-Cam, driven by Harry Mann and Jacquie Oliver, weighed approximately 1,750 pounds and its Lucas fuel-injected Cosworth engine generated 215 horsepower at 8,500 rpm and 132 pounds-feet of torque at 7,200 rpm.

Ford's Lotus-Cortina and Twin-Cam Escort defined dual-purpose road cars in the 1960s and into the 1970s. They could be driven daily, off-road rallied, and road raced with great success. British automotive journalists often referred to the Lotus–Cortina as a "Tin Roof" Lotus 7 and the Twin-Cam Cosworth Escort as a "rocket ship!"

Dean Gregson, High-Performance sales manager at Tasca Ford, raced one of Ford's $1.00 Lotus-Cortinas sold in 1965 to factory-sponsored racers. "The Lotus-Cortina was a great car," said Gregson. "I could eat up Corvettes and Mustangs at Bryar Motorsports Park and Watkins Glen." *Tasca Family Archives*

CHAPTER 8

1967

OK, Now It's Your Move!

Ford calls out the GTO with its hot 390 and 427 Fairlanes, puts a big-block in its Mustang, and wins Daytona 500, Indy 500, the Trans-Am championship, and Le Mans.

Fresh from its unprecedented one-two-three victory at Le Mans, Ford marketers readied their most aggressive advertising campaigns yet for the 1967 model year. Most of the in-your-face advertising focused on the upgraded midsize Fairlane and new 427 options. While the Mustang had built an incredible youth market following, it was restyled, which further enhanced its long-hood/short-deck look. Its platform was reengineered to take a 390 big-block engine—great news for racers and just in time for Chevy's launch of its first pony car, the Camaro.

After changing the title of *CARS* to *Hi-Performance CARS*, I also changed the name of the magazine's annual industry award from "American Classic" to "Top Performance Car of the Year." The recipient was chosen solely on my experiences driving the new models, supported by test-driving input from contributing editor Joe Oldham and managing editor Fred Mackerodt. Unlike other high-profile magazine awards, it was *not* linked to advertising. *Hi-Performance CARS* made its money the old fashioned way—on the newsstand!

The parameters for choosing the award winner started with my definition of *top performance*—the combination of acceleration, braking, handling, midrange response, ride, top speed, and even looks. When we chose the 390 Mustang for the 1967 award, it was based on me spending two days in Dearborn driving the highest-performance Mustangs you could buy on the road course, drag strip, skid pad, and high-speed "soup bowl" at the proving ground. On Ford's drag strip, I ran a best time of 90 miles per hour in 15.2 seconds.

I had originally requested a fastback coupe, but the only Mustang available was a pre-production, non-GT model with GT options, including 390 engine, four-speed, and the excellent Competition Handling Package. The 390/320 four-barrel engine was carried over from the 390/335 big-block available in the 1966 Fairlane. With 10.5:1 compression, the 390 was rated at 320 horsepower at 4,800 rpm and 427 pounds-feet of torque at 3,200 rpm. It was a stout motor that could be brought up to over 400 horsepower by adding key 427 engine components. Because the Mustang platform was changed to accept the 390 engine, installing a 427 would not require major surgery.

Since GT Group-equipped V-8 Mustangs came with power front disc brakes, special handling package, and GT trim, most Mustang buyers either never

Parnelli Jones on his way to winning the Yankee 300 in a Holman & Moody 427 Fairlane at Indianapolis Raceway Park. He also won the Riverside 500 in this car, which was used by Ford in its classic '67 Fairlane advertisement: "427 Fairlane, Available With Or Without Numbers!" *Ford Motor Company*

Top factory drag racer Gas Ronda campaigned a new Mustang powered by an injected 427 SOHC engine. Ronnie Scrima's Exhibition Engineering built the all-new race car, which set a number of records in A/FC, the best being 7.67 seconds at Lions. In 1968, Ronda updated the car by adding a blower. It is shown here at Riverside Raceway. *Ford Motor Company*

The fully detailed R-code 427 dual-quad engine in the one-of-one '67 Galaxie. It's fully documented with a Marti Report. Note the tuned cast-iron factory exhaust manifolds, which deliver header performance without the noise. *Charlie Lillard*

New Jersey–based Downing & Ryan built and raced some of the fastest factory 1966 and 1967 Fairlane Super/Stocks powered by 427 medium-riser dual-quad engines. Here, Jim Downing tests his Super/Stock at Englishtown Raceway in 1967 prior to the NHRA Springnationals. He set the NHRA National Record in S/SB at 11.42 seconds and also ran S/SC.

Factory racer Ed Terry ran the Hayward Ford (Hayward, California) S/SB R-code 427 Fairlane on the West Coast. The factory race cars had 9-inch rears with thirty-one-spline axles, Detroit Lockers, and 4.86 gears. A fiberglass Ram Air induction hood was also part of the package.

Ford followed up its one-two-three win at Le Mans in 1966 with its second win in Roy Lunn's all-new Mark IV in 1967. This is the Gurney-Foyt Mark IV, powered by a 427 Tunnel Port big-block with aluminum heads and dual Holley quads that won. It's on display at the Henry Ford Museum. *Ford Motor Company*

noticed or saw no reason to spend an extra $388.53 for the Competition Handling Package. Checking off that box on the order form transformed a very competent road car into a track-day Mustang. The package included 16:1 quick-ratio steering, 365 pounds-inch-rate front coil springs, 125 pounds-inch-rate rear leaf springs, 35mm adjustable front and rear Koni shocks, 15/16-inch-diameter front sway bar, and a 3.25:1 limited-slip rear.

For a couple of years, Ford and Mercury had been struggling to keep up, both image and performance-wise, with GM's big-engined, slick-styled intermediates, the Chevy SS396, the Pontiac GTO, and the Olds 442. These were the cars that had won over young performance enthusiasts. That would change when Ford decided to make available the venerable dual-four-barrel 427 big-block as an optional engine in 1967 Fairlane and Comet models. Timing couldn't have been better as GM had decided to drop multiple carburetor tri-power in the top performance 1967 GTO and 442. No production GM intermediate model could match the horsepower and torque of the R-code 427 Fairlane.

Ford's advertising agency, J. Walter Thompson, wasted little time in producing advertisements for automotive and even lifestyle magazines featuring the 427 Fairlane. One memorable headline—"How to Cook a Tiger!"—was specifically aimed at the GTO and its Tiger promotions.

Ford and Mercury dealers found it much easier selling 390 Fairlanes and Comets than 427 versions, primarily because of price. The most expensive Fairlane GT convertible had a base MSRP of approximately $3,100. For an extra $264, you could order it with a 390 four-barrel engine. The R-code 427/425 engine added a whopping $1,200 to the price. Since the 390 could take factory 427 speed equipment, the lower cost 390 engine made sense.

Ultra-rare Candy Apple Red '67 Galaxie XL hardtop is one-of-one built with an R-code 427 Medium Riser big-block, four-speed, red interior, and 7-Litre Sports trim. It's big, comfortable, and very fast. *Charlie Lillard*

Ronnie Bucknum drove the Grady Davis Gulf Oil Mustang to a second-place finish at the last race of the 1967 Trans-Am Series at Pacific Raceways, Kent, Washington, giving the Shelby team enough points to cop the SCCA Championship for the second year in a row. *Ford Motor Company*

Another factor was insurance rates that had skyrocketed for cars with large displacement engines.

Even though you could order a 1967 Fairlane with a choice of W-code 427/410 single-four-barrel or R-code 427/425 dual four-barrel engine, the great majority of the 230 427 Fairlanes built were R-code models. Included in 427 Fairlane production were 72 high-content, 500XL models and a single GT hardtop.

Unlike the 427 Fairlane in 1966, the 1967 model came with a hinged steel rather than a lift-off fiberglass hood. With standard dual exhausts with restrictive transverse muffler and 3.89 limited-slip rear, you could expect to run 100 miles per hour in the low 14s. When pro-tuned and equipped with headers and cheater slicks, 427/425 Fairlanes could run 110 miles per hour in the very low 13s.

Mercury was not far behind with 427 midsize models. They committed to a low-volume run of just sixty Comets powered by medium-riser 427/425 engines. Of the sixty, Mercury slipped in twenty-two cheaper, lighter, and shorter Series 202 models. These were a favorite of street and track racers. A one-off Comet 202 sedan was built for Sandy Elliott's drag racing team. At the 1967 NHRA Winternationals, John Elliott set both ends of the national A/SA record and won the NHRA Division 3 Points Championship. He later won his class and lowered the record at the World Finals.

Lincoln-Mercury's Fran Hernandez supported the building of a number of tube-framed, fiberglass-bodied Comet exhibition cars for Jack Chrisman, Pete Gates, Kenz & Leslie, "Dyno Don" Nicolson, and "Fast Eddie" Schartman. These cars were powered by supercharged and injected, as well as naturally aspirated, 427 SOHC engines running on gas and nitro. Fitted with tilt-up, fiberglass Comet replica bodies and Logghe dragster chassis, some weighed just 1,620 pounds. Quarter-mile speeds were in the 190s with mid- to high-7-second elapsed times.

In 1966 when Leo Beebe turned control of the Special Vehicles Activity group over to Jacque Passino, who previously was head of racing, Ford's commitment to competition continued to grow even stronger. Dick Brannan, head of Ford's drag racing team, concentrated his efforts on a 427 Fairlane Super/Stock for 1967. From May 8 through May 12, 1967, drag team member Hubert "Hubie" Platt tested a specially prepared 427 Fairlane at Bristol Dragway in Tennessee. I have a copy of the report drafted by Brannan to SVA: "This vehicle consistently recorded times better than the NHRA National Record."

Jerry Titus was the lead driver on the Shelby Ford Trans-Am Team, winning the most races in the 1967 season and leading Ford and Shelby to their second Trans-Am Championship. Bearing Shelby's Terlingua Racing Team livery, this was one of the four Group II race cars that Shelby kept for Ford's official team. *Ford Motor Company*

Platt's test 427 Fairlane 500, two-door hardtop weighed 3,405 pounds with fiberglass fresh air induction hood, 9-inch rear with thirty-one-spline axles and 4.86:1 rear with Detroit Locker, four-speed Ford transmission, and slicks. The legal NHRA race-prepped medium-riser 427 engine had 13.2:1 compression, "L1/P1" camshaft, and 2-inch ID headers. All tests were run on 103-octane gas plus Goodyear and M&H 15-inch tires ranging in width from 8.90 to 10.50 inches and 29 to 30.3 inches in diameter. Platt made eighteen recorded runs with quarter-mile times ranging from 123.79 miles per hour in 11.42 seconds on M&H slicks to 120.64 miles per hour in 11.76 seconds on Goodyears.

Ford built fifty 427 Fairlanes based on Hubert Platt's test car specs for factory sponsored racers. Platt himself campaigned the *Georgia Shaker* Fairlane with Paul Harvey Ford livery, running consistent low 11.40s at almost 124 miles per hour. At one point, Jim Downing set the NHRA S/SB National Record at 11.42 seconds. Factory racers Ed Terry and Bill Ireland ran dual-quad 427 Fairlanes, while Don McCain campaigned a single-four-barrel, W-code Fairlane and set the S/SD record. At the 1967 NHRA Winternationals, Bill Lawton won B/XS, running 168.22 miles per hour in 8.69 seconds in the Tasca *Mystery 8* Mustang.

Even though all factory drag and NASCAR racing programs were centered around the new 427 Fairlane, Ford still offered customers a choice of W-code or R-code 427 side-oiler engines with four-speed transmissions in the full-size Galaxie. Collector Charlie Lillard owns the rarest 427 R-code, four-speed Galaxie XL hardtop, actually one-of-one built. In the 1967 model year, Ford built almost one million full-size models including 21,053 XL-trim hardtops. Of those XL hardtops, just twenty-one were equipped with R-code dual-quad 427 engines. Eight of those were also optioned with the 7-Litre Sports Package and two painted Candy Apple Red. Only one was equipped with a red vinyl bucket seat interior. That's Charlie Lillard's XL Galaxie, restored and documented with a full Marti Report.

Officially dubbed Mark IV, Ford had its all-new, all-American GT40 endurance racer ready for Le Mans in 1967. Powered by the latest 427 big-block with dual Holleys, two Mark IVs—the J-4 and the J-6—made history. They were raced just once, with Mario Andretti and Bruce McLaren winning the Sebring 12-hour in J-4 and Dan Gurney and A. J. Foyt bringing Ford its second consecutive win at Le Mans in J-6. At Le Mans, Mark Donahue and Bruce McLaren drove their J-5 Mark IV to fourth place. After winning Le Mans for the second time, Henry Ford II announced that Ford was ending its factory endurance racing program.

With Ford ending its participation in endurance sports car racing, budgets were shifted to continue its support of racing cars that looked like cars dealers actually sold. Ford and its dealers had a lot to celebrate in 1967, thanks to the SCCA and Carroll Shelby. Shelby GT350 Mustangs still dominated SCCA B/Production competition and Shelby driver Fred Van Beuren won the B/P crown at the American Road Race of Champions (ARRC) event at Daytona in a GT350.

Both Ford and Lincoln-Mercury Divisions supported SCCA's Trans-Am Series. Shelby represented Ford with Mustangs and Bud Moore Engineering managed a Cougar team. Shelby won the T/A Championship for Ford in 1966 and would go on to take the title in 1967. Bud Moore's Cougars finished the season just two points behind the Shelby-prepared Mustangs.

Shelby's T/A Mustangs were not GT350s. Instead, they were race-prepared notchback Mustangs supplied by Ford. Jerry Titus was Shelby's key driver and won four of the events that led to the championship. He won more races than any other driver in 1967.

Shelby American built a total of twenty-six white, Group II notchback Mustangs for SCCA events, four reserved for Shelby team drivers and twenty-one sold to privateer teams for racing in Trans-Am and/or A/Sedan events. One notchback race car served as the prototype for component testing. Chuck

Mario Andretti won the 1967 Daytona 500 in the Holman & Moody 427 Fairlane powered by the latest big-block with tunnel-port heads and manifold. Ford won six of the eleven major races, including the qualifier and the 500 main event at Daytona and the Riverside 500. *Ford Motor Company*

A. J. Foyt won the 1967 Indy 500 in a Coyote-Ford, averaging 168.98 miles per hour, followed by Ford-powered cars driven by Al Unser, Joe Leonard, Denny Hulme, and Jim McElreath. With three laps to go and leading the field, Parnelli Jones in the STP-Paxton-Turbocar looked as though he would win. However, a transmission bearing failed, and Foyt powered through for the win. *Ford Motor Company*

Cantwell, working with hands-on race car fabricator Jerry Schwartz, managed the project.

The Group II Mustangs and their 289 engines were built at Shelby American's LA Airport complex that included engine dynamometer facilities. I spent a day at the shop in 1967 watching them build the engines as well as Shelby GT Mustangs for stories in *Hi-Performance CARS*. Similar to the engines used in 1965 R-Model Mustangs, the 289 started life as a K-code 289 High Performance and was fitted with machined, big-valve heads; S1CR-6250-2 camshaft and valvetrain; high-rise, dual-quad aluminum intake manifold with Holley 600 cfm carb; finned aluminum Cobra oil pan; and tube headers. I was in the dyno room when one engine was being run and saw ratings range from 415 to 435 horsepower.

Not unlike GT350 Mustangs prepared for competition, the new Trans-Am Mustangs had B-W, T-10 alloy-cased, close-ratio four-speeds; 9-inch rears with Detroit Lockers, adjustable Koni shocks; 1965 R-Model traction bars; and quick-fill, 32-gallon gas tanks. Group II rules prevented Shelby from gutting interiors. The Mustangs had stock dashboards with key R-Model gauges and full door panels with functional windows and cranking hardware. A lightweight, single bucket seat was allowed and, except for removing bumpers, exterior sheet metal essentially remained untouched. For the second year in a row, Ford won the SCCA Trans-Am Championship for cars displacing over 2 liters. Mercury finished second.

Ford's stock car racing program for NASCAR and USAC competition was based on the Fairlane powered by the latest 427 Tunnel Port engine. While Richard Petty won thirty-one races in his Plymouth Hemi and was named NASCAR Grand National Champion, Fords won nine USAC races and ten events in NASCAR's Grand National Division. USAC racers were not allowed to run in NASCAR events unless they were FIA sanctioned. However, Fords won six of the eleven major NASCAR races, including the Daytona 500 Qualifier and main event and the *Motor Trend* 500 at Riverside.

Fred Lorenzen won the Qualifier race at Daytona on February 24, 1967, in a Holman & Moody Fairlane, backed up two days later by another H&M Fairlane

driven to the Daytona 500 win by Mario Andretti averaging 146.93 miles per hour. Lorenzen finished second.

Parnelli Jones drove his H&M Fairlane to wins at the *Motor Trend* 500 and the USAC Yankee 300 at Indianapolis Raceway Park. Mario Andretti finished second in the Yankee 300, which was run on IRP's road course.

It was an all-Ford show at the Indy 500 classic, with the top five slots going to A. J. Foyt in a Coyote-Ford, Al Unser in a Lola-Ford, Joe Leonard in a Coyote-Ford, Denny Hulme in an Eagle-Ford, and Jim McElreath in a Moore-Ford. Foyt recorded an average speed of 168.98 miles per hour and gave Goodyear its first win at the Speedway since 1910.

Jacque Passino's Special Vehicles Activity group celebrated another outstanding year of putting Fords in winner circles and its drivers on podiums at the world's most important racing circuits.

Dan Gurney won the 1967 Belgium Grand Prix at Spa in his Gurney Eagle powered by a Gurney-Weslake engine. The stunning car is shown here driven by son Alex at the Laguna Seca Historics. *M. M. "Mike" Matune Jr.*

1967-1968 Mercury Cougar: The Sign of the Cat!

Actually more of a real GT than pony car, the new Cougar delivered performance plus luxury—and a direct connection to Dan Gurney and Trans-Am racing.

Launched in 1967 under "The Sign of the Cat," the slightly longer and more luxurious Mustang-platform Mercury Cougar was a huge success. It appealed to young adults who wanted a Mustang with more interior room, upscale appointments, and distinctive, up-level styling. Approximately 6 inches longer than the Mustang with a 3-inch-longer (108-inch) wheelbase, the 190-inch long Cougar looked like nothing else in 1967. It delivered Mustang performance and then some!

Right out of the box, the 1967 Cougar won *Motor Trend*'s "Car of the Year" honors. Racing the Cougar in SCCA Trans-Am competition and running against its corporate cousin, Mustang, also raised the vehicle's profile and brought more potential buyers into Lincoln-Mercury dealerships. Fran Hernandez, Supervisor of Lincoln-Mercury's Performance and Evaluation Section, championed a deal with Dan Gurney and Bud Moore Engineering in Spartanburg, South Carolina, to build Trans-Am Cougars and run the racing team. Hernandez and Bud Moore had been working together on NASCAR Comets and track-ready 390 Comet drag cars since 1965.

In 1967, Bud Moore's Cougars collected sixty-two points to Mustang's sixty-four, finishing second in the SCCA Over-Two-Liter class Trans-Am Championship.

After being successfully raced in Trans-Am competition, one of the Bud Moore Cougars went to Tiny Lund for racing in NASCAR's new Grand Touring, or "Baby Grand," Division, the name changed later to Grand American Series. In 1968, Lund won the NASCAR Grand Touring Championship and dominated the series in 1970 and 1971. Lund won 41 of the 109 races in the series' history.

Two of the three No. 98 Bud Moore Trans-Am Cougars driven by Dan Gurney have been restored to original racing specs and are in two major collections— Larry H. Miller Motorsports Park Museum in Toole, Utah, and Beth and Ross Myers' 3Dog Garage in Pennsylvania.

While covering new model introductions, I was able to drive a broad selection of 1967–1968 Cougars on the road course, drag strip, and high-speed oval at Ford's Dearborn Proving Ground. The 390, 427, and 428 models delivered outstanding levels of performance combined with GT ride qualities. Introduced in the 1967 model year in a single hardtop coupe body style, the Cougar offered a variety of engines, from 289 two-barrel to 390 four-barrel and a choice of standard three-speed manual and optional SelectShift three-speed automatic or four-speed manual.

Available in two trim levels, base and XR-7, Cougars could be ordered with a GT Performance Package in either trim. The GT option's primary appeal for enthusiasts was the four-barrel 390 engine and performance-handling package.

One of the remaining No. 98 Trans-Am Cougars, built by Bud Moore Engineering and driven by Dan Gurney. This is the one in the 3Dog Garage collection, here being raced at Laguna Seca Historics. *M. M. "Mike" Matune Jr.*

The author wringing out a preproduction unmarked Cougar with 390 engine on Ford's road course at Dearborn Proving Ground in a photo taken in June 1966 during press preview of 1967 Ford and Lincoln-Mercury vehicles.

Above: Named for Cougar Trans-Am racer Dan Gurney, the XR7-G was the top performance-image model in 1968. Finished in Grecian Gold Poly and fitted with early Rader wheels, it has the ASC-installed Bosch sunroof and vinyl roof covering. Rader wheels were used only on very early production and prototype models, as there were metal-fatigue and air-sealing issues. *Ford Motor Company*

Right: Unique wide taillights on the base-model preproduction '67 Cougar, which featured sequential flashing turn signals borrowed from the Thunderbird.

Some of the key players in Cougar Trans-Am racing in 1967: from left to right, Lincoln-Mercury's Fran Hernandez, drivers Parnelli Jones and Ed Leslie, and Bud Moore. *Fran Hernandez Collection*

The XR-7 trim level was primarily cosmetic. Unique styling touches included hideaway headlamps with vacuum-operated "doors" and Thunderbird-influenced wide taillights with sequential flashing turn signals. The Cougar was basically carried over for the 1968 model year with minor changes. Major performance upgrades included the addition of the new 428-cubic-inch big-block.

Because of the number of Cougar iterations and big-block engine choices, there's a lot of confusion regarding exactly which engines were used in specific models. While there were some real 427 Cougars built, rated at 390 horsepower at 4,600 rpm, in 1967, it's doubtful that any actually reached the public. The 1968 Cougar GT-E 7-Litre model was initially offered with an S-code 427/390 engine. However, after 427 engine production ended in December 1967, GT-E Cougars were powered by 428-cubic-inch engines rated at 335 horsepower at 5,200 rpm.

Lincoln-Mercury took every possible opportunity to tie Cougar Trans-Am racing and high-profile driver Dan Gurney to special models to increase showroom traffic. Gurney participated in promoting the special Cougars, but actually had nothing to do with the design or content of the vehicles.

Also available in the 1968 model year was a far more interesting Dan Gurney model Cougar, the XR7-G. The original concept behind this XR7 version was to give Mercury dealers a special vehicle to compete with Ford dealers selling Shelby Mustangs. The conversion of stock 1968 Mustangs into Shelby GT350s and GT500s was contracted to A. O. Smith Incorporated in Ionia, Michigan.

After leaving LAX, Shelby opened a large race car shop in Torrance, California, and became a board member of Ford's Michigan-based Shelby Automotive,

Inc. It was Shelby Automotive that actually subcontracted the conversion of XR7 Cougars to XR7-G models. Neither Carroll Shelby nor Dan Gurney was involved in the design and content of the XR7-Gs.

In addition to a plethora of cosmetic upgrades, the XR7-G received driving lamps in a custom front valance, nonfunctional hood scoop, hood pins, extraloud horns, and Talbot racing mirrors. When fitted with the 428 CJ engine, XR7-Gs received functional ram-air hood scoops.

XR7-G production was limited with just 619 produced. A total of 188 with S-code 390 engines and automatic transmissions were sold to Hertz. The lowest production 1968 Cougar XR7-G Cougars include 3 428 CJ four-speeds, 11 428 CJ automatics, and 14 390 four-speeds.

According to the Cougar GT-E Registry, a total of 357 GT-E 7-Litre Cougars were factory-equipped with real 427/390 engines and C-6 automatic transmissions. Only 101 "standard-trim" GT-Es were built with 427s. Interestingly, GT-E Cougars with 428/335 Cobra Jet engines are actually rarer as just 37 were produced. Three of the 37 CJ Cougars with standard GT-E trim were built with four-speed transmissions.

The launch of the Cougar in 1967 was incredibly successful. Lincoln-Mercury dealers sold in excess of 150,000, including approximately 27,000 XR7s. Bud Moore, with help from drivers Dan Gurney, Parnelli Jones, Ed Leslie, David Pearson, and Peter Revson, sharpened the Cougar's claws and established the new nameplate as a top-tier racer, capable of winning in SCCA Trans-Am and NASCAR "Baby Grand" competition.

1967 SHELBY GT MUSTANGS:
THE ROAD CARS!

Highly restyled GT350 and GT500 Mustangs offered the best combination of real world performance and Grand Touring qualities of any domestic passenger car in 1967.

Carroll Shelby had even more ambitious plans for his 1967 GT Mustangs than in previous years. He wanted to create a GT that looked like an exciting new car, not a warmed-over production Mustang, and would deliver serious performance. Since Ford was building Mustangs with 390 big-block engines, getting Ford to substitute 427 or 428-cubic-inch engines was doable. Shelby's endgame was to transform the GT's image from racer to road warrior, thus making it more appealing to a larger audience. He knew that the only way to realize his goals was to create not only a unique Shelby Mustang, but also a complete model lineup. He envisioned small- and big-block engine options and choice of body styles—fastback, notchback coupe, and convertible.

The creation of a Shelby Mustang family was Carroll Shelby's master plan for 1967, even though the availability of multiple models might possibly dilute the brand's exclusive image. Shelby American came up with designs

for fiberglass front, rear, and side trim styling that could be applied to all three open and closed models. While the notchback looked nowhere near as exciting as the fastback, it offered potential buyers with families a more functional enthusiast car. A GT convertible was a no-brainer since drop-tops always sold well in key markets, especially California and Florida. With small- and big-block engine choices, Shelby dealers could offer shoppers six different Shelby Mustangs.

Approximately one week before the restyled 1967 Mustang was to start production, Shelby submitted purchase order 2504 on August 9, 1966, for three identical, heavily optioned Candy Apple Red Mustangs—fastback, notchback coupe, and convertible. They were to be powered by Q-code 428-cubic-inch Police Interceptor engines with dual Holley 660-cfm four-barrels. All three cars were ordered with C-6 automatics and would serve as prototypes for the 1967 models. But that was not to be.

Only the fastback was actually prototyped for 1967 Shelby production. Shelby American later converted the notchback and convertible to GT500s for

A rare photo of the one-off supercharged GT500 notchback, *Little Red*, originally ordered to prototype a 1967 coupe and later assigned to Shelby chief engineer Fred Goodell for R&D. The shot was taken at a 1968 Shelby press event on July 6 and 7, 1967, at Riverside Raceway.

internal use. The convertible was assigned to Carroll Shelby as his personal car and the notchback was used to evaluate different powertrains. Eventually the notchback became Shelby American chief engineer Fred Goodell's company car.

According to Brian Styles, current owner of the singular GT500 convertible, "Some time between ordering the three cars on August 9, 1966, and their build in November, Ford put the brakes on the three-model proposal and told Shelby to just stick with the fastback. This was most likely due to the fiberglass fitment problems and cost over-runs. Regardless, the three cars were still built and delivered to Shelby American. The notchback and convertible later received off-the-shelf production fiberglass body parts."

The 1967 Shelby GT350 was produced with the carryover K-code 289/271, boosted to an optimistic 306 horsepower as rated on the 1965 and 1966 models. Unlike the earlier GT350 engines that had tubular headers and low-restriction exhaust systems, the 1967 version utilized the quieter, less efficient factory GT Mustang exhaust with dual resonators and a single transverse muffler. Shelby kept the small-block's solid-lifter valvetrain and added a Cobra high-rise alloy intake manifold with 715-cfm Holley four-barrel. GT350s could be ordered with either Ford four-speed with 3.89 rear or C-4 automatic with 3.50 final gearing.

There was one performance upgrade available for the GT350 carried over from the previous year—a Paxton supercharger boasting a potential 46 percent power increase. Considering that the centrifugal supercharger option cost $550, it is actually hard to believe that twenty-eight customers checked off the supercharger option box on order sheets! A 1967 GT350 carried a base MSRP of $3,995 and if you ordered the supercharger, you'd have a final price of $4,545, or approximately $350 more than a GT500 with a 355-horsepower 428. More than likely, a high percentage of the twenty-eight customers who chose the supercharger rather than stepping up to a GT500 did so to steer clear of insurance rate surcharges for large-displacement engines.

Mustangs ordered for 1967 Shelby conversions were all built at Ford's San Jose plant and shipped in KD, or knock-down, condition to Shelby American's LAX Airport facility without hoods, deck lids, rear seats, and trim. All Shelby-tagged Mustangs were factory equipped with 140-mile-per-hour speedometers and 8,000-rpm tachs.

A Shelby American tech checking out an unfinished '67 Shelby GT Mustang on the LAX facility's makeshift drag strip and skid pad. It's an early production car with center-mounted high-beam headlamps.

GT500 Mustang "donors" were fitted with dual-quad 428 Police Interceptor big-blocks and Ford four-speed manual or beefy C-6 automatics before leaving the plant. To keep costs down, Shelby stayed with the Ford production Traction-Lok limited-slip differential and a 3.50 rear gear on four-speed cars and 3.25 on automatics. Dealers were encouraged to offer GT Mustang buyers interested in racing an optional selection of final drive ratios as well as installation of a gear-type Detroit Locker.

The 335-horsepower 428 engine used by Shelby was the Police Interceptor model with mild hydraulic-lifter cam, dual-point distributor, dual 600-cfm Holley four-barrels on an aluminum intake manifold, and factory cast-iron exhaust manifolds with stock 390 Mustang exhaust system. With typical "Day Two" modifications like tube headers, nonrestrictive exhaust, and tuning, the 428 was probably good for close to 400 horsepower. In stock trim with automatic transmission and cruising gears, it was seriously overcarbureted.

Shelby advertising touted the new GT500 as featuring "a brand-new Cobra Le Mans dual four-barrel engine developed from the V-8 that powered the 1966 Le Mans winners." In truth, there was no connection between the

Either Ford forgot to install a Traction-Lok rear or we blew it during full-throttle starts! This area at Shelby American was used for quarter-mile runs as well as skid-pad testing.

Completed Shelby GT500 #499, left, parked next to a donor Mustang without its deck lid, taillights, and other harvested components. The taillights used on Shelby GT Mustangs have sequential-directional flashing, revealing their '67 Cougar heritage.

consumer 428 with "Cobra Le Mans" valve covers in the GT500 and the 427 engines in the 1966 Le Mans winners. The 428 had merits of its own and was a strong-running, large-displacement engine—bigger than anything you could get in a production 1967 Mustang.

Credit for the 1967 Shelby Mustangs' head-turning styling goes to Pete Brock, who worked with Chuck McHose, a Ford Design stylist on loan to Shelby for the 1967 GT program. The Shelby GT may have had more scoops per square inch of surface area than other car from that era, but stripes, spoiler, and badges seamlessly tied them together. Brock and McHose's styling resulted in the sexiest, most appealing, and highest performing sporty car you could buy in 1967 for under $5,000.

Two styling features on early cars proved to be controversial: the close-spaced, center-mounted high-beam headlamps in the grille and the running lights attached to the upper quarter panel scoops. Some states did not allow center-mounted high beams, forcing Shelby to relocate them to the outer ends of the grille instead. Only the first couple of hundred GTs were produced with side scoops with built-in running lights.

Joe Oldham, wrote about the 1967 GT500 in an article, "Striped Lightning, The Shelby Mustangs" in *Automobile Quarterly*, Volume 16, Number 8: "Anyone stepping into a GT500 and expecting a cataclysm on wheels was in for a rather rude awakening. This was not a racing car at all. In fact, with almost 500 pounds more weight than the 1966 GT350, the 1967 GT500 proved slower than its predecessors."

Oldham added, "The GT500 was an adult sporty car that was a lot more civilized than Shelby had ever dreamed one of his Mustangs could be. It was a smooth GT. 'This is the first car I'm really proud of,' Carroll Shelby told the press at the GT500's introduction at New York's Tavern-On-The-Green restaurant."

Thanks to Shelby American PR manager Dante Cardone, I spent some "all-access" time at the LAX airport facility in 1967. I watched GT Mustangs being built, and actually drove and tested some GT500s before they were shipped to dealers. We didn't have clocks so it was just "seat-of-the pants" driving. The four-speed GT500 felt fast, but not any faster than early GT350s I had driven, but the 428 engines were almost silent compared with solid-lifter 289s used in GT350 Mustangs. I loved the new up-level interior with wood-rimmed steering wheel, extra gauges, and a built-in functional roll bar.

Even though some previous Shelby Mustang standard equipment such as the Monte Carlo bar, tube headers, Koni adjustable shocks, and traction bars were no longer being used, the cars I drove felt more solid and, even with additional weight, handled like sporty grand touring cars. All Shelbys came stock with factory Mustang handling packages plus .94-inch-diameter front antisway bars, export model one-piece cowl-to-shock-tower braces, and adjustable Gabriel shocks. Ford suspension engineer Klaus Arning consulted with Shelby engineers on suspension components and settings.

Whatever the GT500 gave up in acceleration, it more than gained in *real world* ride, handling, and true GT attributes. Shelby had the answer for anyone wanting to buy a GT500 with more performance than stock—order one with a 427 engine. It was not listed as a regular option, but cost an extra $2,000, approximately 45 percent of the total price of a GT500 with mandatory options!

The 427 Shelby GT500 Mustang had few takers. Only two customers ordered GT500s with latest version S-code, single-four-barrel 427/390s. Fred Goodell built a third 427 GT for R&D. It was powered by a lightweight, alloy-head, medium-riser 427 GT40 Mark II engine. Dubbed *Super Snake*, it was used at the Goodyear test track in San Angelo, Texas, for high-speed tire evaluation. It recorded a top speed of approximately 170 miles per hour and average speed of 142 miles per hour for 500 miles. It has survived and is currently in a private collection.

The remaining two customer-ordered, single-four-barrel 427 GT500 Mustangs were a Wimbledon White model with Shelby VIN 1947 ordered for drag racing, and a Dark Moss Green car with Shelby VIN 0289. Frontier Ford Sales in Niagara Falls, New York, originally ordered the green car for Paul Richter. It has been restored and is in Kevin Suydam's exceptional muscle-car collection. It was the first 427 GT500 built and it actually predates Shelby's 427 *Super Snake*. Its MSRP in 1967 was approximately $6,650.

Of the first three 1967 Mustangs Carroll Shelby originally ordered for the GT program, the notchback coupe and convertible were actually the second and third built with Q-code 428 Police Interceptor engines. They became incredibly important vehicles in Shelby Mustang history. Dubbed *Little Red*, the notchback had VIN 0131 and was built on November 8, 1966. In addition to 428 power, the Candy Apple Red coupe was equipped with C-6 automatic, 3.00 rear, air conditioning, and black interior. It is the first and only Shelby GT Mustang notchback.

After Ford limited Shelby to a single model fastback for GT350 and GT500 production, the notchback served as an in-house R&D vehicle and was rarely shown to the press and public. Few photos exist of this car with its combination 1967 and 1968 trim, vinyl roof, and Connolly leather interior. Shelby *did* display the coupe at the 1967 Los Angeles Auto Show to gauge customer reaction and it was shown to the press on July 6 and 7, 1967, at the 1968 model preview at Riverside Raceway. Few journalists at the event cared that much about *Little Red* since it only had a couple of 1968 features and was not part of the model lineup.

Fortunately, I was at Riverside Raceway for the 1967 and 1968 model reveals and managed to get some photos and seat time on the road course. I never opened the hood, but understood at the time that the 428 engine was fitted with a single four-barrel and Paxton supercharger. Most coverage indicates that its engine had two carbs and twin superchargers. Over its lifetime, *Little Red* received a number of naturally aspirated and supercharged engines. It was fast, but rode considerably softer and quieter than the fastbacks we drove. It was the most luxurious Shelby Mustang I had ever driven. Unfortunately, it had a relatively short life of about one year before going to the crusher in November or December of 1967.

Initially assigned to Carroll Shelby as his personal driver, the surviving one-of-one 1967 Candy Apple Red GT500 convertible, Shelby VIN 0139, was later converted into a 1968 styling prototype using preproduction fiberglass body parts fabricated by A. O. Smith in Ionia, Michigan. Between April and June 1967, it was used as a photo car for 1968 Shelby Cobra GT marketing, public relations, and advertising purposes. It retained its original red paint for the first shoot at Malibu Beach, then was repainted Wimbledon White for shoots at the Hollywood Park horse track and other scenic locations.

The convertible appeared in advertisements in *Car Life*, *Playboy*, and *Road & Track* magazines, and in 1968 sales brochures and promotional materials.

This is the red '67 GT500 convertible that was converted into a white 1968 model prototype. After being photographed in Candy Apple Red on the beach, it was repainted Wimbledon White for other shoots and promotions. Here, it sits parked next to a '68 Mustang at a Riverside Raceway press event on July 6 and 7, 1967. Note the Shelby lettering on the prototype's hood: in this shot, only the letters S, H, and B are visible. Neither Shelby nor Ford was paying attention!

Not long after being shown to the press at the 1968 Shelby Mustang introduction at Riverside Raceway, the convertible was returned to Ford Motor Company and was sold at an employee auction. Brian Styles has had the convertible restored to concours-standards twice—first to 1968 prototype specs in 2011 and then, in 2014, to its original 1967 configuration. Debuted at the French Lick Concours in Indiana, the only 1967 GT500 convertible ever built looks exactly the way it did prior to being transformed into a 1968 prototype.

Model year 1967 was very good for Shelby American and Ford. Shelby produced 1,175 GT350s and 2,048 GT500s, not including the one-off convertible and notchback coupe. Overall, dealers sold 283 more Shelby Mustangs in 1967 than they did in 1965 and 1966 combined. However, the relationship between Shelby and Ford would change dramatically for the 1968 model year. Ford wanted more production than Shelby could deliver, as well as more control over design and assembly. Under Ford supervision, 1968 Shelby Mustangs would be produced at the Ford plant in Metuchen, New Jersey, then converted by A. O. Smith and branded Shelby Cobra *GTs*. It would be the beginning of the end of "real" Shelby Mustangs.

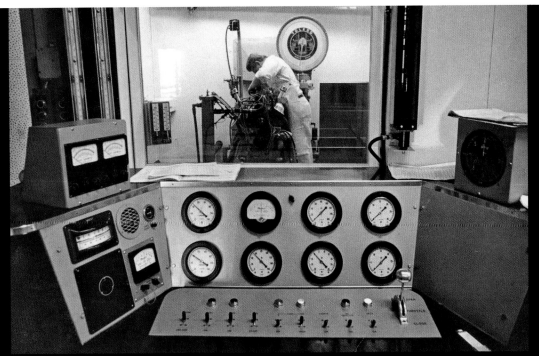

After a spin in GT500 #499, I took some final shots prior to preparation for delivery to a dealer. When shooting at LAX, you never knew what might get into the background!

Up until Carroll Shelby set up his racing operation in Torrance, California, race engines were built in clean rooms and then dyno-tested at the LAX facility. I spent some time in this dyno cell while a dual four-barrel small-block Trans-Am engine was being run. It was a screamer!

GT40 MARK III:
MAYHEM IN MANHATTAN!

In April 1967, Bill Kolb and I tested America's first real supercar for *Hi-Performance CARS*. We dodged New York City taxis, delivery trucks, and the occasional cop car—and frightened women, children, and puppies! It was a glorious day.

Decades before the Z06 Corvette, the Viper, and the Ford GT existed, America's first and only real supercar was Ford's Anglo-American GT40 Mark III. After a trio of GT40s dominated Le Mans in 1966, Ford looked for a repeat performance on the street. Enter the Mark III, a streetable version of the GT40 built to satisfy FIA GT homologation specs.

In 1967, Ford's factory store in Manhattan, Gotham Ford, represented Shelby high-performance cars in New York City. Fortunately, my friend Bill Kolb was manager of everything Shelby and he had a blue GT40 Mark III (M/3 1101) on the showroom floor. It was a Ford-owned prototype, first shown at the New York Auto Show a month earlier. Kolb didn't have any problems sharing its keys with me!

Unlike previous Mark I versions, the new Mark III passed federal regulations for headlamp placement and ground clearance. Kolb was ready to take orders at around $18,500. Since you could buy a GT40 race car for $2,000 less or even a current model Ferrari, Maserati, or Lamborghini for less, finding buyers for a Mark III proved to be an exercise in futility.

Kolb and I spent the morning driving the Mark III around Manhattan, then headed to Randall's Island for a photo shoot. The Mark III had a 306-horsepower Shelby 289 and ZF 5DS-25 five-speed transaxle with 2.50:1 final gearing. It was obviously best suited for the Autobahn—not jousting with taxis and trucks on Manhattan's First Avenue!

He drove while I photographed gawking pedestrians and drivers, not to mention an irate toll taker on the Triborough Bridge who was not happy waiting while Bill tried to slip his hand through the tilt-out side window and then finally opened the door to pay the toll. I took the wheel after the photo shoot.

Here are some of my actual notes from that day:

It was a beautiful spring day and I was cruising along the sun-drenched FDR Drive, playing hero driver in a 175-mph GT40 in midday traffic. It doesn't get any better than this.

Incredible throttle response as long as I keep the Rs up. Braking and handling, superb, like driving a fully sorted-out race car on the street. A little scary.

That red warning light on the dash means I have to turn on the electric cooling fans. Lots to think about when driving a GT40 in traffic. Small outside mirrors do very little.

I think I'm in love. No, lust!

Driving back to Manhattan, I took the FDR Drive and exited at East Sixty-Third Street to play in traffic before returning to Gotham Ford.

"Hey, don't you think it's time to slow down?" barked my copilot. "I think you're getting carried away."

Kolb, who normally treated every traffic light like a drag strip Christmas tree, was not happy. His knuckles were turning a lovely shade of white!

"Why?"

"Because you've been darting in and out of traffic at just under 105 miles per hour for the last three or four minutes and we're going to get nailed—or worse!"

Just 41 inches high, the GT40 Mark III is easily dwarfed by everyday traffic in Manhattan. Ground clearance is problematic with NYC's preponderance of potholes.

Above: Bill Kolb backs the GT40 out of Gotham Ford on First Avenue in Manhattan. Kolb is the Ford factory store's high-performance sales specialist. Note the leftover '66 Shelby GT350 Mustang.

Unfortunately, the small flip-out window within the side glass offers little help for paying tolls. The toll taker on the Triborough Bridge wasn't much help, either; Bill had to open the door.

Frontal styling of the Mark III looks as fresh today as it did almost half a century ago. Ducts in the hood aid cooling of the front-mounted radiator.

The New York Police Department watched us swoop down off the Triborough Bridge on to Randall's Island, figuring we must be breaking some law. They wanted to see our photography permit, and Bill had to sweet-talk them to leave us alone.

There's nothing like a dose of reality to screw up your whole day. I figured I was speeding, maybe 25 or 30 miles per hour over the limit, but it didn't feel like 100-plus miles per hour. The GT40 Mark III proved that it's a race car in street duds and race cars like to run.

From the July 1967 issue of *Hi-Performance CARS*: "At 100 mph, the single Holley four-barrel, 306-horsepower Shelby 289 just loafs along in Third gear. You tend to forget just how fast you are going, as the low semi-reclining driving position minimizes the feeling of speed."

With its wide carpeted sills and doors that contained roof sections, getting in and out of the Mark III was not a pretty sight. Its 8-inch (rear) body extension—needed to make room for FIA-mandated "suitcase" south of the engine—unfortunately took away from the GT40's stunning lines. Extremely limited visibility, approximately 5 inches of ground clearance, and windows with little flaps that tilt open rather than roll down did little for the Mark III's marketing appeal.

By comparison, the GTs from Italy were less race car and more GT—and cheaper and considerably easier to live with. Unlike the competition, the Mark III was a 2,500-pound race car with 45/55 percent front-to-rear weight distribution and very basic street amenities. And there were not many Ford dealers in the country qualified to service a GT40.

Ford's Don Frey, a key engineer in the development of the Mustang and later head of Ford Division, campaigned for a roadworthy GT40 to support the racing program and to serve as a halo car for the Ford brand. The First-Gen street GT40 Mark I was a thinly disguised race car with up-level interior and detuned 289 fitted with Webers, mild cam, and mufflered exhausts. While production records are somewhat murky, it appears that less than a dozen were actually built and marketed at a tick over $15,000.

In 1967, Ford Advanced Vehicles contracted with John Wyer and his partner, John Willment of JW Automotive Engineering, to create a street version of the GT40—a real road-going GT. Wyer, a Brit who had been head of Ford Advanced Vehicles (FAV) along with Roy Lunn, were the GT40's godfathers. By then, JW Automotive Engineering had taken control of FAV in Slough, UK. Dubbed the GT40 Mark III, they chose a 306-horsepower 289 small-block with a single four-barrel carburetor, very similar to the engine used in the 1965–1966 Shelby GT350 Mustangs.

It should be noted that Wyer Ltd. in the UK also continued to construct road-going Mark I GT40s built off real GT40 race cars. Those cars showcased the stunning lines of the original GT40. They didn't have the Mark III FIA updates and extended body. The Mark I had a detuned 335-horsepower GT40 race engine to appeal primarily to enthusiasts who wanted a *real* GT40 they could drive on the street.

A Ford GT40 Mark III ready to be shipped from the United Kingdom. This is one of the later units.

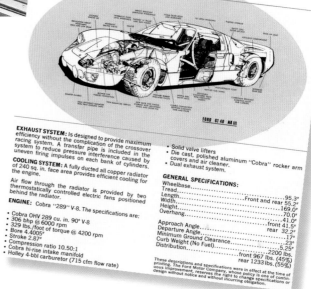

FORD GT40 MARK III

STEERING: Rack and pinion of a new design—available in either right or left drive models. The geometry allows immediate response to the driver's touch.

BRAKES: Disc brakes front and rear, 11.5" dia. front and 11.2" dia. rear. Dual master cylinders have individual large capacity reservoirs. The driver will get a warning from an indicator light on the instrument panel if the reservoirs have low fluid, excessive brake pad wear and/or rapid loss of fluid.

WHEELS AND TIRES: Wheels are 15" Borrani wire spoke with light alloy rims, 6.5" front and 8" rear. Cast magnesium racing wheels are also available in 8.5" front and 10" rear. Tires are Goodyear Wet Weather Racing, 5.80 front and 7.00 rear.

CLUTCH AND TRANSAXLE: A Borg and Beck 8.5"

2-plate diaphragm spring unit clutch combines high torque capacity with low inertia.

ZF 5DS-25 FIVE-SPEED: A fully synchronized transaxle provides a wide variety of final drive and intermediate ratios.

FUEL SYSTEM: Tank capacity is 27.6 gallons, with a tank in the side sills of the car. These tanks are insulated from heat and noise by the polyurethane foam around them.

The fuel gauge will indicate the fuel level in either tank at the flick of a switch on the instrument panel. This switch also controls the electric fuel pump so that the fuel will be pumped from the tank indicated on the fuel gauge. Uniform performance is enhanced with a fuel pressure control device.

EXHAUST SYSTEM: is designed to provide maximum efficiency without the complication of the crossover racing system. A transfer pipe is included in the system to reduce pressure interference caused by uneven firing impulses on each bank of cylinders.

COOLING SYSTEM: A fully ducted all copper radiator of 240 sq. in. face area provides efficient cooling for the engine.

Air flow through the radiator is provided by two thermostatically controlled electric fans positioned behind the radiator.

ENGINE: Cobra "289" V-8. The specifications are:
- Cobra OHV 289 cu. in. 90° V-8
- 306 bhp @ 6000 rpm
- 329 lbs./foot of torque @ 4200 rpm
- Bore 4.4005"
- Stroke 2.87"
- Compression ratio 10.50:1
- Cobra hi-rise intake manifold
- Holley 4-bbl carburetor (715 cfm flow rate)

- Solid valve lifters
- Die cast, polished aluminum "Cobra" rocker arm covers and air cleaner.
- Dual exhaust system.

GENERAL SPECIFICATIONS:

Wheelbase	95.3"
Tread	Front and rear 55.2"
Length	169.0"
Width	70.0"
Height	41.0"
Overhang	front 41.5"
	rear 32.2"
Approach Angle	.23°
Departure Angle	.17°
Minimum Ground Clearance	5.25"
Curb Weight (No Fuel)	2200 lbs.
Distribution	front 967 lbs. (45%)
	rear 1233 lbs. (55%)

These descriptions and specifications were in effect at the time of printing. The Ford Motor Company, whose policy is one of continuous improvement, reserves the right to change specifications or design without notice and without incurring obligation.

Mark IIIs had exhausts somewhat quieter than Mark I GT40 street coupes, along with legal road lighting and ground clearance, and an 8-inch rear extension to make room for "luggage." Windows did not roll down and ventilation was less than desirable. Unfortunately, the Mark III inherited the GT40 race car's wide sills, making the interior cramped and entry/exit difficult. It was a street-legal race car and creature comforts were compromised. Production was to be limited to just twenty. But just seven cars, plus five spare chassis, were actually built.

There were a lot of people at Ford who were not happy with the fit and finish quality of the JWA cars and did not commit to ongoing Mark III development and marketing programs. Ford kept some Mark IIIs for press drives, auto shows, executive loans, and dealer promotions. Ford engineers saw the writing on the wall and knew that the Mark IIIs would not meet 1968 emission and safety standards.

Shortly after we tested the Mark III in 1967, Kolb called and asked if I wanted to buy one. Ford wanted little to do with the Mark III; neither did the public. They had a few GT40s in a warehouse in Secaucus, New Jersey, and offered Kolb a package deal. The cars were not perfect.

"Marty, Ford offered me some 'scratch and dent' Mark IIIs that had been used for auto shows, dealer promotions, and advertising," he said. "We can get them all for around $5,300 each. Are you in?"

While I had fallen in lust with the GT40 Mark III, I figured down the road they would be just used cars and affordable. I passed. Kolb passed as well. We were unquestionably dumb and dumber! Kolb still jokes about the Mark IIIs that got away.

But what happened to the first-built Mark III we drove almost fifty years ago? It was used for promotions by Ford and, in 1968, shipped back to John Wyer in the UK to be brought up to the latest production specs. On September 18,

A GT40 Mark III sales sheet was available at Ford dealers that specialized in high-performance car sales.

1968, it was retrofitted with a four-barrel 302-inch small-block. It also received a NR7 ZF five-speed transaxle with 4.22:1 final drive ratio. On the return trip, it was involved in a bizarre accident where another GT40 Mark III (M/3 1106) was dropped on top of it, flattening its roof. Because damage was so serious, it was shipped to Kar Kraft for restoration.

Upon completion, M/3 1101 passed though a few owners and, in 2005, ended up back in the United Kingdom, where it was converted to right-hand drive and restored to Mark I FIA race specs. Completed in January 2006, it received FIA certification, making it eligible to vintage race in Europe.

CHAPTER 9

1968

Bunkie and the Jets!

In February 1968, GM's Bunkie Knudsen was named president of Ford. A month earlier, 1968½ Cobra Jet Mustangs swept Super/Stock Class and Eliminator titles at the NHRA Winternationals. Total Performance was still alive and well in Dearborn.

Henry Ford II shocked the industry and ruffled quite a few feathers internally when he poached Semon "Bunkie" Knudsen from General Motors before the ink was dry on his resignation papers in February 1968. Knudsen was named president of Ford Motor Company. Some of those feathers belonged to Ford executive vice president Lee Iacocca, who had been on the fast track for the job. Getting Bunkie to cross over to Ford was considered a major coup. His was one of the most prestigious names in the industry and had been a candidate

for the presidency of GM. Unlike most "suits" at his level, Knudsen was a serious car guy and racing enthusiast. When Ed Cole got the nod to run GM in 1967, Knudsen remained executive vice president and head of GM Overseas.

Knudsen was the son of William Knudsen, a former Ford executive and president of GM from 1937 to 1940. After twenty-nine years at GM, Knudsen was not happy being passed over. He entered into negotiations with Henry Ford II in January 1968 and, on February 6, was named president of Ford Motor Company. Knudsen had been a hands-on product guy at GM when he headed Pontiac and Chevrolet divisions, and wasted no time in making changes to products already approved and interfering in areas that fell under Iacocca's control. Almost immediately, Iacocca and Knudsen started getting in each other's faces.

Al Joniec puts the hurt on Dave Wren in his Plymouth to win final round of Super/Stock Eliminations at the 1968 NHRA Winternationals. one of the first fifty Cobra Jets built for drag racing, Joniec ran 120.6 miles per hour in 11.49 seconds to win the gold. *Ford Motor Company*

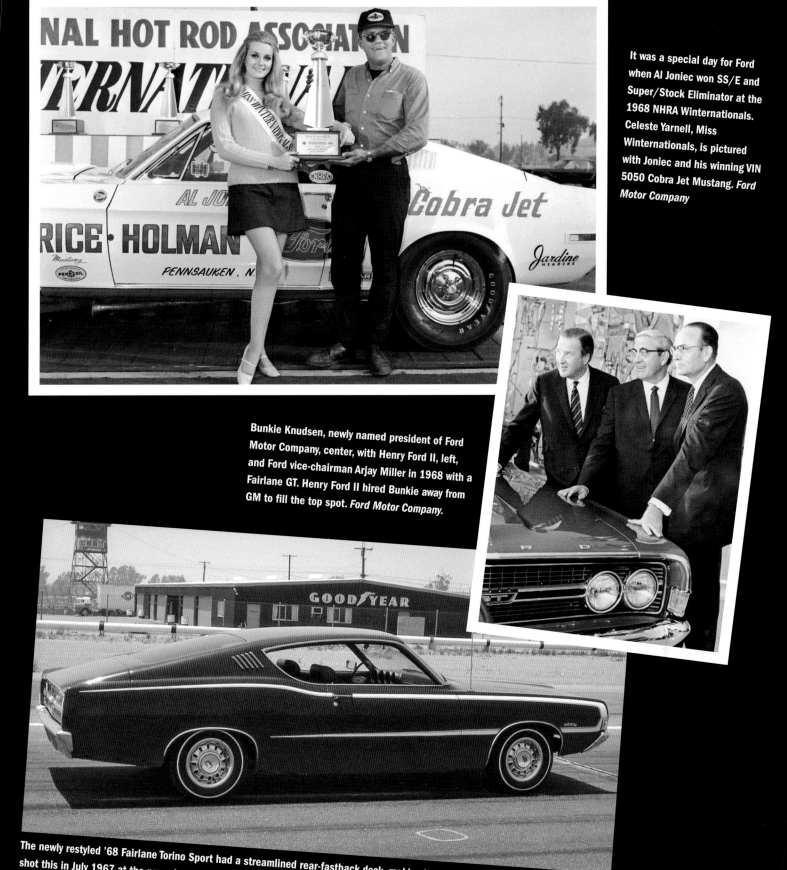

It was a special day for Ford when Al Joniec won SS/E and Super/Stock Eliminator at the 1968 NHRA Winternationals. Celeste Yarnell, Miss Winternationals, is pictured with Joniec and his winning VIN 5050 Cobra Jet Mustang. *Ford Motor Company*

Bunkie Knudsen, newly named president of Ford Motor Company, center, with Henry Ford II, left, and Ford vice-chairman Arjay Miller in 1968 with a Fairlane GT. Henry Ford II hired Bunkie away from GM to fill the top spot. *Ford Motor Company.*

The newly restyled '68 Fairlane Torino Sport had a streamlined rear-fastback deck, making it ideal for high-speed NASCAR tracks. I shot this in July 1967 at the press launch of the Torino at Riverside Raceway. As you can see on the pavement, the area was used for quarter-mile testing.

One of the preproduction '68 Mustang 428 Cobra Jets being tested at the Dearborn Proving Ground. Dynamometer testing revealed over 400 horsepower output when fitted with headers and a low-restriction exhaust system, performance tuning specs and without air cleaner and alternator. *Ford Motor Company*

Rarely does the president of a carmaker get directly involved in performance product and racing decisions. A chief executive who attends NASCAR races and hangs out with car builders and racers at tracks is even more rare. Knudsen did. He brought Larry Shinoda with him, a stylist at GM who had been involved in the design and development of the Corvette Sting Ray. It took little time for Knudsen to bring in his pal, Mickey Thompson, to talk about land speed and endurance racing at Bonneville. Thompson had worked with Knudsen on Pontiac racing projects. Knudsen's mantra once arriving at Ford was, "Build what we race and race what we build." He would become a champion of the Boss 429 engine program.

The big product news for 1968 was the announcement of the availability of 427/390 and 428/335 Cobra Jet engines in Mustangs, Fairlanes, Cougars, and Cyclones. First came the 427 option, available only with automatic transmission and in early-build cars. The 427 was being phased out of production at the end of 1967. While 427 Mustangs were advertised, they could not be ordered at dealerships. A total of 357 GT-E 7-Litre Cougars were built with 427/390 engines with C-6 automatics.

Ford's primary performance car for 1968 was the midyear 428 Cobra Jet Mustang, with four-speed manual or beefed C-6 automatic transmissions. In 1968, the Mustang was pretty much a carryover 1967 vehicle with small trim, suspension, and safety updates, plus important powertrain changes. Ride and handling was improved and, if you ordered a V-8, you could opt for Michelin radial tires for the first time. Gone was the four-barrel 289 small-block, including the venerable 271-horsepower, solid-lifter version, replaced by a new 302 small-block. You could order a 390/325 big-block or wait for the midyear introduction of the potent 428 CJ engine.

Cars tagged for the new CJ option automatically received special attention at the San Jose and Metuchen assembly plants. Those cars were given reinforced front shock towers and 9-inch rears with thirty-one-spline axles, plus four-speed Mustangs were equipped with stagger-mount rear shocks. All CJ Mustangs were factory fitted with a functional fiberglass hood scoop with ram-air induction capability. Under full throttle acceleration, a vacuum-controlled flapper on the

air cleaner assembly opened up, allowing air to go directly to the carburetor, bypassing the air filter. Under normal driving, air was channeled through the air filter.

Before there was a production 428 Cobra Jet, the CJ Mustang was first conceptualized by Bob Tasca, working with John Healey and Bill Lawton, and presented to Ford. Tasca had built his own "Cobra Jet"—a KR-8 "King of the Road" Mustang powered by a 428 engine with 390 GT cam and valvetrain, heads from a low-riser 427, 428 Police Interceptor intake manifold with a 735-cfm Holley, and 390 GT exhaust manifolds. He felt that Ford didn't have a suitable Mustang to compete with Chevrolet's new Camaro, available with a 396/375 solid-lifter big-block. Tasca had built a Mustang that would give any stock Camaro nightmares! Tasca's KR-8 concept was well-received and became the inspiration for the production 428 CJ Mustang.

Prior to regular production, Ford built fifty-four Wimbledon White Mustangs with 428 Cobra Jet engines, specified by DSO-892017, at the Dearborn plant. They were ordered specifically for NHRA Stock and Super/Stock competition. Essentially, they were base SportsRoof Mustangs, not GTs, built without radios and heaters, and with trunk-mount batteries, Police Interceptor drivetrains, and 3.89 limited-slip rears with traction bars. Twenty of them were produced without seam sealers or sound deadening materials. Two different engine packages were employed—one rated at 335 horsepower for C/Stock, the other with horsepower *north* of 360 for Super Stock/E. Distribution of the first Cobra Jet Mustangs included Ford dealers involved in drag racing programs in the US and Canada, with Tasca Ford receiving the most—ten CJs. Approximately ten were also assigned to Dick Brannan's group at Special Vehicles Activity.

Dynamometer testing at Ford revealed that a 335-horsepower CJ engine with headers, open exhausts, maximum tuning specs, and without air cleaner or alternator produced 411 horsepower. A red 1968 Mustang CJ evaluated at the Kingman, Arizona, proving ground clocked a best time of 108-plus miles per hour in 13.4 seconds.

A small fleet of Cobra Jet Mustangs was reserved for the model's California introduction at the AHRA Winternationals at Lions Drag Strip on January 28 and

Bill Lawton testing Tasca Ford's King of the Road 428 CJ concept at Englishtown Raceway Park. The test session took place during a private Ford event for media. Bob Tasca originally came up with the KR-8 Mustang, which became the model for the production Cobra Jet.

Cale Yarborough in the 427-engined Mercury Cyclone built by the Wood Brothers. Cale won the 1968 Daytona 500, averaging 143.25 miles per hour. A Junior Johnson Cyclone and a Holman & Moody Torino took second and third spots. Torinos won the NASCAR, USAC, and ARCA Championships in 1968. *Ford Motor Company*

the NHRA Winternationals at Pomona on February 2 through 4, 1968. Those cars were shipped to Holman-Moody-Stroppe in Long Beach for race prepping. Engines used in the C/Stock Mustangs had "stock" specs with forged 11:1 pistons; 427 steel rods; and .509-inch-lift, 282-degree-duration hydraulic-lifter cams and valve trains; and headers. These cars had 4.44 rears with Detroit Lockers, traction bars, and Goodyear slicks. The modified engines permitted in Super/Stock were built with 11.6:1 pistons; GT40 forged steel rods; deep oil sumps with windage trays; steel cranks; .600-inch-lift, 380-degree-duration solid-lifter cams and Crane valve trains; lightweight valves; and dual-inlet, 735-cfm Holleys on a 427 aluminum intake manifolds. Rear end gearing on the S/S cars was 4.71 with a Detroit Locker and bigger Goodyear slicks.

The Cobra Jet had a less-than-successful launch at the AHRA Winternationals when Hubert Platt red-lighted in his C/Stock Mustang, clocking a 12.62 in the first round of Top Stock. It was another story at the NHRA Winternationals when five Ford Drag Team drivers—Jerry Harvey, Al Joniec, Don Nicholson, Hubert Platt, and Gas Ronda—showed up with six cars for C/SA, SS/E, and SS/EA. Dearborn was there in force to showcase the hottest new "production" pony car. It would be the first NHRA National meet that Ford dominated.

It was Al Joniec, driving the Rice-Holman SS/E Cobra Jet, VIN #5050, that established the new CJ Mustang as the car to beat. Four of the six CJs made it to their respective class finals and Al Joniec beat teammate Hubert "Georgia Shaker" Platt's CJ to win SS/E. He ran 120.6 miles per hour in 11.49 seconds. Following that, he beat Dave Wren's Plymouth for Super/Stock Eliminator.

Bondy Long's *Bowani* crew at the 1968 Daytona 500. Driven by Bobby Allison, the Holman & Moody Torino finished third. John Craft currently owns it. *John Craft Collection*

"My CJ Mustang was capable of running in the low 11s in the 122-mile-per-hour range, though I didn't have to run it that hard to win," said Joniec during a recent interview. "Since it was the official introduction of the Cobra Jet, I didn't want to lower the record and lose any advantage at future events."

However, Joniec ran his Super/Stock CJ at just one more NHRA meet, at Englishtown Raceway Park in New Jersey. He recalled, "There was no way I could make any money running my Mustang in Super/Stock, so I replaced the 428 CJ with the latest 427 with Tunnel Port heads and intake. I ran it as a successful match racer, *Hairy Too*, and in the 3,200-pound class on the NASCAR circuit."

In the 1970s, Joniec's Mustang was converted back to legal NHRA Cobra Jet specs and set a number of records by then-owner Dick Estevez. He set the NHRA SS/FA record at 10.83 seconds, plus records in IHRA competition. The iconic Joniec Cobra Jet has since been restored by Randy DeLisio and is in Nick Smith's outstanding collection.

During the 1968 NHRA season, Cobra Jet Mustangs proved hard to beat. Don Nicholson, driving the Dick Brannan Ford Mustang, consistently ran in the low 11s at speeds up to 125 miles per hour. Barrie Poole in the Sandy Elliott Team CJ Mustang set the record in Canada at 11.87 seconds, later running in the 11.30s on tracks in the United States. Hubert Platt also set a number of records with his CJ during 1968.

Considering the Cobra Jet Mustang was a midyear 1968½ model, Ford did quite well, selling a total of 1,299 CJs, including thirty-four convertibles. Street performance was outstanding and the Mustang made a comeback after being caught short on displacement and power the year before. Ford underrated

the production 428 CJ engines at 335 horsepower, primarily to try to gain an advantage in AHRA and NHRA classifications. It didn't really work.

Streamlined fastback Ford Torinos and Mercury Cyclones, powered by the latest 427 Tunnel Port engines, dominated stock car racing in 1968. Torinos won twenty-one of forty-nine NASCAR Grand National races, with Cyclones picking up six GN wins. At the end of the season, Ford ran a full-page advertisement in enthusiast auto publications that said it all: "Grand Slam! Torino Wins 1968 NASCAR, USAC, and ARCA Championships."

David Pearson nailed down his second NASCAR Championship, winning sixteen races in Holman & Moody Torinos. At the Daytona 500, Cale Yarborough drove the Wood Brothers No. 21 Cyclone to the win, averaging 143.25 miles per hour. LeeRoy Yarbrough, in a Junior Johnson Cyclone, and Bobby Allison, in Bondy Long's Holman & Moody Torino, followed him. For the fifth year in a row, Dan Gurney won the *Motor Trend* 500 at Riverside Raceway. Gurney averaged 100.59 miles per hour on the 2.7-mile road-racing course to take the win, followed by David Pearson, Parnelli Jones, Bobby Allison, and Cale Yarborough in Ford Torinos.

Ford's three-year winning streak at the Indy 500 was interrupted in 1968 by Bobby Unser, who achieved his first of three wins at the Brickyard in Rislone Racing's Eagle-Offy. It was the last race for a front-engine car to be on the starting grid and the first race won by a turbocharged engine.

Finishing second was Dan Gurney, who drove his Olsonite Eagle-Ford powered by a naturally-aspirated, pushrod-design 305-cubic-inch Gurney-Weslake-Ford engine. The next best Ford finish was Denny Hulme, who took fourth place in another Olsonite Eagle-Ford. Gurney later won the USAC Champ

This is the 427 tunnel-port engine for the Bondy Long Torino. It was the highest-power wedge engine Ford used in race cars in 1968 and until the Boss 429 was legal in 1969.
John Craft Collection

Dan Gurney at a Mercury Cougar Trans-Am event in 1968 with a prototype for the 1969 Boss 429 engine. Note the unique valve covers, which never saw production. The engine had a staggered valve layout and "twisted," or crescent-shaped, Hemi combustion chambers. It was a show engine that, judging by the headers, could have been used for marine testing. Early prototype motors had iron heads. *Ford Motor Company*

Car Series Rex Mays 300 at Riverside in his Eagle-Ford. Hard-charging A. J. Foyt posted the first win for Ford's new turbocharged engine at the USAC Hanford 250. It was clear that smaller displacement, high-revving, boosted engines were the future of Indy racing. Ford's new turbocharged engine produced 750 horsepower at 9,500 rpm—an incredible 4.46 horsepower per cubic inch!

After Ford pulled out of GT racing, John Wyer and Jim Willment campaigned JWA GT40-based Mirages. JWA converted the Grady Davis/Gulf Oil Mirages back to lightweight GT40 specs, complete with 289-cubic-inch Gurney-Weslake engines with Weber carburetors. Lucian Bianchi and Pedro Rodriguez drove P/1075, the former M-10003 Mirage, to win Le Mans in 1968. A Gulf Oil/JWA GT40 delivered Ford its third Le Mans win and the 1968 Championship.

Even with a new 302-cubic inch small-block motors with single and twin four-barrel carburetors, Ford and Shelby's Trans-Am effort for 1968 could not stop the Penske/Donahue Z/28 Camaro juggernaut. Mark Donahue, in a Sunoco Blue Camaro, swept the series and gave Chevrolet the Trans-Am Championship in 1968. Jerry Titus and Ron Bucknum drove one of the two Shelby Mustang team cars and won the Daytona 24-Hour, but not much more.

Even with a new president who loved racing, Ford domination in stock car and drag competition, and some fresh products, Ford's 1968 sales of 1.73 million vehicles were just a tiny tick higher than in the previous year. Sales had dropped in 1967 by almost 500,000 from 1966 numbers. Mustang sales in 1968 were 150,000 less than 1967.

Enthusiasts may have had much more to shop for, but insurance rates were putting a damper on the muscle-car marketplace. Robert F. Kennedy and Martin Luther King Jr. were assassinated and the war in Vietnam was escalating. Bunkie Knudsen had his work cut out for him.

Don "Snake" Prudhomme with the Lou Baney–Prudhomme "Shelby Super Snake" fuel dragster, sponsored by Carroll Shelby. The engine is an Ed Pink blown-injected 427 SOHC Ford engine and was first fueler to break the 6-second quarter in NHRA competition. Prudhomme and Lou Baney campaigned the car in 1968 and 1969 seasons and won the 1968 Winternationals. *Ford Motor Company*

The No. 10 JWA Mirage GT40 driven by Paul Hawkins and David Hobbs leads the No. 9 JWA Mirage GT40 driven by Lucian Bianchi and Pedro Rodriguez at Le Mans in 1968. The No. 9 won the race, giving Ford its third win at Le Mans and the World Championship. *Ford Motor Company*

Dan Gurney finished second at the 1968 Indy 500 in his No. 48 Olsonite Eagle-Ford and then went on to win the Rex Mays 300 at Riverside Raceway. He averaged 111.69 miles per hour on the twisty road course in his Eagle powered by a pushrod Ford engine with Weslake heads and injection. Ford-powered cars took the first nine spots. *Ford Motor Company*

Noted Ford race-car restorer Tony Conover restored and races this original SCCA A/Sedan and Trans-Am Mustang. It was owned and raced originally by Ford engineer Bill Clawson, who built and raced the first Ford Trans-Am Mustang in 1965 and later owned the ex-Titus and ex-Follmer Trans-Am Mustangs. *M. M. "Mike" Matune Jr.*

1968 Shelby Cobra GT: Personal Luxury at Warp Speed!

Ford wanted more production; Shelby wanted more performance. The results: Cobra GT Mustangs—from 302 mild to 428 Cobra Jet wild.

I was elated when I returned from Shelby's 1968 GT Mustang press program at Riverside Raceway in July 1967. The Shelby GT line was mildly restyled and packed full of upgraded comfort and convenience features, and power was right on the money. Plus, there was a regular production convertible for the first time. The snake charmer had done it again! I couldn't wait to put together a cover story for the next issue of *Hi-Performance CARS*, November 1967. The cover line, under a shot of me driving next year's Shelby GT Mustang on the track: 1968 Shelby 427 GT500, Hottest Mustang Yet!

Not long after the issue went on sale, we received mail objecting to our featuring a car that didn't exist! There was a lot we came away with from that program that *never* happened—and even more that we didn't know about that *did* happen. Between the long-lead press preview in July, the public announcement of the GT Mustang line in the fall, and a Ford press conference

in the winter of 1967, there were more product and corporate changes at Shelby American than in 1965 to 1967 combined.

I mentioned the hot powerplant choices—427 in the GT500 and supercharged 302 in the GT350—that I found out later you couldn't actually order. The 427 Shelby fastback I had driven at Riverside was a prototype built on a 1967 GT500. And, since I had recently watched GT Mustangs being built at Shelby's LAX Airport facility, I had no reason to think that manufacturing would be relocated to Michigan, which it was. Or that Ford would be more involved in Shelby Mustang design and development to take the lead role in the manufacturing and marketing of the 1968 models.

Then there was the name change from Shelby GT to Shelby Cobra GT. Most of the media community was unaware that Carroll Shelby had sold his Cobra trademark rights to Ford in 1967. Ford wasted no time in utilizing its new purchase. (Years later, the Cobra trademark would be returned to Shelby after a legal battle.) The carryover 1967 roll bar in the coupe and padded roll bar

Pete Disher's rare *Coralsnake* Cobra GT500KR, VIN 03206, is one of three special-paint-option WT-5185 Dark Orange 1968 models built. It's a Shelby Triple Crown Concours winner and the centerpiece of the Coralsnake website. *Pete Disher*

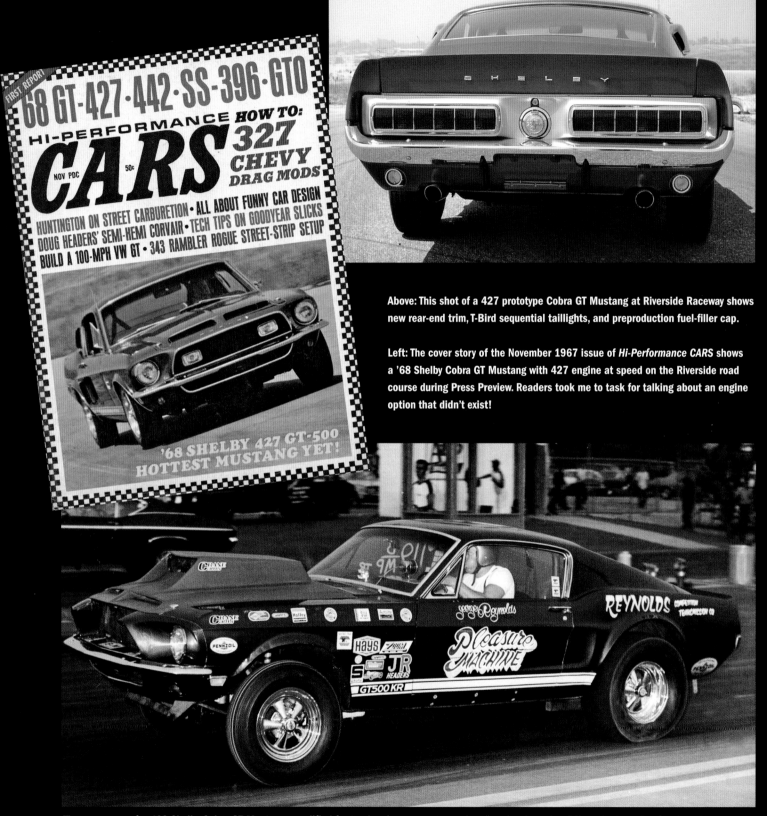

Above: This shot of a 427 prototype Cobra GT Mustang at Riverside Raceway shows new rear-end trim, T-Bird sequential taillights, and preproduction fuel-filler cap.

Left: The cover story of the November 1967 issue of *Hi-Performance CARS* shows a '68 Shelby Cobra GT Mustang with 427 engine at speed on the Riverside road course during Press Preview. Readers took me to task for talking about an engine option that didn't exist!

There were very few '68 Shelby Cobra GT Mustangs modified for track-only use; most were just "weekend warriors." Note the huge Pro Stock–style scoop mated to the stock Shelby scooped hood, the "lightened" front end, the lack of side scoops, and the hefty traction bars. This GT500KR ran in NHRA Modified Production classes.

A 1968 Shelby Cobra GT production at the mini-assembly line at A. O. Smith in Ionia, Michigan. Quality improved through the use of new metal-matched dies for fiberglass pieces. The relationship between A. O. Smith, Shelby Automotive, and Ford was rife with tension, but the process remained in place through 1969 production.

in the convertible suddenly became an "Integral Overhead Safety Bar." That was straight out of Ford Legal, crafted to ward off lawsuits in rollover accidents.

It was a brave new day for everything Shelby. Ford wanted to increase Shelby Mustang production beyond capability of the Shelby American's current LAX facility. There was also talk about the airport not renewing Shelby's lease as part of its expansion. In reality, Carroll Shelby never wanted to be a production car manufacturer. His passion was creating powerful two- and four-seat niche market performance cars with true sports car handling and braking qualities.

I attended Ford's press conference in New York City on December 15, 1967, that focused on the transition of control of Shelby manufacturing and marketing operations. "Carroll Shelby and his Shelby Cobra GT cars will continue to be one of Ford's better ideas," said Ford Division Merchandising Manager William P. Benton. "Shelby American Inc. has been divided into three separate companies—Shelby Automotive, Shelby Parts, and Shelby Racing. Shelby Parts and Shelby Racing are headquartered in a 20,000-square-foot facility in Torrance, California. Ford Division will assist in the management of Michigan-based Shelby Automotive at Mr. Shelby's request. Mr. Shelby will remain on the west coast to direct the parts and racing businesses. As in the past, Shelby Cobra cars will be sold through Shelby-franchised Ford dealers. The number of dealers will be increased from approximately 100 to 150 to provide representation in the top 111 market areas."

Ford wanted to control production costs, something company "bean counters" had been trying to accomplish since the first Shelby Mustang in

The standard engine package in the GT500 was a 360-horsepower Police Interceptor 428 with a single 715-cfm Holley four-barrel and a carryover dual-quad air cleaner that looked like it covered dual quads from the top.

1965. There were also quality control issues that Ford felt could be better dealt with if manufacturing was closer to Ford headquarters. Ford's choice for Shelby Mustang final assembly was the Plastics Division of Tier 1 industry supplier A. O. Smith, a company founded in 1899 and located in Ionia, Michigan. They had been a supplier of lightweight steel chassis to both Ford and GM, and one of two mid-series Corvette Sting Ray body manufacturers. They had fiberglass production capabilities and a mini assembly line at their Ionia location.

The contract between Ford, Shelby, and A. O. Smith was signed in May of 1967, two months before we saw the 1968 models at Riverside. Titled "Basic Program Assumptions For 1968 GT350 and 500 Mustang," original paperwork indicated that there would be three GT350s powered by 302-inch engines and three GT500s powered by 428 engines. The GT350s would be available with carbureted, fuel-injected, and supercharged engines. It was the same for 428 engines used in GT500s.

Communications between Shelby and the media never revealed that fuel injection was being evaluated, yet the program had been going on since mid-1967. Four 1968 Shelbys—two fastbacks, one notchback coupe, and one convertible—were used by Shelby chief engineer Fred Goodell to test a variety of mechanical and electronic fuel-injection systems supplied by Bosch/Bendix, Conolec, and Lucas.

Michigan-based Shelby Automotive, with Carroll Shelby on its board, managed the 1968 Cobra GT Mustang program. All donor Mustangs were built as KD (knock-down) units at Ford's Metuchen plant and shipped by rail to Ionia. Mechanical changes were executed at the plant prior to shipping. A. O. Smith was responsible for the production of fiberglass conversion components—four-piece front end, louvered hood, scoops, rear spoiler and end caps, and taillight panel—using metal-matched dies for high quality. The new design hood utilized a stock Mustang locking mechanism and stylized twist-lock turn-knobs with Dzus fasteners.

Initially, Shelby Cobra GT Mustangs were offered with 302/250 four-barrel and 428/360 Police Interceptor four-barrel engines. Options included a 302/315 supercharged small-block and a 427/400 four-barrel engine. The two optional engines saw service only in prototypes. In May 1968, the 428 engine in GT500 models was replaced by the new, more powerful 428/335 Cobra Jet. The model changed to GT500KR. Some Shelby dealers advertised that the KR model produced 375 horsepower.

Since Ford had been planning the phase-out of the 427 street engine and developing the 428 Cobra Jet in 1967, there was never a business case for using the 427 in a Shelby Mustang. It offered more power and bragging rights than the

more consumerlike 428, but the CJ variant with 427 heads and beefy lower end was not a consumer engine. The CJ offered 427 performance without the complications of adding an optional engine. The 427's costs would never justify the gains.

There are enthusiasts who claim that Shelby built 427 GT500 Mustangs in 1968. The Shelby American Automobile Club is the official keeper of Shelby vehicle production and sales records. According to Rick Kopec, director emeritus of SAAC: "We have no factory information or sales invoices that detail 427 engines installed by the factory in 1968 Shelby Cobra GT Mustangs. This option was considered and planned, but was rejected by the time brochures and specification sheets had been completed and sent to dealers. When a new owner blew an engine and brought the car back to the dealer, it was not unheard of that the owner asked to replace the 428 with a 427. When these cars were purchased later, many thought the 427 engines were original. We know because we had to debunk all of those claims!"

Once Ford plants had tooled up for Cobra Jet Mustang production, the GT500KR replaced the GT500. Shoppers were confused, since the new 428 engine was rated at 335 horsepower and replaced a 360-horsepower engine. And they called it *King of the Road*!

Early advertising for the '68 Shelby Mustang featuring a prototype '67 Shelby convertible that had actually been built in 1966, used with 1967 trim by Carroll Shelby, and later fitted with 1968 model fiberglass. The car was photographed in white and red for advertising and PR. This ad marked the first use of "Integral Overhead Safety Bar" to describe the roll bar.

A one-of-one '68 Shelby Cobra GT500KR Mustang, VIN 04104, originally used as an engineering prototype to evaluate powertrains and big-block supercharging. Painted in special-order WT-6066 Yellow, it was sold by Shelby Automotive without the supercharger and has since been restored. When photos were taken, the Paxton supercharger conversion had not yet been completed. *Kevin Suydam*

The '68 Shelby Cobra GT Mustang had a more luxurious interior, including a swing-away steering wheel option for easier exit. This is the interior of the one-off supercharged KR-500KR. Note the console with extra gauges, including standard Stewart-Warner gauges and two aftermarket gauges installed by Shelby when the car was first supercharged. *Kevin Suydam*

After Cobra Jet Mustangs dominated Super/Stock competition at the NHRA Winternationals in February of 1968, enthusiasts were aware of Ford's underrating of the engine. Documented test results showed that stock GT500s averaged 0-to-60 times in the high 6s and quarter-mile performance of approximately 100 miles per hour in the mid 14s. Similarly equipped KR models sprinted to 60 miles per hour in the mid 6s and covered the quarter-mile in the high 13s at approximately 105 miles per hour.

Bob Tasca first used the tagline "King of the Road" for his KR-8 Cobra Jet concept Mustang, the inspiration for the production 1968½ Cobra Jet.

Shelby had a lot of experience with Paxton superchargers, dating back to the first supercharged Shelby Mustangs in 1966. As in 1967, Shelby intended to offer supercharging on both small- and big-block Mustangs in 1968. The

prototype supercharged GT350 was equipped with the new 302-cubic-inch small-block, boosted by a Paxton centrifugal supercharger force-feeding a sealed Autolite 650-cfm four-barrel. It had been dynamometer-tested at 315 horsepower at 5,000 rpm and 333 pounds-feet of torque at 3,800 rpm. It remained a prototype.

Supercharged 427 and 428 engines had been installed in the 1967 Shelby GT500 notchback, *Little Red*. Shelby engineers built at least two Paxton supercharged 1968 prototypes. One was the first GT500 convertible built, VIN #00056. It was an engineering prototype with a 428/360 engine used to evaluate different engines, induction systems, and drivetrains. It was later sold in original production condition without its supercharger and has since been restored to supercharged prototype specs.

As soon as Cobra Jet engines were available, Shelby Engineering special-ordered (DSO-3037) a KR fastback in optional WT6066 special Yellow paint for supercharger fitment. The goal was to create an ultimate performance GT500KR with a potential horsepower rating in excess of 450. After the supercharger was added, GT500KR VIN #04102 was put on the road with Manufacturer's plate 16-M826. Records indicate it was sold to Courtesy Motors in Littleton, Colorado, without the supercharger. It has been restored and the engine updated with a correct Paxton supercharger. The car is now in Kevin Suydam's collection.

One of the modified 1968 Engineering vehicles survives with its engine intact. EXP-500, a green notchback coupe with black vinyl roof known as the

Left: Testing a prototype '68 GT500 with 427 engine at Riverside. I'm not sure if it was actually any faster than the KR model with Cobra Jet 428 that we drove in mid-1968.

Below: As of May 1968, Shelby Mustang sales materials and catalogs showed availability of either the GT350 small-block or the KR model with 428 Cobra Jet big-block. The KR replaced the normal GT500.

Green Hornet was also used to test a number of powertrains. Originally a 390 Mustang, it was fitted with Shelby Cobra GT fiberglass body parts and a special fuel-injected 428 Cobra Jet backed by a C-6 automatic. It had been equipped with an independent rear suspension with coil-over shocks, reminiscent of IRS setups used on early Shelby Cobra race cars. The rear suspension was changed back to stock using a 9-inch rear with thirty-one-spline axles and locker. More importantly, it was one of Shelby's mules for evaluating fuel-injection systems. In its final iteration, the CJ engine was fitted with a Conolec EFI (electronic fuel injection) system, still on the engine today. It has been restored and is in Craig Jackson's collection.

The *Green Hornet* and *Little Red* served as prototypes for the 1968 GT/CS, or California Special and High Country Special notchback coupes. Essentially sales promotion models for specific regions, they were Mustangs customized with some Shelby Mustang body parts and trim. Built on both GT and base Mustangs, 3,867 California Special models were built at the San Jose plant and distributed to dealers in a few areas. A total of 251 High Country Specials were sold only by Denver dealers. Unlike the Shelby Mustangs, the GT/CS and HCS side scoops were not functional.

For the 1968 model year, Shelby Automotive produced a record 4,450 Shelby Cobra GT Mustangs, in excess of 1,200 more than the previous year. Hertz purchased 225 GT350 fastbacks, two GT500 fastbacks, and one GT500KR convertible, all without special trim. Even with higher insurance rates, Shelby dealers sold 1,053 KR fastbacks and 517 KR convertibles. For the first time, Shelbys could be ordered in standard or six optional colors. A total of 110 fastbacks and 49 convertibles came with special paint.

Even though Carroll Shelby was less involved with 1968 models than he had been in previous years, the Shelby mystique remained strong.

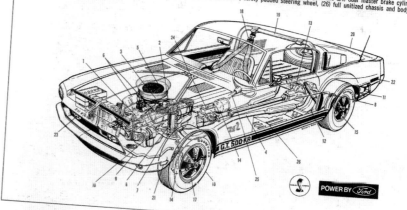

CHAPTER 10

1969

THE HITS JUST KEEP ON COMING!

Boss Mustangs, new racing engines and options, and wins at Daytona, Indy, and Le Mans bolstered Ford's performance image.

It was a banner year for Ford Bosses: Boss 302, Boss 429, and new boss of bosses, Bunkie Knudsen. His passion for racing—and racing what dealers could sell—supported the Boss 429 program, which helped impact Mustang sales.

More importantly, it helped move mainstream Ford Fairlane/Torino and Mercury Montego/Cyclone models like those that dominated NASCAR, USAC, and ARCA.

I presented the 1969 *Hi-Performance CARS* "Top Performance Car of the Year" award to Ford Division General Manager John Naughton, stating: "The Division deserved the award for its attitudes toward and achievements in the

The author presents the 1969 *Hi-Performance CARS* Top Performance Manufacturer of the Year Award to John Naughton, Ford Division general manager, at a special Boss 302 Mustang program in Dearborn.

I shot this at Motion Performance, waiting for my turn to put a new Mach 1 Mustang with 428 CJ power and functional Ram Air Shaker scoop on the Clayton chassis dyno. After tuning, Joe Oldham and Fred Mackerodt tracked it for a test in *Supercars Annual '69*. They ran some 13.70s.

Ford did an excellent job of capitalizing on its racing successes, helping dealers sell cars and parts based on its original "Win on Sunday, Sell on Monday" marketing concept. Ths brochure focused on Torino Cobra and NASCAR, Mach 1 Mustang, and Bonneville records and high-performance engine parts available at dealers. It's surprising to see they used the Mark IV that won Le Mans in 1967 and not the GT40 that won in 1968 and 1969.

1969 PERFORMANCE BUYER'S DIGEST

the cars...the engines...the parts... Ford has everything you need to build your kind of machine

Ever since 1903 when Henry Ford built Old 999 and won his first race, Ford has been building high performance machines. And proving them by winning at Bonneville, Pomona, Indianapolis, Riverside and Le Mans. But there's more to Ford performance than a worldwide winning streak. The same Ford engineers who stretch their minds to win on the tracks are involved in designing performance cars and parts you can buy. And if you don't think that makes for winners on the road, look for this sign which marks your Ford Dealer's Performance Corner and let him prove it. It's the place you've got to go to see what's going on!

REMOVE THIS HANDY GUIDE FOR FUTURE REFERENCE

Ford's Joe Farkas set up this shot to promote David Pearson's 1969 Championship Boss 429 Torino Talladega and some Ford team drivers. Pearson is in front with, left to right clockwise, Cale Yarborough, Richard Petty, LeeRoy Yarbrough, and Donnie Allison. *Ford Motor Company*

The author tracks a preproduction 1969 Cougar Eliminator on the Dearborn Proving Ground road course in June 1968. The Eliminator was available with a 428 CJ or Boss 302 engine and was Mercury's answer to the Boss 302 and Mach 1 Mustang. Note the front spoiler, Ram Air hood, and adjustable wing on the prototype.

high-performance field." In also applauded Ford "for its great new engines, drag racing options, specialty cars, and its continued support of racing."

Mustangs had been on two-year restyling cycles and there were major changes in 1969. Overall length was increased by almost 4 inches and width by approximately 0.25 inch. Curb weight was up by 140 pounds. Leading the charge was the SportsRoof Mach 1 with unique striping and, if ordered, R-code 428 Cobra Jet Ram Air engine with a functional "Shaker" hood scoop.

Once into 1969, the optional 428 Super CJ, with beefed lower end and also rated at 335 horsepower, displaced the 428/335 CJ as the top engine choice. A new "Drag Pack" option included an oil cooler and a 9-inch rear with 3.91 gears and Traction-Lok differential or 4.30 gears with a Detroit Locker. At one point, the SCJ was rated at 360 horsepower.

The Cougar was also restyled for 1969 and lengthened by 3.5 inches and widened by a full 3 inches. Its version of the Mach 1 and Boss 302 Mustangs was the Eliminator with stylish front air dam, rear wing, and scooped hood with click-lock pins. Engine choices included the 428 CJ and new Boss 302.

Two new superperformance Mustangs and a Torino Cobra further enhanced Ford's commitment to enthusiasts. Bunkie Knudsen had fast-tracked the Boss 302 and Boss 429 programs so they could be introduced as 1969½ models.

With the Boss 302, Ford finally had a vehicle to compete with Chevrolet's popular Z/28 Camaro on the street and in Trans-Am racing. Larry Shinoda, who Bunkie brought with him from GM, came up with the Boss 302 name and designed its graphics.

A serious performance car, the Boss 302 Mustang was not available with automatic transmission or air conditioning. Its imposing front spoiler was dealer-installed to avoid damage during shipping. The fiberglass rear wing and backlight louvers were optional. Because of its standard F-60 tires, special fender/wheel well contours were required. Ford engineers, working at Kar Kraft, designed the Boss 302's heavy-duty suspension. Boss 302 Mustangs, priced at approximately $3,500, went on sale in April of 1969 and Ford dealers sold 1,628.

The Boss 302 Mustang showcased the new 302-inch small-block with four-bolt mains; forged steel crank and rods; .524-inch solid-lifter cam; new "Cleveland" canted-valve, big-port heads; and a manually choked, 780-cfm Holley on a high-rise alloy manifold. A factory-installed rev-limiter was set at 6,150 rpm. Like the CJ engine, Ford underrated the Boss 302 at 290 horsepower at 5,800 rpm to avoid insurance company surcharges for 300-horsepower-and-up cars. Stock Boss 302 Mustangs with 3.91 Traction-Lok

Parnelli Jones on August 10, 1969, in a Bud Moore Engineering Boss 302 Mustang at Watkins Glen Trans-Am. Parnelli won T/A races at MIS and Donnybrook, and Ford finished second in the point standings. *Ford Motor Company*

A stock 351 Mustang weighed approximately 3,300 pounds so the race cars were lightened to 2,900 pounds in accordance with SCCA rules. Thin window glass was used as well as aluminum window channel hardware. Engines were mounted lower and set back slightly. Front brakes were almost 12-inch Lincoln discs with four-pot calipers. Other mandatory specs included 8-inch-wide wheels and a maximum engine displacement of 305 cubic inches.

Ford's seven-car Trans-Am "fleet" was race-prepped by Lee Dykstra's group at Kar Kraft, then divided among its factory teams. Three went to Shelby Racing in California, three to Bud Moore Engineering in Spartanburg, and the remaining car to consummate racer Smokey Yunick, in Daytona Beach. Knudsen had a long-standing relationship with Yunick, dating back to his Chevrolet days, so his car was finished and painted with Yunick's gold-trimmed black "Best Damn Garage in Town" livery. Interviews indicate it was originally built with a 429 engine, later swapped for a 302 by Yunick.

Engines for the M-code Trans-Am Mustangs were developed as part of the Boss 302 "Cleveland" engine program. Ford Engine and Foundry personnel, working in leased space at Kar Kraft, developed the new small-block that featured canted-valve, big-port heads. The Boss 302 program development

gears were often quicker and faster than Mustangs with larger engines. Back in the day, well-tuned Boss 302s accelerated to 60 miles per hour in the low 7s with quarter-mile times of high 90s in the low to mid-14s.

Whereas winning at Le Mans and Indianapolis created enviable halos for Ford and its products, winning SCCA Trans-Am and NASCAR/USAC/ARCA events actually helped move the metal! Dealers could sell Torinos, Cyclones, Mustangs, and Cougars on Monday after similar-looking cars won on Sunday.

For the 1969 Trans-Am season, SVA's Homer Perry ordered seven unpainted, four-speed, SportsRoof 351 Mustangs, VIN 48623 to 48629. They were billed to Ford Administrative Service at a total cost of approximately $16,000 and shipped to Kar Kraft on December 3, 1968.

The new Boss 429 motor was homologated for NASCAR after Ford built five hundred Boss 429 Mustangs. The engines were developed by Engine and Foundry, built at a Ford plant, and supplied to Kar Kraft Brighton, where the Mustangs were modified to take the large motors and final-assembled. This photo was taken during early production in 1969. *Ford Motor Company*

Holman & Moody was assigned the Ford Can-Am program and had a number of special lightweight "460" blocks cast for use with Boss 429 heads. Here is Mario Andretti testing the unfinished Can-Am Boss "429er" powered by a 494-inch engine, which was later changed to 477-inch version that put out 659 horsepower at 6,000 rpm. Its best performance was third at Riverside. *Ford Motor Company*

group included Ford racing engine engineer Moses "Mose" Nowland, who said, "We assembled the race-ready Boss 302 engines for the factory teams at Triple E, the Engine-Electrical-Engineering facility in Dearborn, adjacent to the Henry Ford Museum. That's where we built prototype engines for future production and race engines for motorsports teams." Nowland retired as Senior Motorsport Engineer in 2012.

The blueprinted and balanced Trans-Am engine utilized a cross-drilled, forged steel Indy engine crankshaft; .615-inch lift solid cam, GT40-style forged steel rods; headers; and aluminum intake manifold with individual runners and a pair of Holley Dominator four-barrels. Dyno-tested output was 475-plus horsepower at 9,000 rpm. All race engines were assembled with O-ringed cylinder blocks for dry-deck, gasketless sealing. The process utilized gas-filled, stainless steel O-rings around the cylinders and Viton rubber rings around water and oil passage openings.

Moore's Mustangs proved to be faster and more reliable than Shelby's. It was rumored at the time that Shelby either modified or replaced the Ford-supplied engines. Parnelli Jones won at Michigan International Speedway and Donnybrook, and George Follmer took the win at Bridgehampton. Sam Posey won at Lime Rock, posting the only win for Shelby. When championship points were tallied, Ford finished second to Chevrolet—again.

There never was a true business case for building a Boss 429 Mustang. However, the Boss 429 Mustang existed primarily to get its engine homologated for NASCAR so Ford could better compete with Hemi-powered Mopars. In that respect, it was a huge success. The Boss 429, based on the block used in 385-Series 429, 429 CJ and SCJ, and 460 engines, was a dry-deck racing engine with large aluminum heads with staggered valves and crescent-shaped, Hemi-type combustion chambers.

While its formal name was Boss 429, chosen to capitalize on popular youth market lexicon of the day, it was also referenced as "429 Blue Crescent," "429 Shotgun," and "Twisted Hemi." In order to use it in a production car, it was detuned using a small carburetor, mild cam, and restrictive exhausts for a 375

horsepower rating at 5,200 rpm. Torque was a ground-pounding 450 pounds-feet at 3,400 rpm. All Boss 429 Mustangs were equipped with manual, driver-controlled Ram Air induction.

Primarily interested in selling a minimum of 500 cars to be NASCAR legal, Boss 429 Mustang production was assigned to Kar Kraft, while Ford's Engine and Foundry Division developed the Boss 429 engine. Engines were built at the Lima, Ohio, plant and shipped to Kar Kraft. The Boss 429 engine option cost $1,200, which resulted in a Mustang with an MSRP close to $5,000. You could buy a 428 CJ model with all the bells and whistles for just a little over $3,300. With sales running from January to July 1969, the program yielded 857 Boss 429s, including prototypes and two Cougars.

Ford got its NASCAR homologation and those enthusiasts who had to have the most powerful pony car available got what they wanted. The two Boss 429 Cougars, VINs 67772 and 67773, went to drag racers "Dyno Don" Nicholson and "Fast Eddie" Schartman. Kar Kraft billed SVA $8,888.52 for the two conversions on April 30, 1969. Boss 429 Mustangs had KK 429 NASCAR ID tags, with VINs starting with 1201. The standard Mustang Warranty Number plate indicated "Special Performance Vehicle."

Out of the total 1969½ Boss 429 production, 279 received S-code engines with magnesium valve covers and extra-beefy, forged steel NASCAR rods. The

Jack Brabham finished third at the second Can-Am race at Riverside in 1969 in a Holman & Moody–prepared, aluminum-bodied Alan Mann Racing entry. A lightweight Boss Can-Am engine supplied the power. *Ford Motor Company*

Bob Tasca's connections at Ford included Henry Ford II, so it's no surprise that Ford arranged to have his Boss 429 Mustang fitted with a 494-inch Boss engine from Holman & Moody. Tasca used it as the prototype for a line of street Boss Mustangs. His Boss ran 11.0s at 136 miles per hour on street tires. Brent Hajek owns it today. *Ford Motor Company*

Ford's answer to the Road Runner and Super Bee was the Fairlane/Torino/Cobra that came standard with 428 CJ motor and four-speed. Prior to its introduction, I drove this 335-horsepower Ram Air Cobra with manufacturer plates. It could be ordered with a fastback roof, as used in stock-car racing, or a formal roof.

For 1969, Ford tied its drag-racing programs more closely to the marketing of cars and parts with the Performance Car Clinic, which brought factory racers closer to dealers and potential customers. Hubert Platt and Randy Payne campaigned their Mustangs and Torino on the East Coast, while Ed Terry and Dick Wood toured the western states. *Ford Motor Company*

Connie Kalitta was an early adopter of the Boss 429 engine for blown-fuel racing. In 1969, he campaigned both his Bounty Hunter fuel dragster and Mustang Funny Car. Brent Hajek now owns the Mustang. *Ford Motor Company*

rest were fitted with T-code motors with lighter lower end components. All Boss 429s started life as four-speed, 428 CJ SportsRoof Mustangs, shipped to Kar Kraft for body/platform modifications, engine installations, and final assembly. The front spring/shock towers were spaced and inner fenders modified so the Boss 429 engine would fit. Front suspension mounting points were changed and A-arm mounting lowered 1 inch. Engine oil coolers were added and batteries relocated to trunks. Rear ends, with stagger-mount shocks, were available with 3.50, 3.91, or 4.30 Traction-Lok gears.

Stock Boss 429 Mustang real-world performance proved to be less than expected. With a curb weight of approximately 3,800 pounds and a large mass mounted over the front wheels, they did not handle nearly as well as Boss 302 or 428 CJ Mustangs with top suspension options. If you could get the stock tires to hook up, a 3.91-geared Boss 429 was capable of running 102 miles per hour in the low 14s, with 0-to-60 sprints in the low, low sevens. When I first saw the prototypes in Dearborn in November of 1968, engineers claimed quarter-mile times of 106 miles per hour in 13.4 seconds.

Kar Kraft built one drag racing Boss 429 Mustang and shipped it to Holman-Moody-Stroppe in Long Beach, California, for Mickey Thompson to campaign. Driven by Butch Leal, the *War Toy* had twin Holley Dominators, weighed 3,200 pounds, and ran 145 miles per hour in the high 9s in heads-up Super/Stock. Dave Lyall's *Going Thing* Boss 429 Mustang ran consistent 9s in Pro Stock.

The inaugural season for the Canadian-American Challenge Cup Series took place in 1966. Between 1967 and the series end in 1972, there would be a total of fourteen tracks hosting Can-Am races. Dan Gurney posted Ford's one and only Can-Am win during the seven-year series, winning the second race of the opening season at Bridgehampton driving his AAR Lola Mark II powered by a 305-inch, Gurney-Eagle small-block.

Almost from the start, Can-Am was dominated by McLaren-Chevys running all-aluminum, 430- and 496-inch big-blocks with components available from Chevrolet. Exotic Porsche 917s started winning in 1970 and the series became a Chevy-Porsche show. While Can-Am was a low priority at Ford, Special Vehicles Activity did get involved with a Can-Am engine project, the RX-412. After a

A rare photo of an internal Shelby restyling presentation. Stock '69 Mustang with parts to be replaced by Shelby components removed, fully assembled GT500 Mustang and the unique fiberglass conversion parts. Note the support wires hanging from the ceiling. *Ford Motor Company*

The '69 Shelby GT Mustang was the swan song for the Shelby-Ford Mustang relationship. Carroll was less involved than in previous years, and the cars were final-assembled at A. O. Smith. Leftover 1969 models were converted to 1970 models with new Fed-approved numbers by Kar Kraft, as A. O. Smith wanted out of the relationship.

disappointing start with a 344-inch engine, Project RX-412 was reactivated in mid-1969 and focused on lightweight 477- and 494-inch Boss 429s.

Ford produced approximately a dozen lightweight "460" blocks with pressed-in iron cylinder liners, including two cast from magnesium. They were supplied to Holman & Moody for Can-Am race cars and cataloged with SK-number 46020. In 494-inch configuration, the engine was assembled with Boss 429 heads, 4.52-inch pistons, and 3.85-inch stroker crank. While rumored to put out 800 horsepower, the Lucas-injected engine developed 674 horsepower at 7,000 rpm. H&M built a 477-inch version with Lucas injection and an H&M "600" camshaft that generated 659 horsepower at 6,000 rpm and a whopping 577 pounds-feet of torque at 6,000. It replaced the 494-inch first

used in the "429er." Mario Andretti found the smaller-engined racer to be more manageable. Andretti placed third at Riverside in the ex-Shelby McLaren M6B Ford "429er" and, a few weeks later, Jack Brabham posted a third in the Alan Mann Ford. By 1970, both Ford Can-Am cars had retired and Dearborn was out of Can-Am racing.

Holman & Moody used some Boss 429 engines in boats and put a 494-inch lightweight Cam-Am motor into Bob Tasca's one-off Boss Mustang, KK-1214. It ran 11.0s at 136 miles per hour on street tires! It's in the Hajek Motorsports Museum.

In 1968, Plymouth and Dodge introduced bargain-priced Road Runner and Super Bee performance models. Priced at around $3,000 with a 383-inch engine, manual transmission, and "taxi-cab" interior, the low-rent specialty cars were popular with young enthusiasts. For 1969, Ford came up with a better idea—Torino Cobra or, simply, Cobra. With pricing starting at approximately $3,200, you received a standard 335-horsepower 428 CJ engine with four-speed. If you added a few hundred bucks, you could get functional Ram Air induction, limited-slip rear, and some comfort and convenience items.

Ford's factory drag racing efforts in 1969 focused on racers who visited Ford dealers before or after running their cars at nearby tracks. The "Performance Car Clinic" program supported the original "Win on Sunday, Sell on Monday" concept and was welcomed by dealers and enthusiasts. Record-holding drag racers toured with NHRA Super/Stock 428 CJ Mustangs and Torinos. Hubert Platt and Randy Payne handled the east coast, while western states were assigned to Ed Terry and Dick Wood. In addition to S/S cars, Platt and Terry also campaigned a 427 SOHC Mustang.

Clinics included drag racing seminars and proved to be effective marketing tools for both cars and high-performance parts. Ford's performance advertising and marketing tagline was "The Going Thing" and many factory-backed race cars carried that livery.

Shelby's 1969 GT Mustang, with minimal Shelby involvement, served as the swan song for the nameplate. Based on the longer, wider, and heavier Mustang, the new GTs had an all-new look and appealed to an older audience shopping for a sporty luxury car. Ford Design created a new image for the GT using fiberglass front fenders, hood, and deck lid with integral spoiler, and more NACA scoops and air extractors than any one car needed. Its nose was extended and fitted with a grille surround that doubled as a bumper. They carried over the sequential T-Bird taillights, added side scoops, and created what would be the last Shelby Mustang.

Engine choices were limited to a 351/290 Windsor small-block with Autolite four-barrel and Ram Air induction in the GT350. The GT500 had a 428/335 CJ with a 735-cfm Holley on a cast-iron manifold and Ram Air. With an increase in emission devices, the engines barely lived up to their power ratings. Buyers could still choose close or wide-ratio four-speeds or automatics.

Shelby Mustangs came with optional up-level factory interiors with roll bars and consoles with extra gauges. The public had a lot of specialty cars to choose from in 1969 and, with pricing going to over $5,000 for the convertible, sales stagnated. A. O. Smith produced 3,153 Shelby Mustangs, including 3 prototypes and pilot cars, in the 1969 model year. Approximately 150 went to Hertz and another 789 went unsold. When production wrapped up, Shelby pulled the plug on GT Mustangs and his car-building relationship with Ford.

Ford's solution to the leftover problem was to get government permission to add emission devices and assign 1970 VINs. They also decided to cosmetically update the 1970 models with new stripes and Boss 302 front spoilers. By the time 1969 production was over, A. O. Smith was no longer interested in working with Ford. The relationship had deteriorated because of Ford's slow payment of invoices, something that had been problematic since 1968. A. O.

LeeRoy Yarbrough won the Daytona 500 in this Junior Johnson Talladega powered by the tunnel-port 427, as the Boss 429 was not legal until the Atlanta 500 on March 30, 1969. Yarbrough was first driver to win the 1969 NASCAR Triple Crown—Daytona 500, Southern 500, and World 600.

Smith wanted out. Leftover 1969 Shelbys were transported to Kar Kraft for 1970 conversions and original 1969 VIN plates were turned over to the feds for destruction.

During 1969, Special Vehicles Activity's Dick Brannan left Ford to focus on building an aviation business in Atlanta. He returned as a drag racing program consultant later that same year and, in 1970, started driving a Boss 429 Maverick. He continued consulting and racing Fords, ending his career in 1972 when Ford completely stopped supporting racing.

Ford paid a high price to dominate NASCAR and win the Manufacturer's Championship again in 1969. In addition to a mid-season engine change from Tunnel Port 427 to Boss 429, they also had enormous expenses getting mid-season Torino Talladegas and Mercury Spoiler IIs homologated. In a memo dated February 19, 1969, from Special Vehicles Activity to Ford and Lincoln-Mercury Division general managers, Jacque Passino explained the 1969 ½ Talladega and Spoiler II program high-cost overruns: "Timing factors have resulted in unnecessarily high expenditures and interruptions of main line production."

The main reasons for the late initiation of these programs were:

(1) A change in homologation rules requiring the race cars to have exactly the same exterior configuration as the production models.

(2) A strict enforcement of the five-hundred-unit production rule before the vehicles could race.

Both the Talladega and Spoiler II were more aerodynamic than the production Torino and Cyclone in order to be more competitive with Dodge's Charger 500. Based on SportsRoof fastbacks, the Talladega and Spoiler II proved themselves on NASCAR's Super Speedways. The Talladega had a "droop-snoop" extended front end with a tapered panel that ran from the tip of its flat-black hood to the flush Cobra grille. A rear bumper was adapted to work up front and formed an advantageous air dam. Rocker panels were rolled under the car, reducing overall height from 53.5 to 52.6 inches. Because of front-end modifications, overall length was extended by 5.9 inches to 206.

In order to race the new Talladega at Daytona in February of 1969, Ford had to document a minimum of 500 production models. A total of 754 Talladegas, including prototypes, were built with standard 428 CJ engines, C-6 automatic transmissions, flat black hoods, and cloth-vinyl bench seats. Similar Mercury Cyclone Spoiler IIs with large rear wings were also produced at the Atlanta plant. In order to meet NASCAR homologation specs, Mercury added two Spoiler IIs: a Cale Yarborough Edition with a red metallic roof and a Dan Gurney model with a blue roof. Unfortunately, they didn't produce enough Spoiler IIs in time for Daytona.

While the new, more aerodynamic Talladega was legal for Daytona, the Boss 429 engine was not. Ford teams had to run the old Tunnel Port 427s fitted with single Holley Dominator four-barrels. Ford partnered with Holley on the design and engineering of the new 1,000- to 1,100-cfm Dominator, giving them exclusive use of the new carburetor prior to public release.

LeeRoy Yarbrough won the Daytona 500 in a Junior Johnson 427 Talladega, taking the victory with a last-lap pass of race-leader Charlie Glotzbach. Yarbrough, considered one of NASCAR's 50 greatest drivers, went on to win the Southern 500 and World 600 to become the first driver to win NASCAR's prestigious Triple Crown.

In a letter dated March 13, 1969, from Special Vehicles Manager Jacque Passino to NASCAR Executive Manager Len Kuchler—with copies to NASCAR's

William France and Ford and Lincoln Mercury GMs—Ford formally advised NASCAR of its intention to run Boss 429 engines. Passino attached invoices for production Boss 429 Mustangs to prove engine legality and documents to homologate Cyclone IIs with rear wings.

The first appearance of Boss 429 engines and Cyclone Spoiler IIs was at the Atlanta 500 on March 30, 1969. Cale Yarborough won the race in the No. 21 Wood Brothers Cyclone Spoiler II, followed by David Pearson in Holman & Moody's No. 17 Talladega. Yarborough averaged 132.19 miles per hour and led the race for 308 of the 334 laps in the new winged Spoiler II. By the end of the 1969 season, David Pearson had won eleven races in H&M Talladegas to take his third NASCAR Driver's Championship and clinch the Manufacturer's title for Ford. Benny Parsons won his second consecutive ARCA championship driving a Boss 429 Talladega.

For the first time, all thirty-three cars on the starting grid of the 1969 Indy 500 were piston-powered, rear-engined—no turbines or traditional roadsters. The fifty-third American Classic was won by Mario Andretti in the STP Oil Treatment Hawk-Turbo Ford with an average speed of 156.87 miles per hour. He led the field for 116 laps and was followed across the line by Dan Gurney in his Olsonite Eagle-Ford powered by a pushrod 305 engine.

Ford engines, ranging from the Gurney Eagle 305 small-block to the turbocharged 159-inch DOHC and naturally-aspirated 255-inch DOHC engines, ruled the USAC Championship Car Circuit in 1969. Out of nineteen events, Ford-powered cars won thirteen and Andretti won the National Championship.

JWA returned to Le Mans in 1969 with its ex-Mirage GT40s and pulled off something that was never expected—a second straight win with the same car, P/1075, that won Le Mans the previous year. Powered by a 305-inch Gurney-Eagle with Webers, drivers Jackie Ickx and Jackie Oliver defied all odds and beat a Porsche 908 by 300 feet to take the fourth straight Ford win. The 1968 and

Mario Andretti on his way to winning the fifty-third Indy 500 in the STP Hawk-Ford powered by the new turbocharged 159-cubic-inch DOHC V-8. Dan Gurney finished second in his Olsonite Eagle with a pushrod 305-inch small-block. *Ford Motor Company*

1969 Le Mans-winning GT40 is still racing. Owner Rob Walton regularly races P/1075 in historic events.

When Bunkie Knudsen joined Ford in early 1968, racing was a priority. Henry Ford II wanted to win at any cost. But the world was changing and suddenly Washington was all over automakers to improve safety and emissions. New rules and regulations, supported by the Department of Transportation, were coming fast and furious. They would seriously affect R&D budgets. Said Bob Irvin, "Knudsen moved in and started doing things his way. He was almost running the company and [some said] had alienated many other top executives, including HF II who did run the company and was obviously threatened."

The man whose name was on the building had the last word!

Winning Le Mans is cause for celebrating, but winning it two years in a row, like JWA did—with the same car—is beyond belief. Ford GT40 P/1075 was driven by Jackie Ickx and Jackie Oliver for the 1969 win. The same car won in 1968, and it is still being raced in historic events. *Ford Motor Company*

Mickey's Mustangs: Assault on the Salt!

During two trips to the Bonneville Salt Flats, Mickey Thompson and Danny Ongais set 295 land speed records in two stock Mustangs.

Henry Ford II's pursuit of world motorsports domination led Mickey Thompson to Wendover, Utah. At the time, it was a town that time forgot along the Utah-Nevada border and home to the Bonneville Salt Flats. That's where you went, and still go, to break American and International land speed records in the United States. Mickey had done his homework and there were hundreds of records that he felt were ripe for the picking. The experienced drag racer and land speed record challenger was correct.

Had Bunkie Knudsen become president of Chrysler instead of Ford in 1968, we would have been at Bonneville watching Mickey Thompson trying to break records in Dodge Charger 500s. He and Bunkie had been friends since Bunkie was general manager of Pontiac and they partnered on Bonneville and drag racing programs. Before pitching a Mustang Bonneville program to Jacque Passino at SVA, it had already been blessed by the boss.

The Bonneville program started in July of 1968 and continued in September after SCTA Speed Week wrapped up in August. I was "on the salt" a couple of days before and after the final record setting runs on Thursday and Friday, September 18 and 19. With me were Fred Mackerodt, a.k.a. Dilbert Farb, *Hi-Performance CARS'* humor editor, and "Torque East" columnist Joe Oldham. Ford was kind enough to supply a small Cessna with a door removed so we could take overhead action photos. The only problem our pilot had was trying to keep up with Mickey, especially when he was driving the red 427!

There are stock cars and there are *stock* cars. The *stock* Mustangs that Thompson and Ongais drove at Bonneville were the subject of the full-page advertisement that later ran in enthusiast magazines: "1969 Mustangs Shatter 295 Flying and Standing Start Speed and Endurance Records!" These cars were as stock as Holman & Moody NASCAR race cars! In fact, they *were* Holman & Moody race cars, built to NASCAR Baby Grand specs.

Charlie Gray Jr. was SVA's Stock Car Racing Coordinator at the time and remembers the three 1968 Mustangs being shipped to Holman & Moody along with 1969 sheet metal: "The end result was beautiful race cars built especially for Bonneville." A career engineer, Gray retired from Ford in 1991. His last responsibility was Quality Programs Manager for North America.

The three red, yellow, and blue fastback Mustangs at Bonneville were constructed like "half-chassis" NASCAR Torinos, with narrowed and shortened 1965 Galaxie snouts forward of the firewall. Rear ends were swapped for 9-inch H&M full-floaters with Hy-Tuf axles and gearing from 2.50 to 3.00. They were six-point "caged" and had the side drip rails fitted flush with the body. During construction, front ends were dropped 1.5 inches from cowl to the tip of the hood to lower wind resistance at high speeds. Each car was assigned a Holman & Moody VIN plate, the same as used on its NASCAR cars. The only surviving plate, HM8-012-S, is from the red Mustang and reveals that it was a 1968 build, the twelfth of a series of cars delivered in not-track-ready condition.

What really mattered was that those Mustangs were "stock" according to USAC/FIA timer and Chief Stewart Joe Petrali and USAC/FIA's chief observer

Mickey Thompson with three half-chassis Holman & Moody '68 Mustangs with 1969 sheet metal, built for record attempts at Bonneville in July and September 1968. Front to back: red 427 tunnel port, yellow 302 tunnel port, and blue 427 tunnel port. The blue Mustang also ran a supercharged 427 engine. *Ford Motor Company*

Louis T. Torres. Interestingly, the 302- and 427-cubic-inch Tunnel Port engines in the Bonneville Mustangs were not available in production Mustangs nor could they be ordered in any Ford vehicle. Yet they were still considered stock under USAC/FIA rules. Petrali and Torres officiated at the land speed record attempts and certified the records—all 295 of them. In 1968, Bonneville was checked off on Henry Ford II's motorsports domination punch list!

While there were three Mustangs built for the record runs, the red 427 and yellow 302 Mustangs were the ones that set the records. The third Mustang, a blue 427, was run with naturally aspirated and supercharged dual-quad engines. It served primarily as a backup and parts car. The red and yellow Mustangs were fitted with special weight jacks so they could be "preloaded" for running a circle course as well as straightaways. The blue Mustang was strictly a straight-line racer.

Even though the red Mustang had more horsepower, the yellow small-block Mustang was the star of the show. Thompson and Ongais drove it for 24 hours straight, setting in excess of 100 Class C (183-305-cubic-inch) records. They averaged 157.663 miles per hour, a full 17 miles per hour faster than Craig Breedlove in his record-holding AMX. They also drove 405 miles farther than Breedlove when he set the record. Covering 3,783 miles on the 10-mile course, Mickey clocked 166 miles per hour on the last lap.

Powering the yellow Mustang was a 435-horsepower, 302-inch Tunnel Port, blueprinted and balanced for endurance, not necessarily maximum horsepower. It redlined at 7,000 rpm. Like the 535-horsepower 427 Tunnel Port engine in the red Mustang, it had dual 780-cfm Holleys with Autolite part numbers, H&M stainless steel headers, deep sump oil pan with NASCAR oil cooler and pump, and custom CD ignition.

Mike McGuire, a Bonneville racer who worked for Thompson in Long Beach, California, during the late 1960s and early 1970s, recalls, "The Mustangs went to Holman-Moody-Stroppe in Long Beach for engines and then to our shop.

For the program, Ford supplied us with a prototype tractor-trailer that had been wind-tunnel-tested. It still had some tuft strips attached to the cab's mirrors, a trick airfoil behind the cab, and small deflectors on the sides. There was no title, registration, or VIN, just a small brass Ford ID tag!"

The red 427 Tunnel Port Mustang broke standing and flying start records, from 25 to 500 miles, in Class B (305 to 488 cubic inches), but it was plagued with running gear problems. In spite of transmission, dual-disc clutch, and rear end failures, Thompson managed to clock some mid-180-mile-per-hour runs. Cars were often pushed out of the pits to keep clutches from being overworked since final gearing was numerically low. The 427 engine redlined at 6,000 rpm.

Unlike the red and yellow Mustangs, the blue race car was more of a hot rod than an endurance racer. The single-seater started off with a 427 Tunnel Port engine from Holman-Moody-Stroppe, then acquired a 20-percent overdriven GMC-supercharged engine.

As it worked out, the supercharged engine was making too much power for the Mustang and, on acceleration, tended to pull itself loose from its mounts. Fritz Voight solved the problem by installing steel chains from the engine's heads to the chassis rails. The blue Mustang was retired and served as a parts car for the red 427 Mustang that, according to Mike McGuire, "ate transmissions and clutches for lunch and dinner!"

McGuire's responsibilities included delivering the vehicles to Bonneville, setting them up on the salt, and taking care of the red 427 Mustang. After Bonneville, he delivered the red and yellow Mustangs to Ford, dropping them off at Dearborn Steel Tubing. They eventually ended up at Holman & Moody.

Once back in Long Beach, the blue car was used to prototype a Boss 429 engine installation. After its completion, Jacque Passino turned the Boss 429 Mustang program over to Kar Kraft, citing in a memo on September 5, 1968, that reached Bunkie Knudsen, "We're not learning anything here because the car is not a stock Mustang."

Brent Hajek owns the blue 427 Bonneville Mustang restored and shown here with chute at Bonneville in 2008. Hajek, restorer Danny Thompson, and Mike McGuire ran the Mustang at Speed Week to celebrate the fortieth anniversary of Mickey Thompson and Danny Ongais setting 295 land speed records. *Hajek Motorsports Museum*

The blue Mustang ended up going back to Long Beach, and the Boss 429 engine was pulled and replaced by the original supercharged 427. It stayed with the Thompson family and, in 2005, was restored by Mickey's son, Danny, at his Ridgeway, Colorado, shop. A dual-quad 427 Tunnel Port engine replaced the supercharged 427 and its hood was fitted with a Boss 429 Mustang scoop to cover the large section that had been cut out for clearance. It was sold to race car collector Brent Hajek for the Hajek Motorsports Museum in Ames, Oklahoma.

In 2008, Danny Thompson, Brent Hajek, and Mike McGuire ran the restored blue Mustang at Bonneville Speed Week to celebrate the fortieth anniversary of Mickey Thompson setting the records.

In talking with Jim Reep, who worked at Holman & Moody from 1978 to 1981 and is a machinist working in the Charlotte area NASCAR community, "The red and yellow cars without engines landed at Holman & Moody and were converted into legal NASCAR Grand American (Baby Grand) racers. Larry Wallace, H&M's cam grinder and a successful half-mile dirt-track racer, was given the red car."

With a black stripe and No. 49 livery, the red car was sponsored by Dover International Speedway and first driven by Wallace, followed by David Pearson and Bobbie Allison. No. 49 was known as the *Rollins Leasing Special*. Mel Joseph of M. L. Joseph Construction purchased the car from Wallace, then wrecked it and converted it into a dirt-track racer. It was parted out in 1970 and all that remains is its H&M ID plate.

Eventually, the yellow Mustang was sold to NASCAR driver Tiny Lund. He painted it red with No. 97 on the doors and roof for NASCAR Grand American

competition. When Lund passed away, his widow, Wanda, donated it to a local vo-tech school. It has long since fallen off the radar screen. All that remains from the Bonneville record runs is the blue 427 Mustang, restored and owned by Brent Hajek. Ford's mission at Bonneville was to bring land speed records back to Dearborn and supply its advertising agency with material for 1969 Mustang high-performance campaigns and dealer promotions. Mission accomplished!

Goodyear contributed special Bonneville tires for the Mustang record runs. Carroll Shelby Enterprises' Goodyear Western States Racing Tire operation supplied on-site support services.

Ford-Cosworth DFV: The Little Engine That Could!

Debuted in 1967, the DFV 3-liter V-8 was the most successful Formula One engine of all time.

Historically, few pure racing engines or race cars ever win the first time out; even fewer keep up the momentum for years. The Ford-Cosworth DFV engine did! It was purpose-developed and built by Mike Costin and Keith Duckworth at Cosworth Engineering for Colin Chapman's Formula One Team Lotus. The engine program was financed and sponsored by Ford and, at its debut in two Lotus 49s at the third race of the 1967 season, won the pole and the race! At the Dutch Grand Prix on June 4, 1967, in Zandvoort, Graham Hill put his DFV-powered Lotus on the pole and teammate Jim Clark won the race. Clark won three more races in 1967, but reliability issues kept him from rising above third in the 1967 Formula One World Drivers' Championship.

From 1968 to 1974—and in 1976, 1978, 1980, 1981, and 1982—Graham Hill, Jackie Stewart (three times), Jochen Rindt, Emerson Fittipaldi (two times), James Hunt, Mario Andretti, Alan Jones, Nelson Piquet, and Keke Rosberg won Formula One Drivers' Championships in cars powered by Ford-Cosworth DFV engines.

Five chassis builders using DFV engines—Lotus (five times), Matra, McLaren, Tyrrell, and Williams (two times)—won ten Constructors' Championships.

Initially, the 2,992cc, four-cam, four-valve V-8 was rated at 405-408 horsepower at 9,000 rpm. With aluminum heads/block and Lucas Mark 1 timed mechanical fuel injection, the 370-pound, 90-degree engine was named DFV because it was double the displacement of the Cosworth FVA four and also had four valves per cylinder.

Over a period of approximately sixteen years, DFV displacement never changed yet horsepower increased to 450 to 470 at 10,000 rpm in 1971 and 475 to 495 horsepower at 10,800 rpm in 1978. In 1981 and 1982 after working with Judd on new camshafts, horsepower jumped to 510 to 535 at 11,300 rpm! In 1983, Formula One engine rules allowed turbocharging and maximum displacement was limited to 1.5 liters.

A dominant force in Formula One as well as CART and Formula 3000, the 1966 Ford-Cosworth DFV was developed after FIA's announcement in 1965, increasing maximum engine size for Formula One in 1966 from 1.5 to 3 liters. Team Lotus' Colin Chapman needed new engines because his supplier, Coventry Climax, would not be developing larger ones. He already had a relationship with both Ford of Britain and Cosworth. Keith Duckworth was a transmission engineer at Lotus before partnering with Mike Costin and forming Cosworth. Chapman contacted them. The only thing missing was financing.

Funding the project was problematic since neither Cosworth nor Lotus could afford a new engine design and development program. Chapman pitched Ford Motor Company and Aston Martin, and neither was interested. However, Ford of Britain was more receptive since its director of public relations, Walter Hayes, already had a relationship with Chapman and Lotus—they had worked together

Celebrating the production of the four hundredth Ford-Cosworth DFV Formula One engine at Cosworth Engineering in 1986. The men behind the program, left to right, were Cosworth's Mike Costin and Keith Duckworth and VP of Ford Motor Company Walter Hayes. *Ford Motor Company*

Above: The first time out, a Ford-Cosworth Lotus 49 driven by Jim Clark won the 1967 Dutch Grand Prix. Another, driven by Graham Hill, took the pole. *Ford Motor Company*

Right: Legend Jim Clark in Gold Leaf Lotus 49 after winning the first race of the 1968 Formula One season: the South African GP at Kyalami. It was his last F1 race before his death at a Formula Two race at Hockenheim, Germany. *Ford Motor Company*

Right: An Iconic black-and-gold John Player Special Lotus, powered by a Ford-Cosworth DFV engine and driven by Emerson Fittipaldi, leaves the pits at the 1972 Italian GP at Monza. "Emmo" won the race, the 1972 Drivers' Championship, and Lotus-Ford Constructors' Championship in 1972. *Ford Motor Company*

on the Lotus-Cortina. Hayes and Ford of Britain engineer Harley Copp put together a racing engine proposal for presentation to Chairman Stanley Gillen. It was approved and passed on for Dearborn approval. Copp, an American engineer working in the United Kingdom, was a racing enthusiast. He had been instrumental in orchestrating the Ford-Pete DePaolo racing relationship in the mid-1950s.

The plan called for two multi-cam, multi-valve race engines; a four-cylinder FVA for Formula Two; and a V-8 DFV for Formula One. The target date for the DFV engine was the start of the 1967 F1 season. However, it was not ready until the third race and Jim Clark won driving a Lotus-Cosworth.

One of the most respected PR executives in the industry, Hayes became VP and, later, vice chairman of Ford of Europe and VP of Ford Motor Company. Hayes was responsible for the Mustang IMSA GTP racing programs. He retired in 1989 and, in 1990, wrote *Henry: A Memoir of Henry Ford II*.

Few engines have impacted the motorsports world like the Ford-Cosworth DFV.

Denny Hulme checks the fit of the new '71 McLaren F1 race car with Ford-Cosworth DFV power, inboard suspension, and bottle-shape body. Ralph Bellamy, left, designed the new car.

CHAPTER 11

1970

The Best of Times, the Worst of Times!

Ford and Lincoln-Mercury offered shoppers more high-performance choices than ever, but by year-end a black cloud hung over Dearborn.

Bob Dylan had nailed it six years earlier with his anthem, "The Times They Are a-Changin'," the title track of his 1964 album. It could have been Ford's 1970 anthem as well. The only thing constant at Ford in 1970 *was* change.

Since the mid-1960s, Senator Abraham Ribicoff's congressional sub-committee hearings on auto safety and emissions had been pounding away at the Big Three. It didn't take long for the tens of millions of dollars Ford spent annually on racing to come under scrutiny. The pressure was on to get Ford to lower its racing profile and increase its investment in safety and emissions R&D.

Then there was the growth of smaller, more economical imports. They were nibbling away at domestic car sales, especially in the youth market that had embraced high-performance Mustangs. Mustang sales decreased by 17,580 units between 1968 and 1969, and model year sales in 1970 would reveal an incredible drop of almost 110,000 cars!

Buying habits had changed dramatically since the muscle car was the darling of the youth market. In order to be more relevant, Ford would have to develop new, smaller, more economical models incorporating the latest safety and emission control features. This would require huge R&D budgets, leaving little to nothing for racing. And the profits from new models, Maverick in 1970

A ground-pounding '70 Boss 429 Mustang on the Dearborn Proving Ground road course. Driving is Ford PR manager Paul Preuss, whom we asked to drive for photos. This photo was shot in summer 1969 during the Long Lead Press Preview.

Ford's entry in the 1970 Supercar Sweepstakes: a Torino Cobra with standard 429 engine rated at 360 horsepower and Hurst-shifted four-speed. The optional engine was the Cobra Jet Ram Air package with Drag Pack rated at 370 horsepower.

Above: This King Cobra Torino with Boss 429 engine is one of two or three prototypes designed by Larry Shinoda and his team at Ford Design to compete with Mopar Aero cars in NASCAR and built at Kar Kraft but never raced. Photos exist of a yellow, red, and a white one, but one of those could have been a clay mockup. Bud Moore purchased two complete King Cobras from Ford in 1971 for $1,200. *RK Motors, Charlotte*

Left: Bud Moore's Boss 302 Mustangs with 475-horsepower engines, originally driven by George Follmer and Parnelli Jones, shot at Laguna Seca Historics. They won the Trans-Am series championship for Ford. Both Mustangs have been restored to how they were originally raced. *M. M. "Mike" Matune Jr.*

I presented the Top Performance Car of the Year award to Matt McLaughlin, general manager of Lincoln-Mercury, right. He was all smiles when this photo was shot in January 1970. He was later promoted to vice president of sales for the corporation, and on November 20, he was much more somber when announcing Ford's exit from racing.

The Mercury 429 Spoiler was named *Hi-Performance CARS* Top Performance Car of the Year and was featured on the cover of the April 1970 issue. Artist Gary Gretter penned the cover illustration.

and Pinto in 1971, would be considerably less than those generated by topline Mustangs and midsize models.

Contributing to Ford's problem was its market share. Between 1962 and 1969, it had stagnated at approximately 29 percent, even though tens of millions of dollars and dedicated R&D resources kept Fords in winners' circles and its drivers on podiums.

Henry Ford II, recipient of the 1969 Presidential Medal of Freedom from Lyndon Johnson, was under pressure. Late in 1969, he committed resources to support environmental issues and allocated 18 million dollars for cleaning up smokestack emissions at Ford plants. Two months later, he announced massive cuts of over 70 percent in 1970 racing budgets. And that was only the beginning.

By the end of 1970, Ford would be out of racing. On November 20, 1970, Matt McLaughlin, vice president, sales group, announced Ford's withdrawal from all competitive motorsports events. There was an exception, however. There would be limited support of divisional and dealer-related drag racing and off-road events.

Drag racing programs had been extremely cost-effective in creating high profiles for Ford and Mercury brands that gave dealers marketing opportunities. Ford continued its touring Performance Car Clinics in 1970 and increased production of high-performance parts manuals and brochures.

In late 1969, Dick Brannan built a 1970 Maverick Pro Stock powered by a Boss 429 engine. Even though he had left Ford as an employee, he returned later in 1969 as a consultant and continued as a member of the Ford Drag Team until 1972. At the major Pro Stock event of 1970 at Twin City Drag Strip in Oldsmar, Florida, Brannan beat Arlen Vanke to win the Pro Stock Championship. He ran 142-plus miles per hour in 10.10 seconds.

Top East Coast Ford racer Al Joniec built a Pro Stock '70 Maverick powered by a Boss 429 engine in late 1969 and campaigned it under the Rice-Holman Ford banner as in previous years. Dick Brannan built one as well. This shot was taken at Cecil County. *Bob McClurg Photography*

The winged and scooped Cougar Eliminator returned for 1970 in bright colors and with Boss 302, 351, and 428 CJ and Ram Air motors. This shot was taken on the high-speed oval at Dearborn Proving Ground during testing. *Ford Motor Company*

Mustang styling was refreshed for 1970 as was its powertrain option menu. The top image model was the Mach 1 SportsRoof, available with engines ranging from a standard 351 to optional 351/300 four-barrel, 428/335 Cobra Jet, and 428/335 Cobra Jet Ram Air. High-performance 351 engines received canted-valve "Cleveland" heads. Boss 302 and Boss 429 Mustangs were carried over, with the new Boss 429 receiving a solid-lifter valvetrain with the same 375-horsepower rating. Mustangs optioned with 428 engines could also be ordered with optional Drag Packs with either 3.91 gears with Traction-Lok or 4.30 gears with Detroit Locker differentials. Drag Pack engines were also equipped with engine oil coolers and upgraded lower end components.

Ford's big news was in the midsize model lineup, known in the day as supercars. A special Torino Cobra with matte black hood, shaker scoop, and standard 429 Cobra V-8 rated at 360 horsepower was Ford's street version of the H&M Cobra that David Pearson was racing. For 1970, the SportsRoof Cobra had a 1.9-inch wider tread, 1.2-inch lower roofline, and a radical 57.5-degree windshield slope angle—an increase of 6 degrees over the previous year. It could be optioned with Super Cobra Jet 429/370 with Drag Pack gear options, oil cooler, 780-cfm Holley quad, and upgraded lower end.

When we were evaluating new models for *Hi-Performance CARS'* "Top Performance Car of the Year" honors, the Mercury 429 CJ Spoiler impressed us the most for all-around performance. It had an abundance of comfort and convenience features along with a roomy, upscale interior. It delivered true supercar performance and road-holding qualities, and we loved

its new, distinctive look, including rear spoiler. Lincoln-Mercury carried its 1969½ Cougar Eliminator over for 1970 with choice of Boss 302, 351, and 428 CJ powerplants.

What had started four years earlier as an extra class for amateur racers blossomed into one of SCCA's top moneymakers. By 1970, Trans-Am attracted big budgets from carmakers eager to showcase pony cars. Ford, Chevrolet, Dodge, Plymouth, and even American Motors battled for supremacy on twisty road courses.

For 1970, the Automobile Competition Committee of the US (ACCUS) standardized rules for SCCA Trans-Am and NASCAR GT racing so that a car could be legal for both sanctioning bodies. Suspensions could always be changed when Trans-Am cars ran on NASCAR's Super Speedways.

While displacement was still restricted to a maximum of 305 cubic inches, rules were relaxed regarding how displacement was achieved. No longer would a legal engine have to maintain its production bore and stroke. This gave Dodge and Plymouth an opportunity to run their 340-inch engine, destroked to achieve 305 cubic inches. In 1969, NASCAR had permitted destroked engines for the GT Baby Grand Circuit.

Engine rules for 1970 also permitted engines to be bored to meet 305-inch specs, allowing American Motors to run Javelins with 290-cubic-inch engines. Rules regarding carburetion were also changed for 1970. The new standard was a single four-barrel, which made it a little easier for nonfactory racers to compete. In 1969, Trans-Am Mustangs used expensive dual four-barrel manifolds with Holley Dominator carbs.

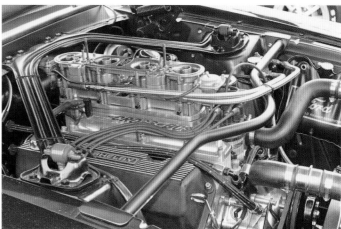

Above: Autolite came up with the Cross Boss intake system with inline four-barrel carbs for racing applications and marketed complete packages for Boss 302 Trans-Am engines and, with an adapter plate, 351 Cleveland motors. Carbs were available with two different throttle-bore dimensions for 850 and 1,425 cfm capacity. There were very few of these built, starting March 1970, and they were initially supplied to factory racers. *M. M. "Mike" Matune Jr.*

Left: A Boss 302 Mustang with new graphics, wing, and backlight louvers at Englishtown Raceway Park. While not announced, some Boss 302s were built with the Drag Pack option, often included when the 4.30 Detroit Locker rear was ordered. Also included was a vertical oil cooler in front of the radiator.

A. J. Foyt won the first race of the 1970 NASCAR season, the 500-miler at Riverside Raceway. He was driving a Jack Bowsher '70 Torino Cobra with new lowered roofline and steeply sloped windshield. Most of the Ford racers campaigned leftover '69 models as racing budgets were severely cut.

For 1970, all teams had to use single four-barrel induction. Autolite introduced its new radical inline Cross-Boss carburetor that, via adapter plates, could be used for single and dual setups. The standard, however, was a single Dominator like the one used on Ford Boss 429 NASCAR engines, flowing over 1,000 cfm. Boss 302 horsepower was still around 475.

Bud Moore Engineering was now Ford's only representative in Trans-Am racing. Moore campaigned three Boss 302 Mustangs—two 1970 models and one reskinned 1969 race car—initially prepared by Kar Kraft and driven primarily by George Follmer and Parnelli Jones. He also still had his leftover 1969 Mustangs and received Shelby's 1969 Boss 302 Trans-Am Mustangs. All were converted to look like 1970 models.

Even with restrictive budgets and the most competitive field since Trans-Am started, Bud Moore's Mustangs outperformed the field. American Motors had Roger Penske and Mark Donahue. Shelby's Phil Remington built Plymouth Barracudas for Dan Gurney's All-American Racers. Keith Black engines powered the Dodge Challenger that Sam Posey drove. After Penske defected to AMC, Chevy fielded a team of Camaros driven by Vic Elford, Jim Hall, Ed Leslie, and Milt Minter.

The eleven-race 1970 series championship went to Ford. It was their third Manufacturers' Championship and Parnelli Jones was named 1970 Trans-Am Champion. According to vintage Mustang Trans-Am enthusiast Mike Durham, "The winningest car was Parnelli's 1969–1970 season racer because it won a lot of races in both seasons, first as a red/black 1969 Mustang and then updated as a School Bus Yellow 1970 Mustang."

Kar Kraft constructed a 1970 Mustang T/A mule with a race engine that became the subject of two how-to books sold by Ford dealers: *Boss 302 Engine Modification* for strip/track and *Boss 302 Chassis Modification*. The purpose was to disseminate proven chassis modification and engine building information to enthusiasts who wanted to field Mustangs for SCCA Trans-Am/Group 2 and drag racing competition.

Race winner Parnelli Jones pulls in for a pit stop during Trans-Am at Laguna Seca on April 19, 1970. Jones and George Follmer, in Bud Moore Boss 302 Mustangs, won six of eleven races in SCCA T/A Series, and Parnelli won the Driver's Championship. Ford won its third Manufacturers' Championship in 1970. Parnelli drove No. 15, VIN 212777, in three of his five victories. *Ford Motor Company*

The Boss Mustang mule, VIN 137143, was ordered with DSO #7842 and sold to Ford Motor Company on November 23, 1969. Painted Grabber Orange, the one-of-one Mustang has survived, has HSR and VSCDC log books, and been updated for safety and performance.

Stock car racing represented a huge investment that actually paid off in sales. Dealers sold on Monday what were full-size and then midsize consumer versions of Fords and Mercurys that won on superspeedways on Sunday.

By cutting budgets, NASCAR teams could not field as many cars. Without sponsorship money, many racers competed only in important events with large purses. Many of the winning Fords and Mercs were leftover 1969 models. In the opening race of the 1970 season, A. J. Foyt took the Riverside 500 in a Jack Bowsher 1970 Ford. The only other win for a 1970 Ford was at the Southeastern 500 at Bristol. Donnie Allison won the race in a Banjo Matthews' Boss 429 Talladega.

Holman & Moody campaigned David Pearson's Boss 429 Ford on a limited schedule and built engines for the Woods Brothers. They also ground cams for other NASCAR teams. After the 1970 season and because of Ford's racing budget cutbacks, Holman & Moody was on its own.

Ford continued winning at the Indy 500. Al Unser Sr. dominated the fifty-fourth annual Brickyard classic, winning the Pole, leading for 190 laps, and taking the checkered flag. He joined his brother, Bobby, as the first duo of brothers to win the 500. It was the first of what would be his incredible four Indy 500 wins. Unser won the race in Parnelli Jones' Vels Johnny Lightning Lola-Ford. He qualified for the pole at 170.22 miles per hour and averaged 155.749 miles per hour for 500 miles. Mark Donahue finished second in Roger Penske's Lola-Ford.

For the first time, all thirty-three cars on the starting grid were turbocharged and Ford 159-inch, DOHC V-8s powered fifteen. Some Ford engines were producing 850 horsepower at 8,500 rpm with 70 to 80 inches of boost!

Even though Ford had revolutionized racing at the Brickyard, its Indy engine program had two strikes against it. The original DOHC engine cost approximately $30,000 to produce and each one sold represented a loss of close to $15,000! While it created a halo for the Ford brand, dealers were not selling Indy race cars.

With racing budgets slashed for the 1970 season and Ford withdrawing from racing almost entirely by the end of the year, the four-cam Indy engine program was killed and all assets given to A. J. Foyt. Development of the original naturally aspirated engine, and the downsized and boosted 159-inch replacement, represented an investment of close to $10 million. Once Foyt started producing engines, cam covers and intake manifolds were cast with "Foyt" logos.

Prior to Henry Ford II pulling the plug on racing, Ford Division chief Lee Iacocca requested internal and racing contractor audits. They were executed by Harold "Red" Poling, tenacious controller of the Product Development Group, who would become president of Ford in 1985 and Chairman/CEO in 1990.

Months of audits revealed financial abuses at its racing contractors, Special Vehicles group and Kar Kraft, its captive skunk works. Iacocca directed Poling to make every supplier account for expenses back to their first contracts and down to the penny. Those audits also exposed Ford employees who had defrauded the company. It was not a pretty picture.

Exactly what drove the audits was never clear. One strong rumor, confirmed by a number of retired Ford managers and a racing contractor, involved a customized Torino. Iacocca was incensed to discover a Candy Apple Red 1970 Torino that was red-flagged. It was in company service and used for personal transportation but had been modified and painted at Kar Kraft, then invoiced at approximately $20,000!

At a company the size of Ford involved in racing and whose chairman and CEO wanted to win at any cost, financial abuses were almost to be expected—but not at the level that was discovered. Misconduct ranged from minor, like the lack of documentation for the gas tank fill-up of a friend's truck that towed a Ford-owned race car when the supplier's truck broke down, to an incredible amount of Ford engines and parts that could not be accounted for.

What angered top brass the most was the exposure of Ford employees who had gamed the system. Results were never released publicly. In talking with people who were there at the time, I discovered some details. Abuses included paving an executive's driveway, personal use of a supplier's airplane, and use of a fast ski boat delivered each summer to an executive's lakefront cottage. Some of those items were billed directly to Ford, others buried in suppliers' books. Supplier contracts would be cancelled and, by year-end, Ford severed its relationship with Kar Kraft. There were no criminal prosecutions.

All Ford Motor Company racing and high-performance engine development projects in 1970 were under the control of Jacque Passino's expanded Special Vehicles organization, so the buck stopped at his office. Approximately one hundred people reported to Passino. The man who headed racing activities and whose guidance turned Henry Ford II's dream of International motorsports domination into reality fell on his sword and abruptly resigned just days before Thanksgiving of 1970. He built his career on racing successes over fourteen years, and still believed that racing improved the breed and was beneficial to the development of cars.

Once cleared of any wrongdoings, Red Poling allowed Special Vehicles' personnel to relocate within the company and appointed SVA chief engineer Hank "Horsepower" Gregorich to head a smaller Special Vehicles organization. Charlie Gray became planning manager and some engineers transferred to the Emissions Labs.

Exact details of what happened during the internal and external audits and the shutdown of Kar Kraft were kept as quiet as possible. Most of the business and automotive media, myself included, were more concerned with how the industry would handle new emissions and safety regulations, the future of performance cars, and the growth of import brands. In December 1970, Lee Iacocca was name president, a position he would hold until July 1978 when, after clashing with Henry Ford II, he was fired!

Al Unser Sr. won his first of four Indy 500s in the No. 2 Lola-Ford campaigned by Parnelli Jones' Vels Johnny Lightning Team. He won the pole and the race in the turbocharged Ford DOHC racecar. Mark Donahue finished second in Roger Penske's Lola-Ford. *Ford Motor Company*

SVA and Kar Kraft: Inside Ford's Skunk Works!

With top race-car builders and drivers, a captive contractor, and unlimited support from its chairman and CEO, Ford's racing operation reflected the uncompromised power of a singular vision—winning. Then in 1970 it all unraveled.

Almost three years before Henry Ford III rejected the AMA racing ban in 1962, Don Frey, a Ford Division executive engineer attached to Product Planning, worked behind the scenes to create a group of like-minded engineers and marketers to support racing activities. His team included Dave Evans, John Cowley, Don Sullivan, and Bill Innes, head of Engine & Foundry. With Lee Iacocca's support, Jacque Passino took over Special Events and became more involved in racing.

Together they created a backdoor access to engines and racing parts, and opened this access to suppliers like Holman & Moody. It was the birth of the Performance and Economy Group at Ford Product Engineering.

This small, stealthy team became visible once Ford started racing in 1962. Dave Evans hired a young Ford engineer Charlie Gray Jr. to coordinate drag-racing activities. Not long after, drag-racing engineer Dick Brannan came aboard and reported to Gray.

By 1964, Leo Beebe was named Special Vehicles manager and Passino became his assistant. John Cowley, Dave Evans, and Ray Geddes coordinated stock car, Indy 500, and Le Mans racing. Over time, a variety of people would sit in the SVA manager's seat: Leo Beebe, John Cowley, Frank Zimmerman, Jacque Passino, Hank Gregorich, and Charlie Gray. Gray moved from drag racing to stock car racing in 1966 and coordinated activities until the end of Ford's racing commitments in 1970.

The year 1964 was pivotal for Special Vehicles Activity. Roy Lunn, chief engineer of Ford Advanced Vehicle Development, moved his GT40 operation in Slough, England, to Dearborn. It came under the auspices of SVA. Once in the

Roy Lunn, left, and Fran Hernandez celebrate Boss 429 Mustang *Job-#1* at Kar Kraft Brighton on January 15, 1969. At this time, Lunn was Kar Kraft's VP of engineering; Hernandez worked for SVA. *Ford Motor Company*

United States, Lunn searched for the right facility to house the project and team. That's when he met Nick Hartman, a friend of GT40 engineer Chuck Mountain and a toolmaker and machine shop owner.

After sitting down with Lunn and his senior engineers Len Bailey, Ed Hull, and Chuck Mountain, Hartman struck a deal to bring the GT40 team into his facility in Dearborn. They decided to name the operation Kar Kraft and it was incorporated on October 5, 1964.

Lunn's GT40 program was Kar Kraft's first major project and paved the way for it to become Ford's skunk works. The actual first assignment was to develop a 427 powertrain and a replacement for the GT40's failure-prone transaxle. This resulted in the Mark IIs that finished one-two-three at Le Mans in 1966.

During the 1960s, just about every domestic carmaker was racing and had contracts with outside racing and engineering shops. Those shops often had dynamometer cells and offered specialized services for both racing and developing future products. And almost all of them catered to multiple clients. But Ford was different. It had Kar Kraft.

Ford's unique Kar Kraft relationship was unlike that of any in the industry. Once up to speed, Kar Kraft offered varied services: design, product development, low-volume manufacturing, race-car building, racing support, and show-car development. It had no other clients, sold a multitude of services, and leased space to Ford for special projects. Kar Kraft and Ford employees staffed it. By the late 1960s, Kar Kraft operations were spread between six buildings, all within reasonable distance of Ford corporate and division offices, manufacturing/assembly plants, and engineering and design centers. As Ford Special Vehicles responsibilities expanded, so did Kar Kraft.

SVA chief Jacque Passino, left, with Marty Schorr at the presentation of *Hi-Performance CARS* magazine's Top Performance Car of the Year for the '67 Mustang 390. Shot in his office at Ford world headquarters.

Larry Shinoda, left, standing, with his design team and the aerodynamic '70 King Cobra prototype, built by Kar Kraft. It was to be Ford's answer to Plymouth's Superbird, but it never got beyond handcrafted prototypes and track testing. *Ford Motor Company*

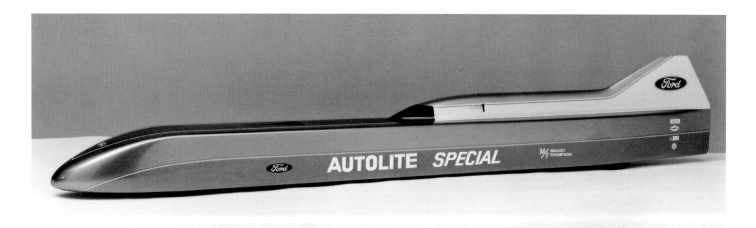

Kar Kraft and SVA's Advanced Concepts Engineering group provided vehicle packaging, aerodynamic design engineering, and partial assembly services for Mickey Thompson's 30-foot land speed record-attempt streamliner. Power came from a pair of 427 SOHC engines generating 2,070 horsepower. *Fran Hernandez Collection*

Larry Parker started his automotive career as an Engineering co-op student at Ford in 1967. "I had great assignments in 1968 through 1970, working for, and with, Ford's top performance and competition engine development engineers."

Parker started working with Advanced Powertrain Research and Mustang and Cougar Vehicle Development, then was assigned to Kar Kraft. From January to July of 1970, he was involved with Boss 429 Mustang homologation, NASCAR engine failure analysis, and 1971 Mustang Boss 351 engine development. He left Ford as an engine engineer in 1984 to pursue industry opportunities and retired as president of Roush Performance Products in 2004. Today, he is an active road racer.

"Working at Kar Kraft was fun and incredibly rewarding, like playing in a gigantic sandbox with other performance-enthusiast engineers and draftsmen," Parker said. "Good thing Ford never discovered that I would have shown up for work every day whether they paid me or not!"

In Kar Kraft, Special Vehicles had a secure, captive organization. According to a 1969–1970 Ford internal presentation, "Kar Kraft was contracted solely to Ford Motor Company and directly responsible to Special Vehicles."

The presentation emphasized that Special Vehicles had "the ability to engineer, build, develop, test, and manufacture a complete vehicle, or any system or components thereof," and also that it was "structured to generate complete product proposals and coordinate total programs with respect to manufacturing, market, and sales."

In 1967, SVA was reorganized with approximately fifty people and divided into four departments reporting to Jacque Passino. John Cowley was Stock Vehicles manager with Homer Perry responsible for Le Mans, Shelby American, and H&M; Charlie Gray coordinating stock car racing; and Chuck Foulger handling drag racing.

Roy Lunn managed Advanced Concepts responsible for Le Mans race cars and Ray Geddes headed GT and Sports Cars, coordinating Shelby American, J. W. Engineering, and Mark III GT40 and Mirage sports-prototype racer activities. Don Wahrman managed Special Events. He was responsible for Indy 500 engine sales and the Mobil Economy Run.

Some of Special Vehicles/Kar Kraft projects included the Boss 429 Mustang, Bill Holbrook's Talladega and Cyclone Spoiler II, Trans-Am race cars, Land-Speed Record cars, Mark II and Mark IV GT40s, Mach 2 Mustangs, presidential

When Kar Kraft locked out Ford on November 16, 1970, one of the Ford properties held hostage was the new Lincoln limo under construction for President Nixon. Once Ford was let in, Fran Hernandez moved it back to Ford for completion. It was then shipped to Hess & Eisenhardt for armoring. *Ford Motor Company*

Designed by Larry Shinoda, the second variant of the "Mach 2" Concept was this slick sports car based on a Pantera platform with a midship-mounted 351 Ford. Shinoda was fired after Bunkie Knudsen and the project died as Lincoln-Mercury announced plans to sell the Pantera in 1971. *Ford Motor Company*

Roy Lunn developed a prototype midship-mounted big-block engine conversion of a '69 Mustang. It was tagged as LID (Low Investment Driveline) and used a 429 engine and transmission facing rearward with a custom 180-degree gearset and driveshaft mating to a standard rear end. A single prototype was built as a possible competitor to the hyped 1971–1972 mid-engined Corvette. Neither actually happened. *Ford Motor Company*

This 1970 photo shows the drafting room of Kar Kraft's 10,000-square-foot Haggerty Road building. Shown are engine engineers Larry Parker, at rear adjacent to secretary, and Denny Wu, opposite. Wu was a brilliant engineer and race-engine tuner, responsible for the 1970 Boss 302 engine improvements. *Ford Motor Company*

limos, midengine Mustang concepts, 1971 Mustang concept prototype, engine packaging services, publication of "how-to" manuals, snowmobile dragster, and off-road Broncos. Kar Kraft was an extension of Ford Motor Company.

In April of 1969, Jacque Passino, now special vehicles manager for the Product Development Group, was assigned additional responsibility for the design and development of all Ford high-performance engines and equipment. According to a Ford press release dated February 15, 1970: "Under the new Special Vehicles alignment, Mr. Passino directs a special engines department and product engineering office in addition to his past duties."

Larry Parker worked with Mose Nowland at Kar Kraft as an engine engineer in 1970 on the Boss 429 Mustang and '71 Mustang Boss 351 projects. He went on to become president of Roush Performance Products. Now retired, he actively races a V-8-powered Brunton Stalker, a modern tribute to the Lotus Seven.

Now with approximately one hundred employees, the new Special Vehicles operation was reorganized again with Henry Gregorich as chief engineer, John Cowley as performance events manager, Fran Hernandez managing sports car teams including SCCA Trans-Am, Charlie Gray heading stock car racing, and Emil Loeffler managing drag racing. Within a year or so, Special Vehicles had doubled in size, scope, and power.

Roy Lunn was noticeably missing from the new Special Vehicles roster. He had left Ford during the first week of January of 1969 to take the position of vice president of engineering at Kar Kraft. "I saw the handwriting on the wall," said Lunn during an interview in 2015. "The future for me at Ford would not include designing and engineering exciting vehicles or high-performance projects. I had the opportunity to go to Kar Kraft and I took it. My plan was to change Kar Kraft from a single-client contractor into a unique company offering specialty services to a variety of domestic and import manufacturers. I was successful in bringing Kar Kraft its second client, BMW."

Lunn could not have foreseen all that would be happening after he left Ford—massive racing budget cuts and financial audits that would find abuses at racing contractors and Special Vehicles that would eventually end the Ford/Kar Kraft relationship. By the time this happened, Lunn had been approached and accepted the position at American Motors of director of engineering at Jeep. He left Kar Kraft for AMC in 1971 and later was promoted to AMC VP of Engineering. He kept his position at Jeep and formed, as president, Renault Jeep Sport which ran AMC and Renault racing in the United States. Lunn retired in 1985 and then came back to take the VP Engineering position at AM General division of AMC to sort out the HMMWV "Humvee" for sale to the US Army. He retired again in 1987.

When Mose Nowland left his home on Monday morning, November 16, 1970, to go to work, he couldn't possibly have imagined how his day would unfold. He was working in leased space in Kar Kraft's Haggerty Road building in East Dearborn. A veteran Ford engine builder who had been involved in the testing and tuning of the 427 NASCAR and Le Mans engines and DOHC Indy racing engines, Nowland was working with Dick Ronzi's group on Boss 302 and 429 race engines. He remembers exactly what happened that day: "I was the first to arrive, around 6:00 a.m., and discovered that my door keys no longer worked. Initially I thought that kids had vandalized the locks. I tried everything and couldn't get in. When I noticed a brand-new, shiny tumbler in the lock, I knew something was really wrong. I hopped the fence to check the rear door and it was the same. We were locked out!"

Nowland continued, "My employees started arriving and so did a Ford security guy. He instructed me to send my men home, then go home myself and wait for a call from one of our bosses, Joe Macura. Joe had also been working at a Kar Kraft building and was locked out. We met a couple of days later and that's when I learned that Ford was withdrawing from racing."

Over the next week or two, Nowland and others got access to Kar Kraft to remove Ford machinery and inventory. What was rarely discussed at the time, and for years to come, was that changing the locks not only kept Ford personnel out, but also held hostage important Ford property, including President Nixon's new stretch limo that was being worked on at Kar Kraft.

Fran Hernandez, SVA's manufacturing liaison to Kar Kraft and coordinator of 1970 Trans-Am racing, moved the limo to the basement at Ford Product Development where it was positioned on a surface plate. It was later moved to Ford's Bohle building where Hernandez, Nowland, and others finished the job before shipping it to Hess & Eisenhardt for armoring. Hernandez continued in supervisory positions at Ford, including presidential limo projects from 1985 to 1988. He retired in 1992 and returned to Ford as a consultant for two more years.

I interviewed the Kar Kraft executive responsible for changing the locks: "We changed the locks because Ford stopped paying our invoices." What he may or may not have known was that Kar Kraft's audits had turned up major financial abuses and Ford was sending in people on Monday to do a physical inventory. And, yes, Ford had stopped paying invoices. After Special Vehicles audits, Jacque Passino resigned. Chuck Mountain, who in 1964 worked for Roy Lunn on the GT40 program and made the Kar Kraft connection, left to take an equity position at Kar Kraft. Henry Gregorich was named director.

Charlie Gray wrapped up all stock car racing business and stayed with what he described as "what was left of Special Vehicles." He added, "I became the planning manager and worked on developing a program for selling performance parts. After a few months, Henry left to become chief engineer of chassis. Special Vehicles was scaled down to department size and I became its manager. Over time, Special Vehicle responsibilities were absorbed into other departments and then disappeared. I moved on to special engines manager and later became advanced large car design manager in the research department."

No longer having Ford's "anchor," Kar Kraft drifted in a sea of controversy before downsizing and completely shutting down. The corporation was dissolved on May 15, 1976. In 1980, Walter Hayes and Michael Kranefuss, with support from Ford executive VP Red Poling, started Special Vehicle Operations, or SVO, racing Mustangs in SCCA Trans-Am and IMSA GT.

A lineup of Boss 429 engines from Ford's Lima, Ohio, plant, awaiting installation in Mustangs at Kar Kraft Brighton. Kar Kraft had the ability to prototype, develop, test, and manufacture limited-production street-legal cars. *Ford Motor Company*

CHAPTER 12

1971

Get 'Em While They're Hot!

It was the first and last year for Boss 351 and 429 CJ/SCJ Mustangs, and the last year for the Torino Cobra, Cyclone Spoiler, and high-compression engines.

Ford's 1971 lineup was revealed to the media at the Dearborn Proving Ground in June of 1970. The Boss 351 Mustang had a separate introduction later in the year at Orange County International Raceway.

Crosstown rival General Motors took the high road for 1971 and lowered compression ratios of engines to run on low-lead and no-lead fuels. Ford stayed the course. Boss 351 and 429 CJ/SCJ engines, with compression ratios averaging over-11:1, required high-octane fuel. Those engines and high-compression ratios would all go away by the time 1972 Fords were introduced.

The Boss 351 Mustang was a late entry in the 1971 lineup, shown to media and the public in November 1970. It turned out to be a one-year-only model; fastback treatment was extreme. Just 1,806 were produced, delivering big-block performance from a superhot small-block. *Ford Motor Company*

Left: Ford prepared the public for new 1971 SportsRoof fastback treatment, first shown on the 1970 Milano Concept that featured Shelby Mustang front-end styling cues. It was a big hit at auto shows. *Ford Motor Company*

Below: *CARS* testers in a Boss 351 Mustang and a 429 CJ Cobra come off the line. A stock small-block Boss 351 Mustang could run 14.10s at over 100 miles per hour, faster than the 429 CJ Cobra and as quick as the 429 CJ Mustang!

Dick Brannan, consultant to Special Vehicles, was one of the last drag racers to be factory supported. This shot of Brannan coming off the line in his Pro Stock Boss 429 Maverick was taken in 1971. In 1972, he ran a Pinto Pro Stock with 351 power, ending Ford sponsorship. *Dick Brannan Collection*

Dan Gurney with the iconic Olsonite Eagle and Gurney-Eagle Conversion kit with Weslake-designed alloy heads for 289-351 small-block Fords. Marketed by Crankshaft Company, the basic four-barrel kit added 75 horsepower and cost under $1,000 in 1971.

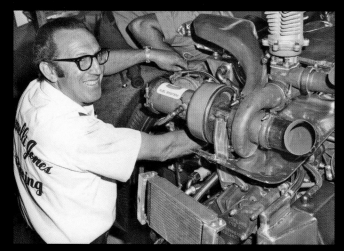

Legendary Indy racing mechanic George Bignotti sets up a turbocharged Ford Model 161 DOHC engine in Parnelli Jones' Lola-Ford. Al Unser Sr. drove it in 1971 for his second win in a row. The engine has unique Bendix fuel injection, developed from an aircraft unit.

Jackie Stewart copped the 1971 Formula One Drivers' Championship driving the Tyrrell-Ford powered by a Ford-Cosworth 3.0 DFV engine. Of eleven races in the series, Ford-Cosworth race cars won seven. Ford of Britain's racing budget was not cut back after Ford withdrew from racing in the United States.

The big news for 1971 was a restyled Mustang: longer, wider, lower, and, unfortunately, heavier. Over six model years, the Mustang gained approximately 500 pounds due to restyling and government-mandated safety updates, including door beams for side impact protection.

While the 1971 Mustang grew by 2 inches, wheelbase increased by 1 inch, width increased by almost 2.5 inches, and front tread width increased by 3 inches, the new Mustang, especially the Boss 351 and Mach I SportsRoof, retained its pony car sex appeal. Fastback SportsRoof models had windshields slanted at a 60-degree angle with slope increased 5.5 degrees. The almost flat backlight offered minimal driver visibility, but made the Mustang look even longer, lower, and wider.

By spreading the front spring towers 3 inches further apart, the new Mustang was able to handle the big 429 CJ and SCJ Drag Pack engines, rated at 370 horsepower at 5,400 rpm and 375 horsepower at 5,600 rpm, respectively. These engines were part of the "385 family" consisting of the Boss 429, 429 Thunder Jet, 429 CJ and SCJ, and 460. The 429s replaced the previous big-block 428 Cobra Jet and offered lightweight, thin-wall-cast, skirtless blocks and round-port heads with canted valves. They were available in Mustang, Cougar, Torino Cobra, and Cyclone Spoiler models.

Although there was just a 5-horsepower difference between the CJ and SCJ Drag Pack engines, the actual differences were considerable. The SCJ engine came with four-bolt mains, solid-lifter valvetrain, forged 11.3:1 pistons, beefier rods, and an aluminum intake manifold with a 780-cfm Holley four-barrel. Induction chores on the hydraulic-lifter CJ engine were handled by a spread-bore 760-cfm Rochester Quadra-Jet on a cast-iron manifold. SCJ Drag Pack Mustangs could be ordered with 3.91 Traction-Lok or 4.11 Detroit Locker gearing, but no automatic transmission. J-code models came with functional Ram Air.

The Mach 1 and Boss 351 Mustangs were not ready when 1971 models were introduced. The Mach 1 had a flat-black, twin-scoop Ram Air hood; blacked out grille; color-keyed urethane front bumper. The short-lived, unique Boss 351 SportsRoof Mustang came even later to the party. Ford had a special press preview for the Boss 351 during the first week of November 1970 at Orange County International Raceway.

I assigned Fred Freel to cover the event, and his story "The Boss Beat Goes On!" ran in the March 1971 issue of *Hi-Performance CARS*. Available only with four-speed, Freel track-tested two Boss 351 Mustangs, one with 3.91 Traction-Lok and the other with 4.11 Detroit Locker rear. Of three passes in each car, his best time in the 3.91 car was 103.21 miles per hour in 14.02 seconds; the 4.11 car ran 102.38 miles per hour in 14.12 seconds. Boss 351 Mustangs came with rev-limiters set at 6,150 rpm.

The subheadline for the story was, "Avoid the last minute rush and check out the Boss 351 Hoss while they are still being built." I had a feeling that the Boss 351 Mustang would never survive Washington's onslaught of emission laws that were strangling high-performance engines. Ford sold 1,806 Boss 351 Mustangs.

New for 1971, the Boss 351, sometimes referenced as the 351 HO, was unique and didn't share much with the available 351 Windsor. Fitted with Cleveland canted-valve heads, similar to those on used the Boss 302, the R-code engine utilized a special four-bolt main bearing block and its heads had polyangle combustion chambers. It also featured a 0.467-to-0.477-inch-lift solid cam and valvetrain, 11.7:1 forged pistons, and an aluminum intake manifold with a 750-cfm Autolite spread-bore carb. The all-new engine generated 330 horsepower at 5,800 rpm and 380 pounds-feet of torque at 3,400 rpm. The Boss 351 was lighter than a 429 CJ model, cheaper to insure, and just as fast! Ford sales were down for the 1971 model year and Mustang numbers dropped off by 41,049 units for a total of 149,678 sold. Between 1969 and 1970, they were off by approximately 100,000 units.

Ford had the right stuff for the supercar marketplace but the marketplace had shrunk. The Torino Cobra and Cyclone Spoiler were carried over with new trim and more weight. You could order either with 370-horsepower 429 CJ, four-speed, or automatic and Traction-Lok gearing. These were more road cars than drag cars, but delivered more solid performance than most of their competitors.

Dan Gurney developed Eagle conversion kits for 289-302 and 351 Ford engines. The kits were announced at the SEMA Show and marketed by Crankshaft Company in Los Angeles. Gurney-Eagle Kits were available with single four-barrel manifold, Webers, or direct-port injection for both street and track use. The basic street kit added 75 horsepower and, in 1971, retailed for $995!

Gurney-Eagle conversions included Alcoa aluminum heads with shallow combustion chambers and $2\frac{1}{32}$-inch intake and $1\frac{5}{8}$-inch exhaust valves, cast by Airplane and Motor Foundry. Kits came with valvetrain assembly, magnesium valve covers and valley cover, external water distribution tubes, and hi-rise aluminum intake manifold. Originally designed by Harry Weslake for Gurney, the heads had trademark heart-shaped combustion chambers and, in race form, accepted Webers or injection bolted directly to the heads. The intake ports allowed for a short, straight, direct injection of fuel and air for maximum efficiency. Racers typically ran Gurney-Weslake or Gurney-Eagle valve covers.

In spite of Ford's withdrawal from just about all motorsports activity, Mustangs wearing familiar Bud Moore Engineering livery could be found dicing it up with other pony cars on SCCA's Trans-Am circuit. Fresh from winning the championship for Ford in 1970, Moore finish the series in second place. AMC clinched the title with Mark Donahue driving a Penske Javelin.

When Henry Ford II announced the end of racing support, except for a small budget for very limited drag racing and off-road events, it did not affect Ford of Britain. Their racing budgets were never curtailed, probably due to his relationship with Walter Hayes and the great job they were doing in Formula One.

With eleven races in the 1971 Formula One season, Ford-Cosworth 3.0 DFV-powered cars—driven by Jacky Ickx, Clay Regazzoni, and Jackie Stewart—won seven! Ford's investment in Formula One continued to pay off in 1971; Jackie Stewart drove a Tyrrell-Ford to win the Drivers' Championship and Tyrrell won the Constructors' Championship.

Ford's withdrawal from racing was really felt in the NASCAR community, especially at Holman & Moody. They continued to build engines for the Wood Brothers and grind cams for a number of teams.

Ralph Moody left H&M in the fall of 1971 and set up a small, independent shop. He prepared the 1969 Cyclone that Bobby Allison drove to win eleven races. The NASCAR organization survived, after carmakers stopped pumping money into stock car racing, by bringing in major sponsorship money from R. J. Reynolds and creating the Winston Cup Series. That relationship lasted until 1999.

Ever-more-restrictive emissions and safety legislation, as well as the DOT coming down on shops and dealerships modifying new cars, signaled that the freewheeling good old high-performance days were coming to an end. One by one, automakers' enthusiast models were phased out and production engines were emasculated by emission controls. Ford high-performance small- and big-block engines were on the endangered species list. By 1974, the Mustang devolved into the Pinto-influenced Mustang II. It wasn't until the 1980s that Ford would actively race under the SVO banner and build high-performance cars once again. In 1982, Ford's advertising tagline "The Boss Is Back!" heralded the Mustang GT as the rebirth of the Boss Mustang.

Conceived in 1991 as Ford's first in-house skunk works, Ford's Special Vehicle Team, or SVT, really started flexing its muscles in 1993 with the SVT Mustang Cobra and F-150 Lightning pickup. And they haven't stopped.

We got a chance to drive the last of the Cyclone Spoilers at the Long Lead media event in June 1970. I loved the way this 429 CJ Spoiler ran, as attested to by the copious rubber deposits I left on the Dearborn Proving Grounds incline section; I had to park it to let the engine cool down!

PANTERA:
DE TOMASO'S MIDENGINE MAGIC!

Built by an Argentine-Italian in Italy for sale by Lincoln-Mercury dealers in the United States, the seductive Pantera had a couple of strikes against it before the first car crossed the pond.

When Lincoln-Mercury revealed the production version of the De Tomaso Pantera—with a suggested retail price of $9,000—to the press on May 18, 1971, at New York City's Waldorf Astoria, it seemed too good to be true. By the time select Lincoln-Mercury dealers were ready to take orders, the MSRP had gone up to $9,995. At approximately half the price of a Maserati Ghibli or Ferrari Daytona, there was nothing like it on the market.

The Pantera boasted a midship-mounted 351 Cleveland engine, five-speed ZF transaxle, cutting-edge steel body styled by Ghia and stamped by Vignale, four-wheel disc brakes, and monocoque platform engineered by Gian Paolo Dallara. It had all the appeal of an Italian exotic only with a powerful American pushrod V-8 and a large dealership network for sales and service. The problem was that early cars were not sorted out, causing warranty costs to skyrocket. Many of the Lincoln-Mercury dealers didn't know how to sell or service a Pantera. It surely had panache and performance, but it was not ready for prime time!

Over approximately five years, Ford would probably lose money on every 1971–1974 Pantera sold in the United States. Fortunately, the Pantera could not meet 1975 Federal emission and safety standards, which gave Ford an easy way out—and they took it. No longer on good terms with Alejandro de Tomaso, Ford swapped the De Tomaso badging with Ghia emblems on the

140 final 1974 GTS models. The last 1974 Ghia Pantera was built on chassis number 7380.

When Ford and de Tomaso parted, Ford sold De Tomaso fifteen Pantera bodies that had been left at Vignale which, like Ghia, was Ford owned. De Tomaso was permitted to continue manufacturing Panteras with Ford-supplied engines, but only for other than US markets. Production finally ended in 1992. Once early quality, safety, and mechanical issues were addressed, Panteras gained respect among enthusiasts. An early Pantera could sprint to 60 miles per hour in about 6 seconds and had a top speed in excess of 150 miles per hour.

The Pantera came to be based on Alejandro de Tomaso's relationship with Ford and Rowan Industries, an international industrial corporation with headquarters in New Jersey dating back to 1959 when De Tomaso Automobili SpA was founded in Modena, Italy. Together with his second wife, Elizabeth "Isabelle" Haskell, an heir to the Rowan Industries fortune, de Tomaso built road and track cars. Both were road racers and came from wealthy families. In 1955, Haskell was the first woman to race at Sebring. She was the granddaughter of Jonathan Amory Haskell, a General Motors director and president of its Export Division from 1920 to 1924. De Tomaso's first production car was the 1964 Vallelunga, powered by a Ford 1.5-liter Cortina engine. It utilized a steel backbone chassis, a design De Tomaso also incorporated into the engineering of the Mangusta, which was powered by a Ford small-block V-8 engine. Other De Tomaso vehicles powered by Ford included the five-place Deauville and two-place Zonda.

In 1972, Ford imported the only FIA Group 4 Pantera built by De Tomaso brought to the United States, shown here at Lincoln-Mercury display at the 1972 New York International Auto Show. It was later sold to racer Warren Tope, son of a Ford executive. Note large riveted fender flares and Le Mans fuel filler mounted behind the side quarter window.

Crisp styling by Tom Tjaarda at Ghia has held up well considering it was first penned in 1969. This is a 1973 model, owned by Archie Urciuoli, restored in 2010 by McLaren and refreshed in 2014 by Automotive Restorations in Stamford, Connecticut. *Archie Urciuoli*

It was the Mangusta that had caught the eye of Lee Iacocca and led to talks between him and de Tomaso regarding a new Ford-powered sports car. They became close friends. Ray Geddes, who had headed Special Vehicles Activity and was a liaison between Ford and Shelby for a number of years, was instrumental in putting together the De Tomaso–Ford partnership. He was later named executive vice president of Ford's new Italian Products Development Group, which included all the De Tomaso properties.

Designed by American Tom Tjaarda at Ghia, the Pantera replaced the stunningly beautiful and somewhat impractical Mangusta. With less rearward visibility than a Ford GT and a clutch from hell, the Mangusta was a four-wheeled piece of art but not a great road car. While the Mangusta had a steel backbone chassis, the new Pantera represented De Tomaso's first use of superior monocoque construction.

With financial help from Rowan Industries, De Tomaso was able to buy coachbuilder Ghia in 1967 and added Vignale in 1969. When the Pantera deal was presented to Ford, Rowan Industries owned 20 percent and Ford invested in an 80 percent stake.

Tracking actual Pantera sales can be confusing. The National Highway Transportation Safety Administration reported that 5,262 were imported by Ford and sold by Lincoln-Mercury dealers between May 1971 and August of 1974. That doesn't take into consideration Panteras imported for sale in Canada. Some sources have reported sales totaling 6,091 units.

On March 18, 1970, Rowan Industries president John C. Ellis and vice president Amory L. Haskell were killed when the company's twin-engine plane crashed on its final approach to Newark Airport. The two men were Isabelle Haskell de Tomaso's brother-in-law and brother. Subsequently, Rowan management was no longer interested in maintaining a financial involvement in the De Tomaso–Ford relationship and sold its interests, including Ghia and Vignale, to Ford. Before the first production Pantera was built in Modena, Ford owned 100 percent of the "partnership."

First shown to the Italian motoring press in Modena in March of 1970, the concept debuted in the US at the fourteenth New York International Auto Show on April 4, 1970. Pantera, Italian for Panther, started selling as a 1971 model at Lincoln-Mercury dealers on May 21, 1971. A total of 1,008 Vignale-bodied 1971 Panteras was sold. A high percentage of these cars were plagued with overheating, faulty air conditioning, and poor fit and finish. There were also serious issues with the Pantera's safety cage, which failed during crash testing. Ford used Holman & Moody on the East Coast and Bill Stroppe on the West Coast to correct the mechanical malfunctions. Later owners would discover rust problems in the rear engine bay compartment due to poor water drainage. Warranty costs soared and Ford ended importation in 1975. De Tomaso continued with the brand and produced a variety of models, some specifically for GT racing, until 1992.

When Ford phased out the 351 Cleveland in the United States, De Tomaso purchased 351 engines from Ford of Australia where they were continuing to develop the engine for racing. Towards the end of Pantera production in the early 1990s, engine displacement dropped to 302 cubic inches. Pantera production from 1970 to 1993 has been estimated at 7,158.

De Tomaso built a limited number of FIA Group 3 and Group 4 Pantera race cars, which were developed by Ferrari racer Michael Parkes. Some were for the 1972 World Endurance Racing Series. The factory offered Group 3 race cars, on special order, into the 1984 model year. A total of 14 FIA Group 4 racers were built over the years.

According to Pantera aficionado Mike Drew, "Ford purchased the only factory Group 4 Pantera exported to the US, chassis number 2344." It was used for the media, marketing events, and auto shows. In 1973, it was sold to Ford vice president Donald Tope's son, Warren. Before being raced by Tope, it had been sorted out at Bill Stroppe's shop and driven by Mario Andretti.

De Tomaso continued to build Panteras that were refreshed with more luxurious interiors, wide-body enhancements, and wings. The Pantera Si, upgraded by Marcello Gandini, was marketed from 1990 to 1993. There were forty-one Si Panteras built with fuel-injected, 5-liter Ford V-8s. Those exported to the United Kingdom were badged Pantera 90. After de Tomaso had exhausted his supply of leftover Vignale bodies in 1977, he sourced bodies from coachbuilders Maggiora, then Embo.

Between 1979 and 1989, many of the Embo-bodied Panteras were brought into the United States as gray-market models by Amerisport, Panteramerica, Stauffer Classics, and Panteras by Wilkinson. They had to be retrofitted to meet EPA and DOT regulations to be legally sold. The last Pantera imported was chassis number 9494, brought in by Amerisport. In 1981, Panteramerica in Santa Monica, California, imported De Tomaso's GTS (formerly Pantera) and GTS-Group 4 models at a starting price of $56,400 and the four-place Longchamp at $59,500.

It was truly unfortunate that by the time the Pantera was sorted out, Ford had bailed out.

FORD'S DNA: INNOVATION THROUGH PERFORMANCE!

Creating a modern GT40 road car was every bit as ambitious as Henry Ford II's desire for international motorsports domination. Both of these goals were attained—and both were historically significant.

The GT40 was a key ingredient in the formula Henry Ford II used to dominate international motorsports and change racing history. Almost four decades later, Henry's nephew, William Clay "Bill" Ford Jr., found new life for the GT40. It was first a concept in 2002, and then it morphed into a modern road car in 2005. The production 2005–2006 Ford GT reinvigorated Ford's historic hallmarks of success: passion, performance, and speed.

On October 30, 2001, Chairman Bill Ford added CEO to his title, the first Ford family member to serve in that position in twenty-two years. The previous CEO, Jac Nassar, had angered dealers, employees, and suppliers and made enemies on Wall Street. Ford was in crisis as sales plummeted for lack of new products. The company's stock had been depressed, and the company was on track to lose $5.45 billion dollars in 2001.

Less than two years away from Ford's centennial, Bill Ford needed an awe-inspiring vehicle to showcase the iconic Blue Oval. Nothing less than a daring, stunning, and aggressively dynamic car would do—a car that shouted horsepower and heritage. It needed to captivate the public and international automotive, business, and lifestyle media. That car was the GT40.

On Sunday, January 6, 2002, at the Detroit Auto Show, Bill Ford revealed the GT40 concept car to the press. With him on stage were Carroll Shelby and a number of iconic racers who had driven GT40s in competition: Bob Bondurant, Phil Hill, Lloyd Ruby, and Sir Jackie Stewart. The concept car captured the spirit of Le Mans 1966 and honored automotive history.

The concept was created in Doug Gaffka's Living Legends design studio, located in two ultra-high-security buildings on Ford's product-development campus in Dearborn. Camilo Pardo was appointed chief designer of the GT40 concept and production Ford GT. He was also an accomplished painter and clothing designer. During the design process, Pardo and his team had a real GT40 Mark I semiroad car, chassis P/1030, on loan to the studio. Its owner took Pardo and his team on "hot laps" at the Dearborn Proving Ground to give them the full GT40 experience.

In July of 2002, Bill Ford announced that the car would go into production as a Ford GT and would be ready for Ford's one hundredth anniversary in June 2003. In May of that year, three functional, preproduction Ford GTs were built, and Bill Ford drove one in the Centennial parade in Dearborn on June 16.

In March of 2004, a fully caged, preproduction build #PB1-1 Ford GT, chassis #0037, was tested by GT team members Mark McGowan and Jeff Porritt at the Nardo Ring in Italy. Hour after hour, the GT was clocked at speeds in excess of 200 miles per hour. It was certified at 209.1 miles per hour, but on one of the runs it hit a top speed of 211.89!

The ultra-high-performance Ford GT is built on an aluminum space frame and sheathed in super-plastic-formed aluminum body panels, except for a fiberglass hood. The rear "clamshell" is of aluminum-over-carbon construction. Power is supplied by a hand-built, aluminum four-cam 5.4-liter, 32-valve V-8 rated at 550 horsepower at 6,500 and 500 pounds-feet of torque at 3,700 rpm. The Lysholm-supercharged, midmounted, dry-sump engine bolts to a six-speed Ricardo transaxle. Top speed is electronically limited to 205 miles per hour. *Car & Driver* test results were published in the January 2004 issue. They recorded 3.3-second 0-to-60 sprints and quarter-mile times of 128 miles per hour in 11.6 seconds.

Ford produced 2,022 GTs for the 2005 model year, followed by 2,011 in 2006. There were no major changes except for two special-edition colors offered exclusively in 2006. First, a Tungsten Grey Metallic was chosen to commemorate the fortieth anniversary of the one-two-three win at Le Mans in 1966; 541 GTs were built in that color. The second special edition for 2006 was the hand-painted Heritage GT with blue-and-orange Gulf Oil livery like the JWA GT40 that won Le Mans in 1968 and 1969. Just 343 Heritage GTs were built.

Since the 1980s, Ford has been racing and marketing naturally aspirated and boosted high-performance Mustangs, some co-branded with Shelby. On January 12, 2015, at the Detroit Auto Show, Bill Ford revealed the 2017 GT, a totally modern, aerodynamic, high-tech road car that will be raced at Le Mans. The carbon-fiber-bodied Gen II Ford GT with a monocoque tub and aluminum subframes will be powered by a race-proven, twin-turbocharged, 600-plus-horsepower, 3.5-liter V-6.

Ford Performance, a new umbrella organization in Dearborn, incorporates SVT, Team RS, and Ford Racing and is under the direction of Dave Pericak. Henry Ford III, great-great-grandson of Henry Ford and Ford Performance global marketing manager, was quoted in *Autoweek*: "One of the things we're trying to do with Ford Performance is really use racing as kind of a laboratory and a test bed for innovation."

Ford's Total Performance future is secure.

Heritage and Horsepower

Ford is returning to Le Mans and building GT supercars in 2016, marking the fiftieth anniversary of its legendary GT40 Mark II one-two-three victory at Le Mans in 1966. Its unprecedented performance was followed in 1967, 1968, and 1969 with Mark IV and GT40 wins. Ford previously celebrated its Le Mans heritage with the 2005–2006 Ford GT.

The new Ford GT, available as a low-volume, ultra-performance supercar, will be represented at the 24 Hours of Le Mans and run the full 2016 schedules of FIA World Endurance Championship and TUDOR United SportsCar Championship racing. Multimatic Engineering and its racing arm, Multimatic Motorsports, will construct street and race-ready Ford GTs.

Seven-time IMSA champions and five-time Rolex 24 of Daytona winners Chip Ganassi Racing with Felix Sabates (CGRFS) will compete in LM GTE Pro with two Ford teams and four GTs. Supporting the Ford GT racing project and Multimatic Motorsports are Roush Yates Engines, Castrol, Michelin, Forza Motorsport, Sparco, and Brembo. The race car has undergone extensive design and testing within Ford and Multimatic, with CGRFS providing input. Roush Yates is supporting development of the 3.5-liter EcoBoost V-6, the most powerful EcoBoost production engine ever.

"As we developed the Ford GT, from the outset, we wanted to ensure that the car has what it takes to return Ford to the world of GT racing," said Raj Nair, Ford Motor Company chief technical officer and group vice president, global product development. "We believe the Ford GT's cutting-edge aerodynamics deliver outstanding levels of downforce for improved stability with minimal drag, and its lightweight composites, including carbon fiber, make for an exceptionally rigid but light chassis. Combined with the power and efficiency of EcoBoost engine technology, the new GT will make for a compelling race car that can once again compete on a global stage."

The all-new Ford GT: America's supercar 2.0!

Ford built 541 Tungsten Grey Metallic '06 Ford GTs to commemorate the fortieth anniversary of the Le Mans win in 1966. The view never changes when you look in the rearview mirror; all you see is the supercharger atop the modular V-8.

Below: Ford will enter a 2016 GT in the 2016 running of the 24 Hours of Le Mans race to commemorate the fiftieth anniversary of its 1966 Ford GT40 one-two-three overall win. *Ford Motor Company*

INDEX

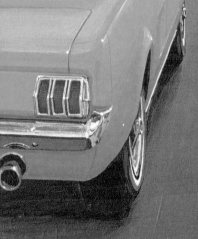